George

Sams **Teach Yourself**

Go

Next Generation Systems
Programming with **Golang**

in **24**

Hours

SAMS   800   A

Sams Teach Yourself Go in 24 Hours
Next Generation Systems Programming with Golang

ISBN-13: 978-0-672-33803-8

ISBN-10: 0-672-33803-3

Library of Congress Control Number: 2017955706

1   17

Trademarks

Warning and Disclaimer

Special Sales

Editor-in-Chief
Mark Taub

Executive Editor
Laura Lewin

Development Editor
Sheri Replin

Managing Editor
Sandra Schroeder

Project Editor
Prathiba.R/
Pearson CSC

Copy Editor
Pearson CSC

Indexer
Pearson CSC

Proofreader
Pearson CSC

Technical Editors
Bala Natarajan
Yoshiki Shibata

Editorial Assistant
Courtney Martin

Cover Designer
Chuti Prasertsith

Cover Image
Ryan McVay/
Getty Images

Compositor
Pearson CSC

Contents at a Glance

Introduction 1

HOUR 1 Getting Started 3
HOUR 2 Understanding Types 13
HOUR 3 Understanding Variables 27
HOUR 4 Using Functions in Go 41
HOUR 5 Using Control Flow 53
HOUR 6 Working with Arrays, Slices, and Maps 71
HOUR 7 Using Structs and Pointers 83
HOUR 8 Creating Methods and Interfaces 101
HOUR 9 Working with Strings 115
HOUR 10 Handling Errors 129
HOUR 11 Working with Goroutines 139
HOUR 12 Introducing Channels 155
HOUR 13 Using Packages for Code Reuse 173
HOUR 14 Naming Conventions in Go 185
HOUR 15 Testing and Performance 199
HOUR 16 Debugging 213
HOUR 17 Using Command-Line Programs 227
HOUR 18 Creating HTTP Servers 243
HOUR 19 Creating HTTP Clients with Go 259
HOUR 20 Working with JSON 273
HOUR 21 Working with Files 289
HOUR 22 Introducing Regular Expressions 305
HOUR 23 Programming Time in Go 317
HOUR 24 Deploying Go Code 329

Index 341

APPENDIX

Online ancillaries: Bonus Hours 25 and 26

Table of Contents

Introduction   1

HOUR 1: Getting Started   3
    Introducing Go   3
    Installing Go   4
    Setting Up Your Environment   8
    Writing Your First Go Program: Hello World   8
    Summary   10
    Q&A   10
    Workshop   11
    Exercises   11

HOUR 2: Understanding Types   13
    What Is a Data Type?   13
    Differentiating Between Static and Dynamic Typing   13
    Implementing Booleans   17
    Understanding Numeric Types   18
    Checking the Type of a Variable   22
    Converting Between Types   23
    Summary   24
    Q&A   25
    Workshop   25
    Exercises   26

HOUR 3: Understanding Variables   27
    What Is a Variable?   27
    Declaring Shorthand Variables   29
    Understanding Variables and Zero Values   30
    Writing a Short Variable Declaration   32
    Styles of Variable Declaration   32

Using Variable Scope 33

Using Pointers 35

Declaring Variables with Constants 38

Summary 39

Q&A 39

Workshop 39

Exercises 40

HOUR 4: Using Functions in Go   **41**

What Is a Function? 41

Defining Variadic Functions 45

Using Named Return Values 46

Using Recursive Functions 48

Passing Functions as Values 49

Summary 51

Q&A 51

Workshop 51

Exercises 52

HOUR 5: Using Control Flow   **53**

Using the `if` Statement 53

Using the `else` Statement 55

Using the `else if` Statement 57

Using Comparison Operators 58

Using Arithmetic Operators 59

Using Logical Operators 59

Using the `switch` Statement 60

Looping with the `for` Statement 62

Using the `defer` Statement 66

Summary 68

Q&A 68

Workshop 69

Exercises 69

HOUR 6: Working with Arrays, Slices, and Maps   **71**

Working with Arrays 71

Working with Slices 73

Working with Maps 78

Summary 80

Q&A 80

Workshop 81

Exercises 81

HOUR 7: Using Structs and Pointers   **83**

What Is a Struct? 83

Initializing a Struct 85

Nesting Structs 89

Creating Default Values for Structs 91

Comparing Structs 93

Understanding Public and Private Values 95

Differentiating Between Pointer and Value References 96

Summary 99

Q&A 99

Workshop 100

Exercises 100

HOUR 8: Creating Methods and Interfaces   **101**

Using Methods 101

Creating Method Sets 103

Working with Methods and Pointers 105

Using Interfaces 109

Summary 113

Q&A 113

Workshop 114

Exercises 114

HOUR 9: Working with Strings   **115**

Creating String Literals 115

Understanding Rune Literals 116

Concatenating Strings 118

Summary 126

Q&A 126

Workshop 127

Exercises 127

HOUR 10: Handling Errors   **129**

Handling Errors and Idiomatic Go 130

Understanding the Error Type 132

Creating Errors 132

Formatting Errors 133

Returning an Error from a Function 134

Errors and Usability 135

Don't `panic` 136

Summary 137

Q&A 137

Workshop 138

Exercises 138

HOUR 11: Working with Goroutines   **139**

Understanding Concurrency 139

Concurrency Versus Parallelism 141

Understanding Concurrency Through a Web Browser 142

Blocking and Non-Blocking Code 144

Handling Concurrent Operations with Goroutines 145

Using Goroutines to Manage Latency 147

Defining Goroutines 152

Summary 153

Q&A 153

Workshop 153

Exercises 154

HOUR 12: Introducing Channels   **155**

Using Channels 155

Using Buffered Channels 159

Blocking and Flow Control 161

Using Channels as Function Arguments 164

Employing the **select** Statement 164

Quitting Channels 167

Summary 170

Q&A 170

Workshop 171

Exercises 171

HOUR 13: Using Packages for Code Reuse   **173**

Importing Packages 173

Understanding Package Usage 175

Using Third-Party Packages 175

Installing a Third-Party Package 176

Managing Third-Party Dependencies 178

Summary 182

Q&A 182

Workshop 183

Exercises 184

HOUR 14: Naming Conventions in Go   **185**

Formatting Code in Go 185

Using **gofmt** 186

Configuring Text Editors 188

Naming Conventions 188

Using **golint** 190

Using **godoc** 192

Automating Workflow 196

Summary 197

Q&A 197

Workshop 198

Exercises 198

HOUR 15: Testing and Performance   **199**

Testing: The Most Important Aspect of Software Development 199

testing Package 201

Running Table Tests 204

Benchmarking in Go 207

Providing Test Coverage 209

Summary 210

Q&A 210

Workshop 211

Exercises 211

HOUR 16: Debugging **213**

Logging 213

Printing Data 218

Using the **fmt** Package 219

Using Delve 221

Using **gdb** 224

Summary 225

Q&A 225

Workshop 226

Exercises 226

HOUR 17: Using Command-Line Programs **227**

Operating with Inputs and Outputs 228

Accessing Raw Command-Line Arguments 229

Parsing Command-Line Flags 230

Working with Types 232

Customizing Help Text 234

Creating Subcommands 235

POSIX Compliance 239

Installing and Sharing Command-Line Programs 240

Summary 241

Q&A 241

Workshop 242

Exercises 242

HOUR 18: Creating HTTP Servers **243**

Announcing Your Presence with the "Hello World" Web Server 243

Examining Requests and Responses 245

Working with Handler Functions 247

Handling 404s 248

Setting a Header 249

Responding to Different Types of Requests 253

Receiving Data from GET and POST Requests 255

Summary 257

Q&A 257

Workshop 258

Exercises 258

HOUR 19: Creating HTTP Clients with Go   **259**

Understanding HTTP 259

Making a GET Request 261

Making a POST Request 262

Gaining Further Control over HTTP Requests 264

Debugging HTTP Requests 265

Dealing with Timeouts 269

Summary 270

Q&A 271

Workshop 271

Exercises 272

HOUR 20: Working with JSON   **273**

Introducing JSON 273

Using JSON APIs 275

Using JSON with Go 275

Decoding JSON 281

Mapping Data Types 283

Working with JSON Received over HTTP 285

Summary 286

Q&A 286

Workshop 287

Exercises 287

HOUR 21: Working with Files   **289**

Importance of Files 289

Reading and Writing Files with the ioutil Package 290

Writing to a File 294

Listing a Directory 295

Copying a File 296

Deleting Files 298

Using Files to Manage Configuration 299

Summary 302

Q&A 303

Workshop 303

Exercises 304

HOUR 22: Introducing Regular Expressions **305**

Defining Regular Expressions 305

Getting Familiar with Regular Expression Syntax 307

Using Regular Expressions for Validation 308

Using Regular Expressions to Transform Data 309

Parsing Data with Regular Expressions 311

Summary 315

Q&A 315

Workshop 316

Exercises 316

HOUR 23: Programming Time in Go **317**

Programming the Element of Time 317

Putting Your Program to Sleep 319

Setting a Timeout 320

Using a Ticker 321

Representing Time in a String Format 322

Working with `Time` Structs 323

Adding and Subtracting Time 324

Comparing Different `Time` Structs 324

Summary 326

Q&A 326

Workshop 326

Exercises 327

HOUR 24: Deploying Go Code   **329**

    Understanding Targets 329

    Reducing the Size of Binaries 332

    Using Docker 334

    Downloading Binary Files 336

    Using `go get` 338

    Releasing Code with Package Managers 339

    Summary 339

    Q&A 339

    Workshop 340

    Exercises 340

Index   **341**

APPENDIX

    Online ancillaries: Bonus Hours 25 and 26

Follow these steps to access the online chapters:

1. Register your book by going to www.informit.com/register, and log in or create a new account.

2. On the Register a Product page, enter this book's ISBN (9780672338038), and click Submit.

3. Answer the challenge question as proof of book ownership.

4. On the Registered Products tab of your account page, click on the Access Bonus Content link to go to the page where your downloadable content is available.

About the Author

George Ornbo is a software engineer, blogger, and author with 14 years of experience delivering software to startups and enterprise clients. He has experience with a broad range of programming languages, UNIX, and the underlying protocols of the web. He is currently working at a Blockchain startup in London.

Dedication

For Bea and Fin. I won a Golden Ticket with you two!

Acknowledgments

Thanks to Laura Lewin and the team at Pearson for giving me the chance to write a second book in the Sams Teach Yourself in 24 Hours Series. Thanks also to Sheri Replin for your amazing work!

Thanks to Bala Natarajan and Yoshiki Shibata for being the technical reviewers of this book. You suggested many excellent improvements throughout the reviews. Any mistakes left in the book are, of course, my own.

Thanks to Robert Griesemer, Rob Pike, and Ken Thompson for thinking again about language design.

We Want to Hear from You!

As the reader of this book, *you* are our most important critic and commentator. We value your opinion and want to know what we're doing right, what we could do better, what areas you'd like to see us publish in, and any other words of wisdom you're willing to pass our way.

We welcome your comments. You can email or write to let us know what you did or didn't like about this book—as well as what we can do to make our books better.

Please note that we cannot help you with technical problems related to the topic of this book.

When you write, please be sure to include this book's title and author as well as your name and email address. We will carefully review your comments and share them with the author and editors who worked on the book.

Email: feedback@samspublishing.com

Mail: Sams Publishing
          ATTN: Reader Feedback
          800 East 96th Street
          Indianapolis, IN 46240 USA

Reader Services

Register your copy of *Sams Teach Yourself Go in 24 Hours* at informit.com for convenient access to downloads, updates, and corrections as they become available. To start the registration process, go to informit.com/register and log in or create an account[*]. Enter the product ISBN, 9780672338038, and click Submit. Once the process is complete, you will find any available bonus content under Registered Products.

---

[*] Be sure to check the box that you would like to hear from us in order to receive exclusive discounts on future editions of this product.

Introduction

Go, or Golang, represents another attempt at language design and is an excellent iteration on C-like programming languages. It provides low-level access to an underlying operating system and has excellent support for networking and concurrency.

Go can be used for a number of purposes, including:

- ▶ Network programming
- ▶ Systems programming
- ▶ Concurrent programming
- ▶ Distributed programming

A number of important Open Source projects have already been created using Go, including Go-Ethereum, Terraform, Kubernetes, and Docker. Go has already made a major impact on Open Source, and success is expected to increase.

Who Should Read This Book?

This book makes few assumptions about programming or computer science experience, but it is helpful to have some basic understanding of programming. As Go is primarily run from the terminal, it is helpful to understand what a terminal is and how to run basic commands. Finally, because Go is often used for systems and network programming, it is helpful to understand a little of how the Internet works, although this is not essential.

Why Should I Learn Go?

If you are interested in creating systems or network-based applications, Go is a great choice. As a relatively new language, it has been designed by experienced and respected computer scientists to respond to the challenges of creating concurrent, networked programs at scale. If you find the syntax of Java or C difficult to program in, Go may offer you a better experience. For programmers with experience of dynamic languages like Ruby, Python, or JavaScript, Go offers the benefits of type safety without the rigidity of traditional languages.

How This Book Is Organized

The book starts with the basics of Go, including setting up your environment and running your first Go program. You are then introduced to some of the fundamentals of the language, including strings, functions, structs, and methods. You will understand how to use Goroutines and Channels, a unique feature of Go that abstracts much of the difficulty of concurrent programming.

You will be introduced to how to debug and test Go code, and will be introduced to some techniques that will help you to understand how to write idiomatic Go code.

You will then understand how to write basic command-line programs, HTTP servers, and HTTP clients; how to work with JSON; and how to work with files.

After learning about Regular Expressions and how to work with time, the book concludes by explaining how to deploy Go applications to production.

Code Examples

Each hour in this book comes with several code examples. These examples help you learn about Go as much as the text in the book. It is highly recommended that you run the code examples as you work through the book. You can download the code examples at https://github.com/shapeshed/golang-book-examples/, or if you already have Go installed, by running `go get github.com/shapeshed/golang-book-examples`.

HOUR 1
Getting Started

What You'll Learn in This Hour:

- ▶ Introducing Go
- ▶ Installing Go
- ▶ Setting Up Your Environment
- ▶ Writing your first Go program: Hello World

During this hour, you understand what Go is and the motivations for creating it. You learn how to install Go and will run your first program. You also learn about the Go Gopher, who will make an appearance now and again throughout this text.

Introducing Go

Go (or Golang) is an open source programming language created at Google in 2007 by Robert Griesemer, Rob Pike, and Ken Thompson. It was announced to the world on the Google Open Source Blog on November 10, 2009. The announcement describes the high-level goals of the language as combining "the development speed of working in a dynamic language like Python with the performance and safety of a compiled language like C or C++."

History of Go

In assessing any language, it is important to understand the motivations of the language designers and the problem the language is trying to solve. Go's creators are heavyweights of computer science. During the 1970s, Ken Thompson designed and implemented the original UNIX operating system, and in this respect alone, his contribution to computer science cannot be overestimated. In collaboration with Rob Pike, he designed the UTF-8 encoding scheme. As well as helping to design UTF-8, Rob Pike helped to develop Plan 9, a distributed, multi-user operating system, and is the co-author of *The Unix Programming Environment*, the canonical expression of the UNIX philosophy. Robert Griesemer is a Google employee with a deep understanding of language design who worked on code generation for Google's V8 JavaScript engine that powers both the Chrome web browser and Node.js.

Go was designed by computer science heavyweights for the requirements of Google. It took two years to design the language, and the team brought years of experience and a deep understanding of programming language design. They took inspiration from Pascal, Oberon, and C, as well as the convenience of dynamic languages. As such, Go is an expression of language design by experienced computer scientists, designed for one of the biggest Internet companies on the planet. All of Go's creators have talked of their motivation to create Go as a reaction to their frustration with C++. According to Rob Pike, Google I/O 2012, Meet the Go Team:

> "We were doing a lot of C++ development and the joke, but there is a lot of truth in it, is that we got tired of waiting for the compilations."

You don't need to understand the history of language design to use Go. It is enough to know that years of experience and a deep understanding of the strengths and weaknesses of other programming languages have gone into the design and implementation of Go. In part a reaction to frustrations with C++, Go offers a modern programming language that can be used to create performant web servers and systems programs.

Go Is a Compiled Language

Go uses a compiler to compile code. A compiler takes code and compiles it into binary (or byte code) format. During the compilation of code, a compiler can check for errors, make performance optimizations, and output binaries that can run on different platforms. To create and run a Go program, a programmer must go through the following steps.

1. Create a Go program in a text editor.
2. Save the file.
3. Compile the program.
4. Run the compiled executable.

This is different from languages like Python, Ruby, or JavaScript, where there is no compilation step. You will understand the strengths and weaknesses of using a compiler in Hour 2. There is no need to install a compiler, as Go ships with a compiler.

Installing Go

Go is available for FreeBSD, Linux, Windows, and macOS. If you are running a recent version of any of these platforms, it is highly likely that Go is supported. For the latest on requirements on these platforms, refer to the system requirements on the Go website. Where possible, using an operating system package manager to install Go is recommended for general usage.

Go may be installed using a download from the Golang website. If you are getting started, it is recommended that you use the installers available. There is no installer available for Linux, but

Go is generally available in distribution package managers, or if you are a more experienced Linux user, you can build Go from the source code. For Windows and macOS, simply download the file, double click, and complete the installation process. You will see a standard installer window, as shown in Figure 1.1.

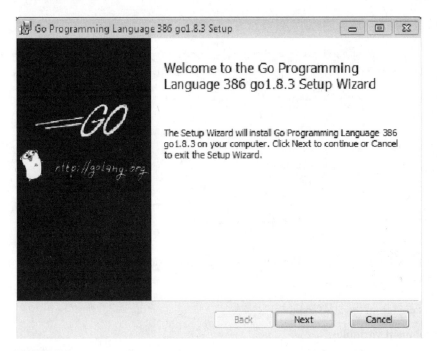

FIGURE 1.1
Running the Go Installer on Windows. (Source: Microsoft Corporation)
https://golang.org

Installing on Windows

Once the installer has completed, open a command prompt and type **go version**. If you see a response with the version number, Go was installed correctly (see Figure 1.2).

FIGURE 1.2
Verifying that Go is installed on Windows. (Source: Microsoft Corporation)

To complete the installation, the directory structure for Go projects needs to be created. To do this, open a command prompt from the Start menu and create the directories (see Figure 1.3).

```
mkdir %USERPROFILE%\go
mkdir %USERPROFILE%\go\bin
mkdir %USERPROFILE%\go\pkg
mkdir %USERPROFILE%\go\src
```

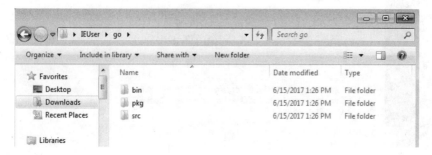

FIGURE 1.3
Creating the Folder Structure for Go Projects. (Source: Microsoft Corporation)

With these folders created, the GOPATH environment variable can be added. Add an environment variable on Windows:

1. Click Control Panel from the Start menu.

2. Search **environment variables**.

3. Click Edit environment variables for your account (see Figure 1.4).

4. Click **New**.

5. In Variable name, enter **GOPATH**.

6. In Variable value, enter **%USERPROFILE%\go**.

7. Click **Save**.

FIGURE 1.4
Setting the GOPATH on Windows. (Source: Microsoft Corporation)

If you have a command prompt open, close and reopen it. At the prompt, type the following to check that the GOPATH variable was set:

```
echo %GOPATH%
C:\Users\george\go
```

Installing on macOS or Linux

Once the installer is complete, open a command prompt and type **go version**. If you see a response with the version number, Go was installed correctly, as shown in Figure 1.5.

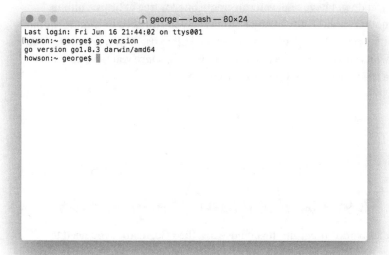

FIGURE 1.5
Verifying That Go Is Installed on macOS. (Source: Apple, Inc.)

To complete the installation, the directory structure for Go projects needs to be created. To do this, open a command prompt from the start menu and create the directories.

```
mkdir $HOME/go
mkdir $HOME/go/bin
mkdir $HOME/go/pkg
mkdir $HOME/go/src
```

To set the GOPATH variable, edit your .bashrc file (or equivalent if you are running another shell) and add the following to it. You will find your .bashrc file in your home directory.

```
export GOPATH=$HOME/go
```

Reload your shell or close and reopen the terminal. At the prompt, type the following to check that the GOPATH variable was set.

```
echo $GOPATH
/home/george/go
```

Setting Up Your Environment

Go is opinionated about how your work environment is configured. As an open source project, code sharing is also important. To enable code sharing in the future it is recommended that you create a Github account. If you do not have one, you can create one for free at https://github.com/. If you prefer to use another service, like Gitlab or Bitbucket, you will need to change "github.com" in the commands that follow to the URL of the service you wish to use. If you are not familiar with Git or GitHub, do not worry; this will be covered later in the book. Once you have created your Github account, create the folders to hold your source code as follows.

```
// Linux / macOS
mkdir -p $GOPATH/src/github.com/[your github username]

// Windows
mkdir %GOPATH%\src\github.com\[your github username]
```

Writing Your First Go Program: Hello World

It is time for the famous "Hello World" program! If you have installed Go, all that you need to create a Go program is a text editor and your brain. You may already prefer a text editor, but some editors you may wish to consider include Sublime, Textmate, Notepad++, Atom, Vim, or Emacs. Programmers are notorious for engaging in heated debate about which text editor is best, but if you are just starting out pick one that you feel comfortable with. Go requires no special text editor, so if you just want to experiment with Go the default text editors on your operating system will work.

Listing 1.1 shows the Go Hello World program. This simple program prints a line of text to the terminal.

LISTING 1.1 Hello World

```
1:  package main
2:
3:  import (
4:      "fmt"
5:  )
6:
7:  func main() {
8:      fmt.Println("Hello World!")
9:  }
```

Saying "Hello World!"

In this example, you run your first Go program!

1. Create a folder to hold the program and change into that directory.

```
// Linux / macOS
mkdir -p $GOPATH/src/github.com/[your github username]/hello
cd $GOPATH/src/github.com/[your github username]/hello

// Windows
mkdir %GOPATH%\src\github.com\[your github username]\hello
cd %GOPATH%\src\github.com\[your github username]\hello
```

2. Open hour01/example01 in the code examples for this book.

3. In the hello folder that you just created, create a file called `main.go`.

4. Copy the contents of hour01/example01 into `main.go`. You can also use Figure 1.1 to copy the code.

5. Within the hello folder, run `go build`.

6. Within the hello folder, run `./main` on Linux or macOS or `main.exe` on Windows.

7. You should see "Hello World!" printed to the console.

8. Congratulations! You just ran your first Go program!

DID YOU KNOW?

Most Languages Have a "Hello World" Example

"Hello World" is a simple programming example that is used to showcase the syntax of a programming language. It is often used to check that installations are running correctly and is used as the first introduction to a language. It can be a useful way to quickly compare programming languages.

Compiling and Running Programs with Go Run

Go offers a shorthand for compiling and running a file because this is a common step during development. The following code compiles a program and runs it in one step.

```
go run main.go
```

Unlike `go build`, there is no executable file created. As such, `go build` is a convenient way of developing Go code, because there is no need to have separate compilation and execution steps. Furthermore, there is no need to run `go clean` to clean up executable files.

Meet the Gopher

The Go programming language has a mascot! The Go Gopher, shown in Figure 1.6, appears at conferences, documentation pages, and blog posts. It was created by Renee French, a talented author and illustrator who is married to Rob Pike, one of the co-creators of Go.

FIGURE 1.6
The Go Gopher (by Renee French).

Summary

During this hour, you learned some of the motivations behind Go and who created it. You installed Go and ran your first program. You learned the difference between **go build** and **go run** and even met the Go Gopher. Not bad for an hour!

Q&A

Q. Why was Go created when there are so many other languages?

A. Go is a reaction to traditional languages, like Java and C++, which can be cumbersome, slow, and heavy. Taking some inspiration from dynamically typed languages, like Python, the language designers wanted to create a language that was easy to work with, but could scale to large teams working on high traffic production systems.

Q. The executable file that the compiler outputs is huge, while the source code file size is tiny. Why is that?

A. The compiler binary file needs to include everything it needs to execute the program. The downside of this is that it results in a large file in relation to the source code. The upside is that there are no dependencies to install when you want to run the program.

Q. Should I use `go build` or `go run`?

A. When developing it is recommended to use `go run`. When you are ready to share your program, use `go build`.

Workshop

The workshop contains quiz questions and exercises to help you solidify your understanding of the material covered. Try to answer all questions before looking at the "Answers" section that follows.

Quiz

1. What are the things you need to run a Go program?

2. Can you explain the difference between `go build` and `go run`?

3. What is the Go Gopher?

Answers

1. Aside from a computer, all you really need is a terminal and a text editor.

2. The `go build` command compiles an executable binary that can be used to run the program. The `go run` command compiles the program and then runs it in one step.

3. The Go Gopher is Go's mascot. You will meet the Go Gopher across the Go ecosystem.

Exercises

1. Modify the "Hello World" program and change the text to something you would like to say. Run the program by using `go build` and then running the executable. Change the text again and run the program using `go run`. Do you understand the difference between the two approaches?

2. Perform an Internet search for 'Hello World' programs in a variety of other languages. Can you see any similarities between the Go example and other programming languages?

3. If you have time, watch Rob Pike's introduction to the Go programming language that he gave in 2009. It outlines many of the design goals of Golang. The video is available on YouTube (https://www.youtube.com/watch?v=rKnDgT73v8s).

HOUR 2
Understanding Types

What You'll Learn in This Hour:

- ▶ What is a data type?
- ▶ Differentiating between static and dynamic typing
- ▶ Implementing Booleans
- ▶ Understanding numeric types
- ▶ Checking the type of a variable
- ▶ Converting between types

Go is a statically typed language and this is an important concept to understand, particularly if you do not have a computer science background, or have worked with dynamic languages like Python or JavaScript. This hour introduces you to data types and allows you to understand the difference between strongly typed and dynamically typed languages. You learn how Go's type system works and are introduced to the basic types.

What Is a Data Type?

Data types allow programming languages, compilers, databases, and code execution environments to understand how to operate on and process data. If a data type is a number, for example, it is often possible to perform mathematical operations on it. Programming languages and databases frequently extend functionality and performance to programmers based on data types. Most programming languages also feature standard libraries to work with common data. Databases also offer query languages that allow programmers to interact with and query data based on underlying data types. Whether data types are explicitly declared or not, they are an important construct of programming and computing in general.

Differentiating Between Static and Dynamic Typing

Languages are said to be "strongly typed" if a compiler throws an error when types are used incorrectly. Languages are said to be "dynamically typed" (also known as "loosely typed" and "weakly typed") if a runtime converts types from one type to another in order to execute the program, or if the compiler does not enforce the type system. Whether one is better than the other is the source of much debate; formal computer scientists value the correctness and safety of a strongly typed language while others value dynamically typed languages for simplicity and speed of development.

Some advantages of using a statically typed language include:

▶ Better performance than dynamically typed languages.

▶ Bugs can often be caught by a compiler.

▶ Code editors can offer code completion and other tooling.

▶ Better data integrity.

Some advantages of using a dynamically typed language include:

▶ It is often faster to write software using a dynamically typed language.

▶ There is no need to wait for a compiler to execute code.

▶ Dynamically typed languages are generally less rigid, and some argue that they are more open to change.

▶ Some argue there is a shorter learning curve.

Go has a concept of types that is either explicitly declared by a programmer or is inferred by the compiler. During this hour, types are explicitly declared to help your understanding. Listing 2.1 shows a string being used to print a message to the terminal.

LISTING 2.1   Introducing Types

```
 1:  package main
 2:
 3:  import (
 4:      "fmt"
 5:  )
 6:
 7:  func sayHello(s string) string {
 8:      return "Hello " + s
 9:  }
10:
11:  func main() {
12:      fmt.Println(sayHello("George"))
13:  }
```

Do not worry if you do not fully understand Listing 2.1. The important part is the declaration of the `sayHello` function. In the parameter declaration, the function takes a single argument of s that is specified as the type `string`. The return value from this function is also specified as a `string`. Thus, when a compiler compiles the program it can check that any argument passed to the function is a `string`. If the argument is not a `string` the compiler will throw an error. This is highly desirable, as it can mean that the error may never reach customers of a product.

To compare strongly and dynamically typed languages, we will look at an example from JavaScript, a widely used dynamically typed language. Do not be concerned if you are not familiar with JavaScript. The point is to examine the difference in how types are handled.

The simple function shown in Listing 2.2 takes two values, adds them together, and then returns the result.

LISTING 2.2   Simple JavaScript Function

```
1:   var addition = function (a, b) {
2:        return x + y;
3:   };
```

If the function is given two numbers, it works fine.

```
addition(1,3)
4
```

If, however, the function is passed a number and a string, something strange happens:

```
addition(1,"three")
1three
```

In this case, the function has returned a string. Why? Although JavaScript has a concept of types, it is largely permissive in the way that they may be used. In this example, JavaScript performs type coercion on the number value and converts it to a string. The string "1three" is returned. While the flexibility of JavaScript is attractive, it can lead to subtle and at times catastrophic runtime bugs.

Suppose that the addition function is being used in a program to take some input and save it to a database. Databases generally have a concept of data types, and many have the concept of an integer. An integer is a whole number that can be negative or positive. If a database has defined a database field as an integer, it expects an integer.

The JavaScript addition function can return a string or an integer. If a string is passed into the function, a string will be returned. If this value is used to insert data into a database filed that expects an integer, an error will be thrown. Even worse is that this error is a runtime error, meaning the error will directly affect users of the program. Unless the error is handled, the error is likely to cause the program to crash.

Comparing the same function in Go, you can see that the data types of arguments and the return value are declared.

Listing 2.3 shows an example of types in Go. The function declares that only two values of int are accepted by the function and that the data type int will be returned. Without even looking at the implementation of the function, it is possible to see that it takes two integers and returns an integer. If a programmer makes the mistake of passing a string to this function, a compiler will catch the error.

LISTING 2.3   **Types in Go**

```
 1:  package main
 2:
 3:  import (
 4:      "fmt"
 5:  )
 6:
 7:  func addition(x int, y int) int {
 8:      return x + y
 9:  }
10:
11:  func main() {
12:      fmt.Println(2,4)
13:  }
```

Listing 2.4 shows an example of an incorrect type being passed to a function. In this example, a compile time error is thrown instead of a customer experiencing a potential software crash.

LISTING 2.4   **Passing an Incorrect Type**

```
 1:  package main
 2:
 3:  import (
 4:      "fmt"
 5:  )
 6:
 7:  func addition(x int, y int) int {
 8:      return x + y
 9:  }
10:
11:  func main() {
12:      var s string = "three"
13:      fmt.Println(addition(1, s))
14:  }
```

Attempting to run this program results in a compiler error. This also provides useful information on why the error was thrown. In this case, a string was used where an `int` was expected.

```
cannot use s (type string) as type int in argument to addition
```

The Go compiler can also catch other common errors like passing too many or too few arguments.

TRY IT YOURSELF ▼

Passing an Incorrect Type

In this example, you will understand how Go's compiler enforces the type system.

1. Open hour02/example04.go from the code examples for this book.

2. From the terminal, run the program with `go run example04.go`

3. You should see an error as follows:

```
./example04.go:11: cannot use s (type string) as type int in argument to addition
```

Implementing Booleans

With a basic understanding of types, it is now possible to explore how Go implements some of the fundamental data types. The first is Boolean. A Boolean may be either true or false, but nothing else. Although some other languages permit the values 1 and 0 to represent true and false, Go does not. A Boolean value can be declared as follows.

```
var b bool
```

If the variable is not assigned a value, it will be false by default. Listing 2.5 shows a Boolean variable being initialized and then printed to the terminal.

LISTING 2.5 Declaring a Boolean Type Variable

```
 1: package main
 2:
 3: import (
 4:     "fmt"
 5: )
 6:
 7: func main() {
 8:     var b bool
 9:     fmt.Println(b)
10: }
```

Booleans may be reassigned after they have been created (see Listing 2.6), and they are an extremely useful programming construct.

LISTING 2.6   Reassigning A Boolean Type Variable

```
 1:   package main
 2:
 3:   import (
 4:       "fmt"
 5:   )
 6:
 7:   func main() {
 8:       var b bool
 9:       fmt.Println(b)
10:       b = true
11:       fmt.Println(b)
12:   }
```

▼ TRY IT YOURSELF

Declaring and Reassigning a Boolean Type Variable

In this example, you understand how to initialize and reassign a Boolean type variable.

1. Open hour02/example06.go in the code examples for this book.

2. From the terminal, run the program with `go run example06.go`

3. You should see the Boolean type being reassigned.

   ```
   false
   true
   ```

Understanding Numeric Types

Numbers are fundamental to programming. However, without a computer science or mathematics background, some terms may seem confusing. You may have heard of floats, integers, unsigned integers, 8-bit, 64-bit, bigint, smallint, tinyint. These are all types of integer or number. To understand what these terms mean, know that numbers are stored internally on computers as bits. Bits are just a series of Boolean values and are either 1 or 0. One bit is either a 1 or a 0. For 4-bit integers, compare the raw bits with the decimal representation. In Table 2.1, it is possible to see that there are 16 numbers in total for 4-bit numbers.

TABLE 2.1   4-Bit Unsigned Integers

Binary	Decimal
0000	0
0001	1
0010	2
0011	3
0100	4
0101	5
0110	6
0111	7
1000	8
1001	9
1010	10
1011	11
1100	12
1101	13
1110	14
1111	15

Signed and Unsigned Integers

For signed integers, one of the bits may be used as a sign to represent its value. This is commonly a negative sign: –. Table 2.1 represented unsigned 4-bit integers where the values ranged from 0 to 15. Signed integer values can be either negative or positive, so the range is –8 to 7. Table 2.2 shows 4-bit signed integers.

TABLE 2.2   4-Bit Signed Integers

Binary	Decimal
0000	0
0001	1
0010	2
0011	3
0100	4

(Continued)

Binary	Decimal
0101	5
0110	6
0111	7
1000	−8
1001	−7
1010	−6
1011	−5
1100	−4
1101	−3
1110	−2
1111	−1

DID YOU KNOW?

Numbers Depend on a Computer Processor

The maximum numbers that can be used on a computer depends on the underlying architecture of a computer processor. Most computers today are 64-bit and can support unsigned integers up to 9223372036854775807. Some of the first microprocessors contained just four bits, meaning only signed integers between −8 and 7 could be represented!

Declaring an integer in Go is as follows:

```
var i int = 3
```

Using the `int` type is a signed integer, and as such positive and negative numbers are supported. Depending on the underlying architecture of a machine, `int` can either be a signed 32-bit integer or a signed 64-bit integer. Unless you are working with really big numbers, or have particular performance concerns, you can just use `int` without really worrying about what the compiler does.

Floats

Floats (or floating-point numbers) are numbers that have values either side of a decimal point. Examples of floating point numbers are 11.2, 0.1111, 43.22. Integers can only be whole numbers, so to work with fractions of whole numbers, you must use floats. Depending on the size of the number, floats in Go can either be 32-bit or 64-bit. For most modern CPUs, using `float64` is recommended.

```
var f float32 = 0.111
```

Strings

The string type is any sequence of characters that can be numbers, letters, and symbols. Some simple examples of strings are:

- cow

- $^%$

- a1234

Strings are implemented in almost all programming languages. They typically store pieces of data that include numbers, letters, or symbols. Initializing a string in Go is straightforward.

```
var s string = "foo"
```

The string type can also be empty, and this can be a useful programming construct to add data to a string from other variables or to hold temporary data.

```
var s string = ""
```

After a string variable is created, data may be added to a string but the value of the variable may not be overwritten. The following is permitted in Go where an empty string is initialized and then the string "foo" is added to it.

```
var s string = ""
s += "foo"
```

It is not possible to perform mathematical operations on a string, even if it looks like a number. In this case, it should be converted to a number type.

Hour 9, "Strings," covers strings.

Arrays

An array is another data type that is common to almost all programming languages. It is a slightly more sophisticated type in that it forms a collection of elements. To represent the members of a band, for example, an array of strings is a good choice. When initializing an array, both the length and type of an array must be specified.

```
var beatles [4]string
```

In this example, the number within the brackets represents the length of the string and is immediately followed by the type, which in this case is a string.

```
beatles[0] = "John"
beatles[1] = "Paul"
beatles[2] = "Ringo"
beatles[3] = "George"
```

Hour 6 covers arrays in more detail.

NOTE
_____

Arrays Start from Zero

You may have noticed that, in the variable declaration, the array length is given as "4", but that when accessing elements within an array, the index only goes up to "3". This may be confusing initially, but occurs because all counts in arrays start from zero.

_____

Checking the Type of a Variable

Occasionally, it may be necessary to check the type of a variable. This can be achieved with the `reflect` package in the standard library. This allows the underlying type of a variable to be accessed. For the majority of the time, the compiler will catch incorrect types. Using the `reflect` package (as shown in Listing 2.7) can be useful for debugging or if there is a requirement to verify the underlying type.

LISTING 2.7   Type Checking with the `reflect` Package
_____

```
 1:  package main
 2:
 3:  import (
 4:      "fmt"
 5:      "reflect"
 5:  )
 6:
 7:  func main() {
 8:      var s string = "string"
 9:      var i int = 10
10:      var f float32 = 1.2
11:
12:      fmt.Println(reflect.TypeOf(s))
13:      fmt.Println(reflect.TypeOf(i))
14:      fmt.Println(reflect.TypeOf(f))
15:  }
```

Checking Types

In this example, you understand how to check a type with the `reflect` package.

1. Open hour02/example07.go in the code examples for this book.

2. From the terminal, run the program with `go run example07.go`

3. You should see the types printed to the console.

```
string
int
float32
```

Converting Between Types

A common programming task is to take data in one type and convert it to another. Typically, this occurs when reading data from the network or a database. Go provides good support within the standard library for converting between types. For converting to and from strings the `strconv` package provides a full set of methods for type conversion.

Suppose that the variable s exists as a type string with the value `true`. To complete Boolean comparisons, the string must be converted into a Boolean type.

```
var s string = "true"
b, err := strconv.ParseBool(s)
```

The variable b is now a Boolean type. Similarly, a Boolean value can be converted to a string.

```
s := strconv.FormatBool(true)
fmt.Println(s)
```

Listing 2.8 shows an example of converting a Boolean type to a string.

LISTING 2.8   Converting and Checking Types

```
1:  package main
2:
3:  import (
4:      "fmt"
5:      "strconv"
6:      "reflect"
7:  )
8:
9:  func main() {
```

```
10:        var b bool = true
11:        fmt.Println(reflect.TypeOf(b))
12:        var s string = strconv.FormatBool(true)
13:        fmt.Println(reflect.TypeOf(s))
14:    }
```

▼ TRY IT YOURSELF

Converting Types

In this example, you learn how to convert a type using the `strconv` package.

1. Open the file hour02/example08.go in a text editor and try to understand what the example is doing.

2. From the terminal, run the program with `go run example08.go`.

3. You should see the types printed to the console showing that the Boolean type has been converted to a string type.

   ```
   bool
   string
   ```

TIP

Understanding Data Structures

Misunderstanding data types is a common source of bugs in programming. When working with a data source, take some time to understand data types before using them. If the data source is a database, look at the database schema and the data types in use. It could save you significant time debugging!

Summary

During this hour, you were introduced to data types. You learned the difference between strongly typed and dynamically typed languages as well as some pros and cons of these. You were introduced to some basic data types in Go before learning how to check the data type of a variable and convert between types. You have covered a lot in this hour, including some fundamentals of computing. In fact, it is time for a high five from a Gopher!

Renee French

Q&A

Q. Why is the string "1234" a string and not a number?

A. Regardless of whether a string looks like a number, it is a string type. To use it as a number, it must be converted to a number type.

Q. Can an array hold more than one data type?

A. Yes. Examples of this will appear in Hour 6.

Q. I'm familiar with languages like C. Do I need to worry about memory allocation in Go?

A. Go takes care of initializing memory and performs garbage collection. Although normal rules around memory usage apply, you do not need to manage it directly.

Workshop

The workshop contains quiz questions and exercises to help you solidify your understanding of the material covered. Try to answer all questions before looking at the "Answers" that follow.

Quiz

1. What are the strengths and weaknesses of using a strongly typed language?

2. Can you explain the difference between an unsigned integer and a signed integer?

3. How can you check the type of a variable?

Answers

1. A strongly typed language gives better data integrity, and often a compiler can catch bugs before the code is executed. Using a strongly typed language can be slower to develop and more rigid than using dynamic typing. Go is partly a reaction to strongly typed languages that are overly rigid and slow to compile. It aims to combine the speed and flexibility of dynamically typed languages with the performance and integrity of statically typed ones.

2. An unsigned integer has no "sign" to take up bytes. In a 4-bit integer, an unsigned integer has 16 possible numbers and can only be positive. A 4-bit signed integer still has 16 possible numbers, but they can be either negative or positive.

3. A type can be checked using the `reflect` package. For a refresher, refer to Listing 2.6.

Exercises

1. List the number types that you can recall from this chapter. Are you happy that you can explain to yourself the differences between types? Go back and refresh your understanding if necessary.

2. Create a short program that converts a `string` type variable to an `int` type variable and back again.

3. If you have time, watch Gary Bernhardt's talk titled *WAT*. It is a humorous look at dynamically typed languages, including JavaScript (https://www.destroyallsoftware.com/talks/wat). Take it with a pinch of salt!

HOUR 3
Understanding Variables

What You'll Learn in This Hour:

- ▶ What is a variable?
- ▶ Declaring shorthand variables
- ▶ Understanding variables and zero values
- ▶ Writing a short variable declaration
- ▶ Which style of variable declaration is best
- ▶ Using variable scope
- ▶ Using pointers
- ▶ Declaring variables with constants

Variables are a fundamental part of writing computer programs. During this hour, you learn about how to create variables and use them in Go programs. You are introduced to styles of declaring variables in Go and how variables are scoped.

What Is a Variable?

If you program in any language, it will not be long before you reach for a variable. A variable is simply a reference to a value, and is one of the foundations of being able to construct programming logic. In Go, declaring a variable can be achieved in a number of ways. In Hour 2, you learned how Go is a statically typed language. As such, when variables are declared, they either explicitly or implicitly are assigned a type. In Listing 3.1, a variable is initialized with the name of s type of `string`.

LISTING 3.1   Declaring a String Variable

```
 1:  package main
 2:
 3:  import (
 4:      "fmt"
 5:  )
 6:
 7:  func main() {
 8:      var s string = "Hello World"
 9:      fmt.Println(s)
10:  }
```

Listing 3.1 can be explained as follows:

1. A variable is initialized by using the `var` keyword.

2. The variable is assigned the name `s`.

3. The variable is assigned the type of `string`.

4. The = assignment operator signifies that the variable should be assigned a value of whatever is to the right of =.

5. The string literal `Hello World` is assigned to the variable `s`.

6. The `fmt` standard library package uses the variable name `s` as a reference to the value of `s` and passes it to the `PrintLn` method.

7. The value of `s` is printed.

In Listing 3.1, the assignment of a value occurred inline with the initialization of the variable. It is equally valid to declare a variable and assign a value to it later. In Listing 3.2, a variable is initialized and then assigned a value later in the code.

LISTING 3.2   Assigning a Value after Initializing a Variable

```
 1:  package main
 2:
 3:  import (
 4:      "fmt"
 5:  )
 6
 7:  func main() {
 8:      var s string
 9:      s = "Hello World"
10:      fmt.Println(s)
11:  }
```

As you learned in Hour 2, the type of a variable is important as it defines what values may be assigned to it. A variable with the type of `string`, for example, cannot be assigned an integer value. Similarly, a Boolean value cannot be assigned the value of a string type. If an incorrect value is assigned to a variable type, a compile time error will be thrown. In Listing 3.3, a string is assigned to a variable with the type `int`.

LISTING 3.3   Assigning an Incorrect Type to a Variable

```
 1:  package main
 2:
 3:  import (
 4:      "fmt"
 5:  )
 6:
 7:  func main() {
 8:      var i int
 9:      i = "One"
10:      fmt.Println(i)
11:  }
```

Running this example results in a compile-time error, because the code is trying to assign a string value to an integer type. Because the word "One" is not an integer type, it cannot be assigned to a variable with the type of integer.

```
go run example03.go
# command-line-arguments
./example03.go:7: cannot use "One" (type string) as type int in assignment
```

Declaring Shorthand Variables

Go supports several shorthand ways of declaring variables. Variables of the same type may be declared and assigned values on the same line, as shown in Listing 3.4.

LISTING 3.4   Shorthand Variable Declaration

```
 1:  package main
 2:
 3:  import (
 4:      "fmt"
 5:  )
 6:
 7:  func main() {
 8:      var s, t string = "foo", "bar"
 9:      fmt.Println(s)
10:      fmt.Println(t)
11:  }
```

Variables of different types may also be declared using the syntax in Listing 3.5.

LISTING 3.5   Shorthand Variable Declaration for Different Types

```
 1:   package main
 2:
 3:   import (
 4:       "fmt"
 5:   )
 6:
 7:   func main() {
 8:       var (
 9:           s string = "foo"
10:           i int = 4
11:       )
12:       fmt.Println(s)
13:       fmt.Println(i)
14:   }
```

After a variable is declared with a type, it is not possible to declare it again. Although reassigning the value is allowed, declaring a variable again is not permitted and results in a compile time error.

```
var s int = 1
fmt.Println(s)
// This is not permitted
var s string = "Hello World"
```

Understanding Variables and Zero Values

When a variable is initialized, it is assigned a value in Go. This value is known as a zero value. This is different from other languages where variables that are not assigned a value have the value of nil or undefined. Listing 3.6 demonstrates how variables are assigned a default value on initialization. What the value is depends on the type of the variable.

LISTING 3.6   Variable Zero Values

```
 1:   package main
 2:
 3:   import (
 4:       "fmt"
 5:   )
 6:
 7:   func main() {
 8:       var i int
 9:       var f float
```

```
10:        var b bool
11:        var s string
12:        fmt.Printf("%v %v %v %q\n", i, f, b, s)
13:    }
```

Initializing Variables with Zero Values

In this example, you will understand how Go initializes variables without values.

1. Open hour03/example06.go from the code examples for this book.

2. From the terminal, run the program with `go run example06.go`.

3. You should see the zero values for the variables printed to the console.

```
go run example06.go
0 0 false ""
```

The fact that Go makes this design decision is an important point to note when working with variables. Before too long, it is likely that you will need to check whether a variable has been assigned a value. Remember that checking whether a variable is `nil` will not work in Go. Instead, the default value should be checked. For a string, type the zero value after initialization is `""`. As such, for a variable with the type `string` the zero value of `""` can be checked to see if a value has been assigned (see Listing 3.7).

LISTING 3.7 Checking for Zero-Valued Variables

```
1:  package main
2:
3:  import (
4:      "fmt"
5:  )
6:
7:  func main() {
8:      var s string
9:      if s == "" {
10:          fmt.Printf("s has not been assigned a value and is zero valued")
11:      }
12:  }
```

Go forbids a `nil` value to be assigned when a variable is initialized. This causes a compile time error.

Writing a Short Variable Declaration

Where variables are declared with a function, Go supports a further shorthand version known as a short variable declaration. A short variable declaration is written as shown in Listing 3.8.

LISTING 3.8   Declaring a Variable in Short Variable Form

```
 1:   package main
 2:
 3:   import (
 4:       "fmt"
 5:   )
 6:
 7:   func main() {
 8:       s := "Hello World"
 9:       fmt.Println(s)
10:   }
```

Listing 3.8 can be explained as:

1. A variable is declared with the variable name s. Note the var keyword and type is not given.

2. The := short variable assignment operator indicates that short variable declaration is being used. This means that there is no need to use the var keyword or declare the variable type. It also means that the value to the right of := should be assigned to the variable.

3. The "Hello World" string literal will be assigned to s.

When using short variable declaration, the compiler infers the variable type, so there is no requirement to set it explicitly. Note that short variable declaration may only be used inside a function.

Styles of Variable Declaration

You may have noticed that Go offers several ways to declare a variable. For completeness, here are the ways that a variable can be declared:

```
var s string = "Hello World"
var s = "Hello World"
var t string
t = "Hello World"
u := "Hello World"
```

Which style should be used? There is some constraint enforced by the language here. It is not possible to use short variable declaration outside a function, but otherwise, anything goes.

Of course, how you use variables is a question of style and how you are using them. For declaring and assigning variables on the same line, the convention that the Go language authors mostly use in the standard library packages is short variable declaration inside functions to omit types outside of functions. The generally accepted way is to use short variable declaration, as shown in Listing 3.9. If you look at the Go source code, you see that short variable declaration is the most common way of declaring a variable.

LISTING 3.9   Idiomatic Variable Declaration

```
 1:  package main
 2:
 3:  import (
 4:      "fmt"
 5:  )
 6:
 7:  var s = "Hello World"
 6
 7:  func main() {
 8:      i := 42
 9:      fmt.Println(s)
10:      fmt.Println(i)
11:  }
```

TRY IT YOURSELF ▼

Idiomatic Variable Declaration

In this example, you will understand idiomatic variable declaration in Go.

1. Open hour03/example09.go from the code examples for this book. Try to understand the different types of variable declaration.

2. From the terminal, run the program with `go run example09.go`.

3. You should see the zero values for the variables printed to the console.

```
Hello World
42
```

Using Variable Scope

The term *scope* refers not to where a variable is declared but rather where it can be referenced. The Go language is *lexically scoped* using *blocks*. At first, this jargon can seem daunting, but it is important to understand how this works. The word *lexical* is an adjective meaning "relating to the vocabulary of a language." This means Go defines where variables can or cannot be referenced. This is useful when programming because, depending on the context of where a variable is used, it is possible to be certain of the reference. A block is defined in Go as "a possibly empty sequence of declarations and statements within matching brace brackets."

In plain English, this can be explained as:

► Brace brackets { } in Go denote a block.

► A variable declared within brace brackets { } may be accessed anywhere within the block.

► Brace brackets within brace brackets denote a new block, known as an inner block.

► Inner blocks can access variables within outer blocks.

► Outer blocks cannot access variables within inner blocks.

In short, every inner level (or block) can access its outer levels, but outer levels cannot access inner levels.

► Listing 3.10 shows that the structure of the program and the scope of variables is defined by brace brackets. Any new pair of brace brackets denotes a new block.

► The indentation of code reflects the level of block scope. For each block, the code is indented.

► Variables from outer blocks may be referenced within inner blocks.

LISTING 3.10   Lexical Scoping in Go

```
1:   package main
2:
3:   import (
4:       "fmt"
5:   )
6:
7:   var s = "Hello world"
8:
9:   func main() {
10:      fmt.Printf("Print 's' variable from outer block %v\n", s)
11:      b := true
12:      if b {
13:          fmt.Printf("Printing 'b' variable from outer block %v\n", b)
14:          i := 42
15:          if b != false {
16:              fmt.Printf("Printing 'i' variable from outer block %v\n", i)
17:          }
18:      }
19:  }
```

Note that the s variable is not within brace brackets but is available in inner blocks. This is because Go also considers a file a block, so anything outside of the first level of brace brackets in a file is available within all blocks.

Understanding Variable Scope

In this example, you will understand variable scope in Go.

1. Open hour03/example10.go from the code examples for this book. Try to understand the different types of variable declaration.

2. From the terminal, run the program with `go run example10.go`.

3. You should see variables from different scopes printed to the terminal.

```
Printing 's' variable from outer block Hello world
Printing 'b' variable from outer block true
Printing 'i' variable from outer block 42
```

Using Pointers

Pointers are another important point to grasp in relation to variables. When a variable is declared in Go, it is allocated a position in the computer's memory. This allows the value of the variable to be stored, modified, and retrieved. The address of the memory location on the computer may be retrieved by preceding a variable name with an ampersand & character. Listing 3.11 shows the memory location of a variable being printed to the terminal.

LISTING 3.11   Assigning a Value after Initializing a Variable

```
 1:  package main
 2:
 3:  import (
 4:      "fmt"
 5:  )
 6:
 7:  func main() {
 8:      s := "Hello World"
 9:      fmt.Println(&s)
10:  }
```

Running this code returns a sequence of letters and numbers that reference the memory location rather than the value of the variable.

Using a Pointer

In this example, you understand how to use a pointer.

1. Open hour03/example11.go from the code examples for this book.

2. From the terminal, run the program with `go run example11.go`.

3. You should see a memory location printed to the console.

   0xc42000e230

The sequence of numbers is in base 16 format. Do not worry if you do not understand what base 16 is. It is enough to understand that each variable has a different memory address where the value of the variable is stored. In Listing 3.12, an integer variable is passed to another function and the memory address of both variables is printed. Do you think the memory address will be the same?

LISTING 3.12   Passing Variables as Values

```
 1:  package main
 2:
 3:  import (
 4:      "fmt"
 5:  )
 6:
 7:  func showMemoryAddress(x int) {
 8:      fmt.Println(&x)
 9:      return
10:  }
11:
12:  func main() {
13:      i := 1
14:      fmt.Println(&i)
14:      showMemoryAddress(i)
15:  }
```

When this program is run, two memory addresses are shown.

```
go run example12.go
0xc42000a2e8
0xc42000a320
```

When a variable is passed to a function, a new memory allocation is made, and a copy of the value is written to it. There are now two instances of the variable in different memory locations. Generally, this is undesirable because it uses more memory, and there are now multiple copies of the original variable, making it easy to introduce bugs. To account for this, Go offers pointers. Pointers point to the memory location of a variable and are a type in Go. They are declared using the asterisk character immediately before the variable name. The previous example may be modified to use a pointer, as shown in Listing 3.13.

LISTING 3.13   Passing Variables as Pointers

```
 1:  package main
 2:
 3:  import (
 4:      "fmt"
 5:  )
 6:
 7:  func showMemoryAddress(x *int) {
 8:      fmt.Println(x)
 9:      return
10:  }
11:
12:  func main() {
13:      i := 1
14:      fmt.Println(&i)
14:      showMemoryAddress(&i)
15:  }
```

When this program is run, two memory addresses are shown:

```
go run example13.go
0xc42000a2e8
0xc42000a2e8
```

The modifications to the code may be explained as follows:

▶ The value passed to the showMemoryAddress is modified from i to &i. The preceding ampersand & means reference the memory address where the variable value is stored.

▶ The type of the first argument of the showMemoryAddress function is changed from an int to a *int. The preceding asterisk means that the type is now a pointer to an integer, rather than an integer.

▶ When the variable is printed within the showMemoryAddress function, there is no need to use an ampersand as it is a pointer.

What if the variable value of a pointer needs to be used rather than the memory address? This can be referenced by preceding a variable name of any pointer type with an asterisk.

```
func showMemoryAddress(x *int) {
    fmt.Println(*x)
    return
}
```

By using an asterisk, the value, rather than the memory address, is printed.

Declaring Variables with Constants

Constants represent values that do not change during the life of a program. They can be useful for declaring variables that never change. Once a variable has been initialized, it can be referenced but never changed. Listing 3.14 shows a constant being initialized and printed to the console.

LISTING 3.14 Declaring a Constant

```
 1:  package main
 2:
 3:  import (
 4:      "fmt"
 5:  )
 6:
 7:  const greeting string = "Hello, world"
 8:
 9:  func main() {
10:      fmt.Println(greeting)
11:  }
```

Attempting to change the value of a constant during a program results in an error. Listing 3.15 shows an example of attempting to change the value of a constant.

LISTING 3.15 Attempting to Change a Constant

```
 1:  package main
 2:
 3:  import (
 4:      "fmt"
 5:  )
 6:
 7:  const greeting string = "Hello, world"
 8:
 9:  func main() {
10:      greeting = "Goodbye, cruel world"
11:      fmt.Println(greeting)
12:  }
```

Running Listing 3.15 results in an error.

```
go run example15.go
# command-line-arguments
./example15.go:10: cannot assign to greeting
```

Summary

Much was covered in this hour. You learned many of the fundamental building blocks of Go, including how to declare a variable, including shorthand syntax. You learned about zero values in Go and how Go assigns default values to types. You learned about short variable declaration and preferred style for using variables. You learned about constants for values that never change. You learned the important concept of scope and where variables can be referenced. Finally, you learned about pointers and how variables are stored in memory.

Q&A

Q. There seem to a be a lot of styles of declaring a variable in Go. How do I know what to use?

A. A good way to understand Go conventions is to look at the source code of Go itself at https://golang.org/src/. Pick a package name you are familiar with and look through the code for examples of variables.

Q. Is it not dangerous to not declare a variable type? Maybe the compiler will get it wrong?

A. The Go compiler is great at dynamically inferring variable types if they are not explicitly declared. In the unlikely event that the compiler has a problem it will tell you.

Q. Memory is relatively new to me. Where can I learn more about this?

A. This lecture from Professor Mehran Sahami at Stanford University explores how memory works when programming (https://www.youtube.com/watch?v=W8nNdNZ4OEQ). Although it is focused on Java, much of it is relevant to Go.

Workshop

The workshop contains quiz questions and exercises to help you solidify your understanding of the material covered. Try to answer all questions before looking at the "Answers" section that follows.

Quiz

1. When can a short variable declaration := not be used?

2. What denotes a block in Go?

3. What is the purpose of a constant?

Answers

1. A short variable declaration may not be used outside of a function.

2. A block in Go is denoted by brace brackets {}. For completeness, there is also a file level block, package level block, and a universe block.

3. A constant is a value that should not change while the program is running. Examples of a constant include a tax code or a commission rate. These values should not change without the program being recompiled.

Exercises

1. Create a short program where you create a string variable and print it. On a new line, change the value of the string to something else and print it. Finally, on a new line, change the value of the string to an integer value like 42. What happens? Why does it happen?

2. To help cement your understanding of scope, modify example 10. Try to use a variable from an inner block in an outer block. What happens, and why? Reference some variables from an outer block within inner blocks and print them. Do you feel comfortable that you understand variable scope?

3. From memory, explain what happens when a variable is passed to a function. What does this mean in terms of memory? Why should you use pointers?

Using Functions in Go

What You'll Learn in This Hour:

► What a function is
► Defining variadic functions
► Using named return values
► Using recursive functions
► Passing off functions as values

Functions represent another core construct of not just Go but programming in general. During this hour, you learn about using functions in Go, beginning with a simple function that returns a single result. You will see how Go can return multiple results, accept a varying number of arguments, and how it displays some features that make it look somewhat like a functional programming language.

What Is a Function?

At a high level, a function takes an input and returns an output. As data flows through a function, it is transformed. A good example of this is a simple function to sum two numbers. This takes two numbers, adds them together, and returns the result. In this trivial example, the two numbers are said to be the inputs and the result of the sum is said to be the output.

```
func addUp(x int, y int) int {
    return x + y
}
```

Function Structure

Functions in Go give information to both the compiler and programmer about what the function will accept as an input and what to expect as an output. The first line of a function provides this information and is known as the function signature. Returning to the addUp function, this can be used to examine the structure of a function in Go.

```
func addUp(x int, y int) int {
    return x + y
}
```

The `func` keyword signifies that this is the beginning of a function. Next comes the name of the function. This is optional, but allows the function to be called (or used) elsewhere. The set of brackets declares the expected variables for this function. In this case, it is two numbers of the type `int` (a signed integer of at least 32 bits in size). After the closing bracket comes the return value, which is also an `int`. The opening brace signifies the start of the function body, which is terminated by the closing bracket. If the function signature declares a return value, the function body must end in a terminating statement. There is usually but not always a return value.

Returning a Single Result

Remember that at a basic level, a function takes an input and returns an output. An example of this is discovering whether a number is odd or even. Before implementing a function, it is useful to think for a moment about what the function does, what the inputs are, and what the return value will be. This helps in the design of functions and can also inform how to test a function. Programming languages often offer many ways to solve a problem, so being clear about the inputs and outputs of a function makes the implementation of the function less important from a design perspective.

For a function to discover if a number is odd or even, the following assumptions can be made about the function:

▶ The function takes a single argument that is an integer.

▶ The function returns a Boolean value that will be true if the integer is even and false if it is not.

Earlier, you learned about function signatures where the expected input and output types are declared. By taking a moment to think about the structure of the function, the function signature can now be written.

```
func isEven(i int) bool {
}
```

The function takes an input of an integer and returns a Boolean value with a name of `isEven`. With the function signature specified, the implementation can now be written. The function must assess whether an integer value is even, and return a Boolean. One way to achieve this is to use the modulus operator `%`. This takes an integer to the left of the operator, divides it by the number to the right of the operator, and returns the remainder. The function implementation can now be written.

```
Func isEven(i int) bool {
    return i%2 == 0
}
```

In designing functions, a programmer is limited only by the language and imagination. There are some important considerations to be aware of when writing more complex pieces of software or working in a team.

▶ The function does one thing and does it well. Software will inevitably change, and having many short functions that are composed together makes it easier for software to respond to change. This also helps to test individual functions and the software as a whole.

▶ Maintenance. If you are working in a team, do you think the function is easy to read and understand? If it is not, it may be overly complex or require some documentation. Remember that it may be you that revisits the function in the middle of the night in twelve months' time!

▶ Performance. Sometimes, the performance of a function is of paramount importance. A well-defined function allows programmers to change the implementation of a function and to run objective benchmarks on the performance of a function. In the isEven function, a caller of the function is not interested about the implementation so long as the function implements the function signature. This allows the implementation to be easily changed.

Listing 4.1 shows a function being declared and called.

LISTING 4.1   Calling a Function

```
 1:  package main
 2:
 3:  import "fmt"
 4:
 5:  func isEven(i int) bool {
 6:      return i%2 == 0
 7:  }
 8:
 9:  func main() {
10:      fmt.Printf("%v\n", isEven(1))
11:      fmt.Printf("%v\n", isEven(2))
12:  }
```

To call (or use a function), the function can be referenced by name and given any arguments it is expecting. In Listing 4.1, the isEven function is called twice, and the result is printed to the terminal. There is no limit to the number of times a function can be called.

Creating and Calling a Function

In this example, you will understand how to create and call a function.

1. Open hour04/example01.go from the code examples for this book.

2. Read the code and try to understand what it is doing.

3. From the terminal, run the program with `go run example01.go`.

4. You should see the following text printed to the terminal showing the function was called twice.

```
False
True
```

Returning Multiple Values

Go functions can return multiple results by declaring multiple return values in the function signature. This allows the terminating statement to return more than one value. In the following example, the function signature declares that the function takes no arguments and returns an int and a string. The return statement returns multiple values, separated by a comma.

```
func getPrize() (int, string) {
    i := 2
    s := "goldfish"
    return i, s
}
```

When calling the function, return values can be directly assigned to variables and used as expected.

```
func main() {
    quantity, prize := getPrize()
    fmt.Printf("You won %v %v\n", quantity, prize)
}
```

Listing 4.2 shows function returning multiple results.

LISTING 4.2   Returning Multiple Values from a Function

```
1:  package main
2:
3:  import "fmt"
4:
5:  func getPrize() (int, string) {
```

```
 6:        i := 2
 7:        s := "goldfish"
 8:        return i, s
 9:    }
10:    func main() {
11:        quantity, prize := getPrize()
12:        fmt.Printf("You won %v %v\n", quantity, prize)
13:    }
```

Defining Variadic Functions

Variadic functions are defined as a function of indefinite arity. In plain English, this means that they accept a variable number of arguments. In Go, it is possible to pass a varying number of arguments of the same type as referenced in the function signature. The syntax to specify this is three dots (. . .). In the following example, the function signature accepts an arbitrary number of arguments of the type int.

```
func sumNumbers(numbers ...int) int {
```

The function will accept one or more integers. It may be used to sum any number of integers and will return a single integer. Within the function, the numbers variable contains a slice of the argument. Do not worry if you do not know what a slice is; this is covered in Hour 6, "Working with Arrays, Slices, and Maps." The implementation of the function to sum any number of integers looks like this.

```
func sumNumbers(numbers ...int) int {
    total := 0
    for _, number := range numbers {
        total += number
    }
    return total
}
```

The function may now be used to sum a set of integers.

```
func main() {
    result := sumNumbers(1, 2, 3, 4)
    fmt.Printf("The result is %v\n", result)
}
```

Listing 4.3 shows variadic function being used to sum multiple numbers.

LISTING 4.3   Using a Variadic Function

```
 1:  package main
 2:
 3:  import "fmt"
 4:
 5:  func sumNumbers(numbers ...int) int {
 6:      total := 0
 7:      for _, number := range numbers {
 8:        total += number
 9:      }
10:      return total
11:  }
12:
13:  func main() {
14:      result := sumNumbers(1, 2, 3, 4)
15:      fmt.Printf("The result is %v\n", result)
16:  }
```

▼ TRY IT YOURSELF

Understanding Variadic Functions

In this example, you will understand how to use variadic functions.

1. Open hour04/example03.go from the code examples for this book.

2. Read the code and try to understand what it is doing.

3. From the terminal, run the program with `go run example03.go`.

4. You should see the following text printed to the terminal showing the function was called twice.

   `The result is 10`

5. Change the number of arguments passed to function and run the program again.

Using Named Return Values

Named return values allow a function to assign values to named variables before they are returned. This can be useful to make a function more explicit or readable. To use named return values, the function signature declares the variables as part of the return values.

```
func sayHi() (x, y string) {
```

This declares that there will be two values returned that are both of the type `string`. The signature also specifies variable names (x and y) that can be used to assign values within the function body.

```
func sayHi() (x, y string) {
    x = "hello"
    y = "world"
    return
}
```

Within the function, body values are assigned to the named variables before the terminating return statement. If you use named return values, there is no need to explicitly return the variables. This is known as a naked return statement.

```
func main() {
    fmt.Println(sayHi())
}
```

Calling the function returns the named variables in the order that they were declared.

```
hello world
```

Listing 4.4 shows an example of named return values.

LISTING 4.4   Named Return Values

```
 1:  package main
 2:
 3:  import "fmt"
 4:
 5:  func sayHi() (x, y string) {
 6:      x = "hello"
 7:      y = "world"
 8:      return
 9:  }
10:
11:  func main() {
12:      fmt.Println(sayHi())
13:  }
```

Understanding Named Functions

In this example, you will understand how to use named functions.

1. Open hour04/example04.go from the code examples for this book.

2. Read the code and try to understand what it is doing.

3. From the terminal, run the program with `go run example04.go`.

4. You should see the following text printed to the terminal.

   ```
   hello world
   ```

Using Recursive Functions

Although a simple concept, recursive functions are a powerful programming construct. Recursive functions are functions that can call themselves indefinitely or, more usually, until a particular condition is met. To use recursive functions, a function calls itself as the result value of a terminating statement.

```go
func feedMe(portion int, eaten int) int {
    eaten = portion + eaten
    if eaten >= 5 {
        fmt.Printf("I'm full! I've eaten %d\n", eaten)
        return eaten
    }
    fmt.Printf("I'm still hungry! I've eaten %d\n", eaten)
    return feedMe(portion, eaten)
}
```

In this example, the important thing to note is the last line of the function body. Instead of returning a value, the function calls itself and the function will be executed again. Typically, recursive functions call themselves until a particular condition is met. In this example, if the `eaten` variable is 5 or more, the function returns and stops calling itself.

Listing 4.5 shows an example of a function calling itself until a condition is met.

LISTING 4.5 Recursive Functions

```go
1:  package main
2:
3:  import "fmt"
4:
5:  func feedMe(portion int, eaten int) int {
6:      eaten = portion + eaten
```

```
 7:        if eaten >= 5 {
 8:            fmt.Printf("I'm full! I've eaten %d\n", eaten)
 9:            return eaten
10:        }
11:        fmt.Printf("I'm still hungry! I've eaten %d\n", eaten)
12:        return feedMe(portion, eaten)
13:    }
14:
15:    func main() {
16:        fmt.Println(feedMe(1, 0))
17:    }
```

Understanding Recursive Functions

In this example, you will understand how to use recursive functions.

1. Open hour04/example05.go from the code examples for this book.

2. Read the code and try to understand what it is doing.

3. From the terminal, run the program with `go run example05.go`.

4. You should see the following text printed to the terminal.

```
I'm still hungry! I've eaten 1
I'm still hungry! I've eaten 2
I'm still hungry! I've eaten 3
I'm still hungry! I've eaten 4
I'm full! I've eaten 5
```

Passing Functions as Values

Go has some features of functional languages, such as being able to pass functions as arguments to other functions. Although this may seem like an inception-like scenario, it offers powerful functionality. In essence, Go treats functions as a type like any other, so it is possible to assign functions to a value and call them at a later date. In the following example, a function is assigned to a variable fn.

```
func main() {
    fn := func() {
        fmt.Println("function called")
    }
    fn()
}
```

► A function is assigned to the variable `fn` using the shorthand variable assignment from Hour 3, "Understanding Variables."

► The function is declared and prints a line to show that it has been called.

► The function is called using `()` after the variable name.

Remember that functions are a type in Go, so they may be passed to another function. The previous example can be extended to pass the `fn` variable to another function where it is called, as shown in Listing 4.6.

LISTING 4.6 Passing a Function as an Argument

```
 1:  package main
 2:
 3:  import "fmt"
 4:
 5:  func anotherFunction(f func() string) string {
 6:      return f()
 7:  }
 8:
 9:  func main() {
10:      fn := func() string {
11:          return "function called"
12:      }
13:      fmt.Println(anotherFunction(fn))
14:  }
```

Note that the function signature contains a sub function signature. This shows that the function argument will be a function that will return a string. The receiving function still needs to declare what the return type will be (and it could be anything). In this case, it is also a string.

▼ TRY IT YOURSELF

Understanding Functions as Values

In this example, you will understand how to use functions as values.

1. Open hour04/example07.go from the code examples for this book.

2. Read the code and try to understand what it is doing.

3. From the terminal, run the program with `go run example07.go`.

4. You should see the following text printed to the terminal showing that the function was called after being passed as an argument.

```
function called
```

Summary

During this hour, you learned about how to use functions in Go. You learned about function signatures and basic functions. You saw how to return a single result, and then learned how to return multiple results before moving on to understand how to use variadic functions and named return values. Finally, you learned how functions can call themselves and how Go supports passing functions as arguments to other functions.

Q&A

Q. Can I modify the number of arguments and types for a function after it is declared?

A. No. Once a function is declared, the compiler takes the function signature and uses it to verify that the number of arguments and types are correctly used.

Q. Should I use named return functions?

A. *Named return functions* can be used for short functions but can make code more difficult to read; and in some cases, they are more prone to bugs. There is nothing bad about writing more verbose code, but only if it enhances maintainability and readability.

Q. Why are shorter functions favored?

A. Shorter functions have several advantages. They are more readable, easier to test, and allow the programmer to focus on the function doing one thing and doing it well. A single, large function can become monolithic and difficult to change.

Workshop

The workshop contains quiz questions and exercises to help you solidify your understanding of the material covered. Try to answer all questions before looking at the "Answers" section that follows.

Quiz

1. How many return values can a function have in Go?

2. What do you call a function that calls itself?

3. Can functions be passed as arguments in Go?

Answers

1. A function in Go can have one or more return values. Furthermore, the return values can be of different types.

2. A function that calls itself is known as a *recursive function*.

3. Yes, functions in Go can be passed as arguments to functions. Functions are considered a type like any other and may be passed around accordingly. Go is said to have "first-class functions" because functions may be passed as arguments to functions.

Exercises

1. Without writing any code, design a function to convert centigrade to Celsius. What are the inputs and outputs?

2. Write a function that calls itself ten times, then exits.

3. Write a function that takes two arguments and returns three.

HOUR 5
Using Control Flow

What You'll Learn in This Hour:

▶ Using `if`, `else`, and `else if` statements
▶ Using comparison operators
▶ Using arithmetic operators
▶ Using logical operators
▶ Using the `switch` statement
▶ Looping with `for` statements
▶ Using the `defer` statement

During this hour, you learn about control flow and how the flow of execution of code is determined. This allows you to construct programs that respond to data in different ways. To support this, you learn about the `if` statement and how to build up logic using comparison, methodical, and logical operators. You will understand how to use loops and to iterate over blocks of code multiple times. Finally, you are introduced to `defer` that allows a function to be executed after another function has finished.

Using the `if` Statement

The `if` statement is present in almost all programming languages and represents an important component of creating computer programs. In simple terms, an `if` statement evaluates a condition and then does something if it is true. The "if this then that" paradigm is allows programs to respond to data in different ways and for programmers to build up logic that can respond to different conditions. From command line programs to modern day computer games, the humble `if` statement powers both complex and simple logic trees. As you might expect, an `if` statement is simple to write in Go, as shown in Listing 5.1.

LISTING 5.1 `if` Statement

```
1:  package main
2:
3:  import (
4:      "fmt"
5:  )
6:
7:  func main() {
8:      b := true
9:      if b {
10:         fmt.Println("b is true!")
11:     }
12: }
```

Listing 5.1 can be explained as:

- A variable b is initialized and assigned the value of `true`. The type is inferred to be Boolean.

- An `if` statement evaluates whether b is `true`.

- Because the `if` statement evaluates to `true`, the code within the curly brackets is executed.

- A line is printed to the terminal to show that b is true.

▼ TRY IT YOURSELF

Using a Simple `if` Statement

In this example, you will understand how to use an `if` statement.

1. Copy the code in Listing 5.1, which is also available as example01.go in this book's code examples.

2. Read the code and try to understand what it is doing.

3. From the terminal, run the program with `go run example01.go`.

4. You should see the following text printed to the terminal.

   ```
   b is true!
   ```

If the value of b is changed to `false`, the `if` statement will evaluate to false and will not execute the code within the curly brackets, as shown in Listing 5.2.

LISTING 5.2   An `if` Statement that Evaluates to False

```
1:   package main
2:
3:   import (
4:       "fmt"
5:   )
6:
7:   func main() {
8:       b := false
9:       if b {
10:          fmt.Println("b is true!")
11:      }
12:  }
```

Multiple `if` statements can be run one after the other, and they will be evaluated in the order that they appear in the source code.

An `if` statement will always evaluate a Boolean expression and execute code within curly brackets if true; it will not if it is false. The simple `if` statement is a powerful paradigm, and it is possible to build sophisticated programs with just the `if` statement.

TRY IT YOURSELF ▼

Understanding an `if` Statement that Evaluates to False

In this example, you will understand what happens when an `if` statement evaluates to false.

1. Copy the code in Listing 5.2. This is also available as example02.go.

2. Read the code and try to understand what it is doing.

3. From the terminal, run the program with `go run example02.go`.

4. You should not see anything printed to the terminal, as the Boolean expression evaluated to false.

Using the `else` Statement

The `else` statement provides code to be executed if it is reached. It does not evaluate anything, so it will always be run if it is reached. If any of the statements that precede an `else` statement are true, it will not be run. `else` statements in Go follow the closing brackets of other statements and generally are the last statement in a block. The `else` statement basically says, "If nothing else is true, run this."

An `else` statement can be used to account for a scenario where preceding `if` statements do not evaluate to true. Listing 5.3 shows an example of an `else` statement being used.

LISTING 5.3   An `else` Statement

```
1:  package main
2:
3:  import (
4:      "fmt"
5:  )
6:
7:  func main() {
8:      b := false
9:      if b {
10:          fmt.Println("b is true!")
11:      } else {
12:          fmt.Println("b is false!")
13:      }
14:  }
```

If the `if` statement evaluates to true, the `else` will not be executed. An `else` statement represents a scenario that should be run if all the proceeding statements evaluate to false. If any of the proceeding statements are true, it will be ignored.

▼ TRY IT YOURSELF

Using an `else` Statement

In this example, you will understand how to use an `else` statement.

1. Copy the code in Listing 5.3. This is also available as example03.go in the code examples for this book.

2. Read the code and try to understand what it is doing.

3. From the terminal, run the program with `go run example03.go`.

4. You should see the following text printed to the terminal:

   `b is false!`

5. Change the value of b to be `true` and run the example again. Note how the `else` statement is ignored.

Using the else if Statement

There are frequently times where multiple Boolean expressions should be evaluated, one after the other. For these scenarios, the else if statement can be used. The else if statement allows subsequent Boolean expressions to be evaluated if previous Boolean expressions evaluate to false. This logic says that if the previous if or else if statement are false, try this other one. The else if statement immediately follows the closing bracket of an if or else if statement and provides another Boolean expression. It is possible to have multiple else if statements one after the other. Listing 5.4 shows an example of an else if statement.

LISTING 5.4   An else if Statement

```
1:   package main
2:
3:   import (
4:       "fmt"
5:   )
6:
7:   func main() {
8:       i := 3
9:       if i == 3 {
10:          fmt.Println("i is 3")
11:      } else if i == 2 {
12:          fmt.Println("i is 2")
13:      }
14:  }
```

Listing 5.4 can be explained as follows:

▶ A variable i is initialized and assigned the value of 2.

▶ The first if statement evaluates whether i is equal to 3. It is not, so the next line is ignored.

▶ The else if provides a second Boolean statement to evaluate whether i is equal to 2.

▶ As i is equal to two, the next line is executed and a line is printed to the terminal.

The fundamental difference between the else and the else if statement is that the else if statement allows a Boolean condition to be evaluated. The else will always execute the code if it is reached.

Using an `else if` Statement

In this example, you will understand how to use an `else` statement.

1. Copy the code in Listing 5.4. This is also available as example04.go in the code examples for this book.

2. Read the code and try to understand what it is doing.

3. From the terminal, run the program with `go run example04.go`.

4. You should see the following text printed to the terminal:

   ```
   i is 2
   ```

5. Change the value of `i` to be `3` and run the example again. Note how the `else if` statement is ignored as the first `if` statement evaluates to true.

Using Comparison Operators

Boolean evaluations simply return true or false but can be made to make more complex evaluations with comparison operators. These allow any data type to be compared with another of the same type and to return true if it matches the comparison and false if it does not. Some common comparisons that are made in programming include:

▶ Does one string match another?

▶ Are two numbers the same?

▶ Is one number greater than another?

▶ Is one number less than or equal to another?

Table 5.1 shows the comparison operators available in Go.

TABLE 5.1 Comparison Operators

Characters	Operator
==	Equal to
!=	Not equal to
<	Less than
<=	Less than or equal to
>	Greater than
>=	Greater than or equal to

An important point about comparison operators in Go is that they must be of the same type. It is not possible to compare a string with an integer, for example.

Using Arithmetic Operators

For any statement that offers a Boolean evaluation, it is possible to use basic arithmetic to enhance logic and evaluation. Arithmetic operators are frequently combined with a comparison operator to create a Boolean statement to manage control flow.

Some common arithmetic comparisons that are used in Boolean statements include:

▶ Does the sum of two numbers equal a particular number?

▶ Is the difference between two numbers greater than a particular number?

▶ Is one number divided by another equal to a particular number?

Table 5.2 shows commonly used arithmetic operators in Go.

TABLE 5.2   Arithmetic Operators

Character	Operator
+	Sum (also known as addition)
−	Difference (also known as subtraction)
*	Product (also known as multiplication)
/	Quotient (also known as division)
%	Remainder (also known as modulus)

Like comparison operators, arithmetic operators must compare the same type.

Using Logical Operators

Along with comparison and arithmetic operators, logical operators can be used to support control flow. Logic operators support three types of comparison.

Some common logical comparisons that are used in Boolean statements include:

▶ Are two variables both true?

▶ Does either of two variables evaluate to true?

▶ Is a variable not equal to a number?

Table 5.3 shows commonly used logical operators in Go.

TABLE 5.3 Logical Operators

Characters	Operator
&&	AND - if both conditions evaluate return true
||	OR - if either condition evaluates return true
!	NOT - if a condition does not evaluate return true

Using the `switch` **Statement**

Switch statements are an alternative way to express lengthy `if else` Boolean comparisons, as shown in Listing 5.5. Many programmers favor using `switch` statements over `if else` for readability, and at a compiler level the resulting code is also likely to be more efficient. For all but a few `if else` comparisons, the `switch` statement offers more readable code and better performance.

LISTING 5.5 A `switch` Statement

```
1:   package main
2:
3:   import (
4:       "fmt"
5:   )
6:
7:   func main() {
8:       i := 2
9:
10:      switch i {
11:      case 2:
12:          fmt.Println("Two")
13:      case 3:
14:          fmt.Println("Three")
15:      case 4:
16:          fmt.Println("Four")
17:      }
18:  }
```

Listing 5.5 can be explained as follows:

▶ A `switch` statement declares the variable to be evaluated as `i`.

▶ A series of case statements declare Boolean expressions that should be evaluated in relation to the variable `i`.

▶ If an expression is found to be true, the code within the expression is evaluated.

► If an expression is found to be not true, execution passes onto the next case statement.

► In this case, because `i` is equal to `true`, the word "Two" will be printed to the terminal.

Using a `switch` Statement

In this example, you will understand how to use a `switch` statement.

1. Copy the code in Listing 5.5. This is also available as example05.go in the code examples for this book.

2. Read the code and try to understand what it is doing.

3. From the terminal, run the program with `go run example05.go`.

4. You should see the following text printed to the terminal:

   Two

5. Change the value of `i` to be 3 and run the example again. Do you understand how a `switch` statement works?

`switch` offers a more succinct way to write `else if` conditions and can also support a default case to be executed if none of the case statements return true. This is similar to `else` conditions. Within a `switch` statement, the `default` keyword can be used to indicate a condition that should be executed if none of the cases match. Although a default condition is normally written as the last statement, it can appear anywhere within a switch statement. Listing 5.6 shows a default case being used within a `switch` statement.

LISTING 5.6 Adding a Default Case to a `switch` Statement

```
1:   package main
2:
3:   import (
4:       "fmt"
5:   )
6:
7:   func main() {
8:       s := "c"
9:
10:      switch s {
11:      case "a":
12:          fmt.Println("The letter a!")
13:      case "b":
14:          fmt.Println("The letter b!")
15:      default:
16:          fmt.Println("I don't recognize that letter!")
17:      }
18:  }
```

▼ TRY IT YOURSELF

Adding a Default Case to a `switch` Statement

In this example, you will understand how to use a default case to a `switch` statement.

1. Copy Listing 5.6. This is also available as example06.go in the code examples for this book.

2. Read the code and try to understand what it is doing.

3. From the terminal, run the program with `go run example06.go`.

4. You should see the following text printed to the terminal:

   `I don't recognize that letter!`

5. Change the value of s to be a and run the example again. Is the default case executed?

Looping with the `for` Statement

A `for` statement allows a block of code to be repeatedly executed. This is commonly known in programming as a loop, where a section of code is repeatedly executed until a certain condition is no longer true. A simple example of this is taking a number and incrementing it by 1 until it reaches a certain number (see Listing 5.7).

LISTING 5.7   Single Condition `for` Statement

```
 1:  package main
 2:
 3:  import (
 4:      "fmt"
 5:  )
 6:
 7:  func main() {
 8:      i := 0
 9:      for i < 10 {
10:          i++
11:          fmt.Println("i is", i)
12:      }
13:  }
```

Listing 5.7 can be explained as follows:

▶ A variable i is initialized and assigned the value of 0.

▶ A `for` statement evaluates whether i is less than 10.

▶ If the Boolean statement evaluates to true, the code within the `for` statement is executed.

► The i variable is incremented using the ++ increment operator.

► The value i is printed to the terminal.

► The execution returns to the Boolean expression, and i is evaluated as to whether it is less than 10.

► When i is no longer less than 10, the Boolean expression evaluates to false and code within the `for` statement is no longer executed and the loop stops.

Understanding the `for` statement

In this example, you will understand how to use a `for` statement.

1. Copy Listing 5.7. This is also available as example07.go in the code examples for this book.

2. Read the code and try to understand what it is doing.

3. From the terminal, run the program with `go run example07.go.`

4. You should see the following text printed to the terminal:

```
i is 1
i is 2
i is 3
i is 4
i is 5
i is 6
i is 7
i is 8
i is 9
i is 10
```

5. Note how the code loops until the value of i is no longer less than 10.

A `for` **Statement with** `init` **and** `post` **Statements**

As well as single conditions, the `for` statement can specify an `init` statement that will be run the first time, a condition to test, and a `post` statement. These are separated by a semicolon and allows iteration (or looping) code to become much shorter.

► `init` statement. This is run only once before the first iteration.

► Condition statement. This is a Boolean statement that will be evaluated on each iteration.

► `post` statement. This is evaluated after each iteration.

Listing 5.8 shows `init` and `post` statements being used with a `for` statement.

LISTING 5.8 A `for` Statement with `init` and `post` Statements

```
 1:  package main
 2:
 3:  import (
 4:      "fmt"
 5:  )
 6:
 7:  func main() {
 8:      for i := 0; i < 10; i++ {
 9:          fmt.Println("i is", i)
10:      }
11:  }
```

Listing 5.8 can be explained as follows:

▶ A variable `i` is initialized and assigned the value of 0.

▶ A `for` statement evaluates whether `i` is less than 10.

▶ If the Boolean statement evaluates to true, the code within the `for` statement is executed.

▶ The `i` variable is incremented using the ++ increment operator.

▶ The value `i` is printed to the terminal.

▶ The execution returns to the Boolean expression, and `i` is evaluated as to whether it is less than 10.

▶ When `i` is no longer less than 10, the Boolean expression evaluates to false and code within the `for` statement is no longer executed and the loop stops.

If you want to run this example, it is available as example08.go in the books, code examples.

`for` **Statements with a** `range` **Clause**

A `for` statement can also accept a data structure to loop over. In the following example, an array is created to hold a series of numbers. You learn about arrays in Hour 6, but in short, slices hold a sequence of grouped data types. Listing 5.9 shows a `for` statement with a `range` clause.

LISTING 5.9 A `for` Statement with a `range` Clause

```
 1:  package main
 2:
 3:  import (
 4:      "fmt"
```

```
 5:  )
 6:
 7:  func main() {
 8:      numbers := []int{1, 2, 3, 4}
 9:      for i, n := range numbers {
10:          fmt.Println("The index of the loop is", i)
11:          fmt.Println("The value from the array is", n)
12:      }
13:  }
```

Listing 5.9 can be explained as follows:

▶ The variable `numbers` is initialized and assigned a slice that contains four integers.

▶ The `for` statement assigns an iteration variable to the variable `i`. This will hold the index of the iteration. This is updated at the end of each loop.

▶ The `for` statement assigns an iteration variable to the variable n. This will hold the value from the slice for the iteration in the loop. This is also updated at the end of each loop.

▶ Within the loop, the value of each of these variables is printed.

A `for` statement with a `range` clause can be used to loop over most data structures in Go without needing to understand the length of the data.

TRY IT YOURSELF

Using a `for` Statement with a `range` Clause

In this example, you will understand how to use a `for` statement with a `range` clause.

1. Copy the code in Listing 5.9. This is also available as example09.go in the code examples for this book.

2. Read the code and try to understand what it is doing.

3. From the terminal, run the program with `go run example09.go`.

4. You will see the following text printed to the terminal:

```
The index of the loop is 0
The value from the slice is 1
The index of the loop is 1
The value from the slice is 2
The index of the loop is 2
The value from the slice is 3
The index of the loop is 3
The value from the slice is 4
```

Iteration Starts from 0

The iteration variable starts from zero and is incremented by one each time. If you want to do something at a particular iteration, make sure that you count from zero and not 1!

Using the `defer` Statement

Defer is a useful feature of Go that allows a function to be executed after a surrounding function returns. This can be triggered by a `return` statement or if a function has reached the end of the function body. The `defer` statement is typically used for cleanup operations or to ensure that operations like network calls have completed before running another function. Listing 5.10 shows a defer statement that will execute when the surrounding function returns.

LISTING 5.10   Executing a `defer` Statement

```
 1:   package main
 2:
 3:   import (
 4:       "fmt"
 5:   )
 6:
 7:   func main() {
 8:       defer fmt.Println("I am run after the function completes")
 9:       fmt.Println("Hello World!")
10:       }
11:   }
```

Listing 5.10 can be explained as follows:

- ► A `defer` statement is given a function to execute once the function completes.

- ► "Hello World!" is printed to the terminal and the function completes.

- ► Once the function has completed, the function given to the `defer` statement is executed.

Understanding `defer` Statements

In this example, you will understand how to use a `defer` statement:

1. Copy the code in Listing 5.10. This is also available as example10.go in the code examples for this book.

2. Read the code and try to understand what it is doing.

3. From the terminal, run the program with `go run example10.go`.

4. You should see the following text printed to the terminal:

```
Hello World!
I am run after the function completes
```

Listing 5.11 shows multiple `defer` statements and the order that they will be executed in.

LISTING 5.11   Multiple `defer` Statements

```
 1:  package main
 2:
 3:  import (
 4:      "fmt"
 5:  )
 6:
 7:  func main() {
 8:      defer fmt.Println("I am the first defer statement")
 9:      defer fmt.Println("I am the second defer statement")
10:      defer fmt.Println("I am the third defer statement")
11:      fmt.Println("Hello World!")
12:      }
13:  }
```

Listing 5.11 can be explained as follows:

▶ Three `defer` statements are each given a function to execute once the function completes.

▶ "Hello World!" is printed to the terminal and the function completes.

▶ Once the function has completed, the `defer` statements execute their functions in the reverse order that they were declared in the script.

Working with Multiple `defer` Statements

In this example, you will understand how multiple `defer` statements work.

1. Copy the code in Listing 5.11. This is also available as example11.go in the code examples for this book.

2. Read the code and try to understand what it is doing.

3. From the terminal, run the program with `go run example11.go`.

4. You should see the following text printed to the terminal:

```
Hello World!
I am the third defer statement
I am the second defer statement
I am the first defer statement
```

Summary

During this hour, you learned how to use control flow to construct logic. You learned how to construct execution flows using `if`, `else if`, and `else` statements. You then saw how comparison, arithmetic, and logical operators can be used to construct Boolean expressions to construct control flow. You were introduced to the `switch` statement as an alternative to `if`, `else if`, and `else`. You learned about the `for` statement and how to loop over blocks of code repeatedly based on a single condition, a `for` clause or `range` clause. Finally, you learned about `defer`, which allows a function to be executed after the containing function returns. You should have everything you need to construct basic control flow and much more!

Q&A

Q. Can I use more than one type of operator (e.g., comparison and arithmetic) to construct a Boolean expression?

A. Yes. A Boolean expression can be constructed with any number of operators. For example, it is possible to create a Boolean operator that returns true if a number is less than 4 (using a comparison operator) and not 1 (using a logical operator).

Q. Should I use `else if` or `switch`?

A. Both `else if` and `switch` are valid ways to create control flow. Many programmers find a `switch` statement easier to read than an `else if` chain. As such, using `switch` is recommended.

Q. Why would I want to use a `defer` statement over just using normal control flow?

A. Some examples of using `defer` include closing a file after it has been read, handling a response from a web server after it has been received, and requesting some data from a database when a connection has been established. When a function needs to run after something else has completed, `defer` is a good option.

Workshop

The workshop contains quiz questions and exercises to help you solidify your understanding of the material covered. Try to answer all questions before looking at the "Answers" section that follows.

Quiz

1. If there are two `if` statements and the first one evaluates to true, will the second be evaluated or ignored?

2. Can you explain what the `OR` logical operator does?

3. In what order are multiple `defer` statements executed once a function returns?

Answers

1. A second `if` statement will be evaluated regardless of the outcome of the first statement. To prevent the second `if` statement from being evaluated if the first one is true, it should be changed to an `else if` statement.

2. The OR logical operator will return true if either expression it is given returns true.

3. Multiple `defer` statements are executed in reverse order. This means the `defer` statements closest to the end of the function will be executed first.

Exercises

1. Write a program to evaluate an integer variable with a value of 88. Write an `if` statement to evaluate whether the number is less than 200 and print a line to the terminal if this evaluates to true.

2. Create an `if` statement to evaluate whether a number is greater than 5 and less than 10.

3. Create a `for` statement to loop over some code 20 times and then exit. Which of the three `for` statement variants did you choose? Why?

HOUR 6
Working with Arrays, Slices, and Maps

What You'll Learn in This Hour:

▶ Working with arrays
▶ Working with slices
▶ Adding and removing elements from a slice
▶ Working with maps

In this hour, you are introduced to some of the fundamental building blocks of Go. You learn how to initialize and assign values to elements in an array. You also learn about the difference between arrays and slices in Go. You learn how to add and remove elements from a slice before being introduced to maps. By the end of this hour, you will understand three data structures that are commonplace in Go programming.

Working with Arrays

An *array* is a data structure that is a collection of other pieces of data. An array is commonly used in programming to logically group pieces of data. Arrays are frequently used to store a numerically indexed group of data and represent a fundamental building block of programming.

To create an array in Go, the length and data type must be declared when initializing an array variable:

```
var cheeses [2]string
```

This may be explained as follows:

▶ The `var` keyword initializes a variable with the name of `cheeses`.

▶ An array is assigned to the variable and is given the length of two.

▶ The array is given the type of the type of string.

With the variable initialized, strings may now be assigned to the elements of the array:

```
cheeses[0] = "Mariolles"
cheeses[1] = "Époisses de Bourgogne"
```

The bracket after the variable name represents the position in the array that the value should be assigned to. The index starts at zero rather than one, so to access the first element of an array the index is "0". To access the second element of an array, the index is "1", and so on.

To print the values of an array, the variable and the index value can be used:

```
fmt.Println(cheeses[0])
fmt.Println(cheeses[1])
```

Furthermore, to print every element of an array, the variable name on its own can be used.

```
fmt.Println(cheeses)
```

Listing 6.1 shows an array being initialized and printed to the terminal.

LISTING 6.1   Initializing an Array

```
 1:   package main
 2:
 3:   import (
 4:       "fmt"
 5:   )
 6:
 7:   func main() {
 8:       var cheeses [2]string
 9:       cheeses[0] = "Mariolles"
10:       cheeses[1] = "Époisses de Bourgogne"
11:       fmt.Println(cheeses[0])
12:       fmt.Println(cheeses[1])
13:       fmt.Println(cheeses)
14:   }
```

Understanding how to Initialize an Array

In this example, you will understand how to initialize an array, assign values to elements, and print elements from an array.

1. Open hour06/example01.go from the code examples for this book.

2. Read the code and try to understand what it is doing.

3. From the terminal, run the program with `go run example01.go`.

4. You should see the following text printed to the terminal:

```
Mariolles
Époisses de Bourgogne
[Mariolles Époisses de Bourgogne]
```

Once the length of an array has been initialized, it is not possible to add more elements beyond the length that has been defined. Suppose that an additional value is added to the `cheeses` array at position three. What do you think will happen?

```
cheeses[2] = "Camembert"
```

Because the `cheeses` array has been declared to have two elements, it is not possible to assign a value to element three, and a compile time error is thrown.

```
./example02.go:9: invalid array index 2 (out of bounds for 2-element array)
```

Working with Slices

Arrays are an important part of Go, but it is much more common to see and use slices in Go. A *slice* is defined as a "contiguous segment of an underlying array and provides access to a numbered sequence of elements from that array." As such, slices provide access to parts of an array in sequential order. Why then do slices exist? Why not just use arrays?

Using arrays in Go has some limitations. You saw in the `cheeses` array that it was not possible to add additional elements to the array. Slices offer more flexibility than arrays in that it is possible to add, remove, and copy elements from a slice. Slices can be considered a lightweight wrapper around arrays that preserves the integrity of the array type but makes arrays easier to work with.

To declare an empty slice with a length of 2, the syntax is

```
var cheeses = make([]string, 2)
```

This may be explained as follows:

▶ The `var` keyword initializes a variable with the name of `cheeses`.

▶ To the right of the equals sign, the Go builtin `make` initializes a slice with the first argument representing the data type and the second argument representing the length. In this example, the slice contains two string elements.

▶ The slice is assigned to the `cheeses` variable.

With the slice initialized, values may now be assigned to it in the same way as working with an array.

```
cheeses[0] = "Mariolles"
cheeses[1] = "Époisses de Bourgogne"
```

Printing the values of a slice is also directly equivalent to working with an array.

```
fmt.Println(cheeses[0])
fmt.Println(cheeses[1])
```

So far, slices look similar to arrays. What is different about slices, however, is the ability to add and remove elements.

Adding Elements to a Slice

Go offers the builtin function `append` as a way to extend the length of a slice.

```
cheeses := append(cheeses, "Camembert")
fmt.Println(cheeses[2])
```

`append` resizes the array if necessary, but abstracts this complexity from the programmer. In this example, the slice is resized from two to three elements, and the value "Camembert" is assigned to the newly created element at index 2. In terms of the programming interface, programmers can just reference the element by the newly created index. The array has been resized and the value applied in a single line of code.

Listing 6.2 shows an additional element being added to a slice.

LISTING 6.2   Adding an Additional Element to a Slice

```
1:   package main
2:
3:   import (
4:       "fmt"
5:   )
6:
7:   func main() {
```

```
 8:         var cheeses = make([]string, 2)
 9:         cheeses[0] = "Mariolles"
10:         cheeses[1] = "Époisses de Bourgogne"
11:         cheeses = append(cheeses, "Camembert")
12:         fmt.Println(cheeses[2])
13:  }
```

TRY IT YOURSELF ▼

Understanding how to Add an Element to a Slice

In this example, you will understand how to add an element to an existing slice:

1. Open hour06/example03.go from the code examples for this book.

2. Read the code and try to understand what it is doing.

3. From the terminal, run the program with `go run example03.go`.

4. You should see the following text printed to the terminal:

   ```
   Camembert
   ```

The `append` function is also a variadic function. You learned about variadic functions in Hour Four and understood that variadic functions can take a varying number of arguments. This means that it is possible to append many values to a slice by using the `append` function.

```
cheeses := append(cheeses, "Camembert", "Reblochon", "Picodon")
```

This resizes the `cheeses` slice accordingly and assigns the values into the newly created elements as expected.

Listing 6.3 shows multiple elements being appended to a slice.

LISTING 6.3   Appending Multiple Elements to a Slice

```
 1:  package main
 2:
 3:  import (
 4:      "fmt"
 5:  )
 6:
 7:  func main() {
 8:         var cheeses = make([]string, 2)
 9:         cheeses[0] = "Mariolles"
10:         cheeses[1] = "Époisses de Bourgogne"
11:         cheeses = append(cheeses, "Camembert", "Reblochon", "Picodon")
12:         fmt.Println(cheeses)
13:  }
```

▼ TRY IT YOURSELF

Adding Multiple Elements to a Slice

In this example, you will understand how to add multiple elements to a slice.

1. Open hour06/example04.go from the code examples for this book.

2. Read the code and try to understand what it is doing.

3. From the terminal, run the program with `go run example04.go`.

4. You should see the following text printed to the terminal:

   [Mariolles Époisses de Bourgogne Camembert Reblochon Picodon]

Deleting Elements from a Slice

To delete an element from a slice, the `append` builtin may also be used. In the following example, the element at index 2 is to be deleted:

```
cheeses = append(cheeses[:2], cheeses[2+1:]...)
```

Checking the length of `cheeses` before and after the element has been deleted shows that it has been correctly resized. Furthermore, the ordering is correctly maintained.

Listing 6.4 shows an element being deleted from a slice.

LISTING 6.4   Deleting an Element from a Slice

```
 1:   package main
 2:
 3:   import (
 4:       "fmt"
 5:   )
 6:
 7:   func main() {
 8:       var cheeses = make([]string, 2)
 9:       cheeses[0] = "Mariolles"
10:       cheeses[1] = "Époisses de Bourgogne"
11:       cheeses[2] = "Camembert"
12:       fmt.Println(len(cheeses))
13:       fmt.Println(cheeses)
14:       cheeses = append(cheeses[:2], cheeses[2+1:]...)
15:       fmt.Println(len(cheeses))
16:       fmt.Println(cheeses)
17:   }
```

Copying Elements from a Slice

To copy all or some of the elements of a slice, the builtin function `copy` may be used. To copy elements from one slice to another, a slice must be initialized with the same type. It is not possible, for example, to copy elements from a slice of strings into a slice of integers. Listing 6.5 shows an element from one slice being copied to another.

LISTING 6.5   Copying Elements from One Slice to Another

```
 1:  package main
 2:
 3:  import (
 4:      "fmt"
 5:  )
 6:
 7:  func main() {
 8:      var cheeses = make([]string, 3)
 9:      cheeses[0] = "Mariolles"
10:      cheeses[1] = "Époisses de Bourgogne"
11:      var smellyCheeses = make([]string, 2)
12:      copy(smellyCheeses, cheeses)
13:      fmt.Println(smellyCheeses)
14:  }
```

The `copy` function makes a copy of elements in the new slice, so if at a later date the elements in one slice are modified this will have no effect on the other slice. It is also possible to copy single elements or a range of elements into a new slice. In the following example, the element at index 1 will be copied.

```
copy(smellyCheeses, cheeses[1:])
```

TRY IT YOURSELF ▼

Understanding how to Copy Elements from One Slice to Another

In this example, you will understand how to copy elements from one slice to another.

1. Open hour06/example06.go from the code examples for this book.

2. Read the code and try to understand what it is doing.

3. From the terminal, run the program with `go run example06.go`.

4. You should see the following text printed to the terminal:

   ```
   [Mariolles Époisses de Bourgogne]
   ```

Working with Maps

Arrays and slices are a collection of elements that may be accessed by an index value. A map is an unordered group of elements that is accessed by a key rather than an index value. While the word *array* is common to most programming languages, a map can often be known as associative array, dictionary, or hash if you have experience in other programming languages. Maps can be very efficient in looking up pieces of information, as the data can be retrieved directly through the key. In simple terms, maps can be considered a collection of keys and values.

An empty map can be initialized in a single line of code.

```
var players = make(map[string]int)
```

This may be explained as follows:

▶ The `var` keyword initializes a variable with the name of `players`.

▶ To the right of the equals sign, the Go builtin `make` initializes a map, with the key type being a string and the value type being an integer.

▶ The empty map is assigned to the player's variable.

Key value pairs can now be assigned into the empty map.

```
players["cook"] = 32
players["bairstow"] = 27
players["stokes"] = 26
```

The bracket after the variable name represents the key value. To the right of the equals sign is the integer value that will be assigned to the key.

To print the value of a key in a map, the key is referenced to retrieve the value.

```
fmt.Println(players["cook"])
fmt.Println(players["stokes"])
```

Just as with arrays and slices, to print every key value pair of the map, the variable name on its own can be used.

```
fmt.Println(players)
map[cook:32 bairstow:27 stokes:26]
```

Listing 6.6 shows a map being initialized and values being added into it.

LISTING 6.6   Initializing a Map

```
 1:  package main
 2:
 3:  import (
 4:      "fmt"
 5:  )
 6:
 7:  func main() {
 8:      var players = make(map[string]int)
 9:      players["cook"] = 32
10:      players["bairstow"] = 27
11:      players["stokes"] = 26
12:      fmt.Println(players["cook"])
13:      fmt.Println(players["bairstow"])
14:  }
```

Elements can be added dynamically to a map, and there is no need to resize it. This is an example of one feature of Go where the behavior of the language is more like a dynamic programming language like Ruby or Python than a C-like language.

Deleting Elements from a Map

To delete elements from a map, the delete builtin function can be used.

```
delete(players, "cook")
```

To remove a key value combination from the map, pass the map and the key name to the delete function. In Listing 6.7, the element with the key cook is removed from the map.

LISTING 6.7   Removing an Element from a Map

```
 1:  package main
 2:
 3:  import (
 4:      "fmt"
 5:  )
 6:
 7:  func main() {
 8:      var players = make(map[string]int)
 9:      players["cook"] = 32
10:      players["bairstow"] = 27
11:      players["stokes"] = 26
12:      delete(players, "cook")
13:      fmt.Println(players)
14:  }
```

▼ TRY IT YOURSELF

Understanding how to Delete an Element from a Map

In this example, you will understand how to delete an element from a map.

1. Open hour06/example08.go from the code examples for this book.

2. Read the code and try to understand what it is doing.

3. From the terminal, run the program with `go run example08.go`.

4. You should see that the map contains two key value pairs:

```
map[bairstow:27 stokes:26]
```

Summary

This hour introduced you to arrays, slices, and maps. You learned how to initialize and assign values to elements in arrays. You saw how it is difficult to resize arrays and how slices offer a convenient alternative. You learned about slices and understood how to add and remove elements from a slice. Finally, you were introduced to maps that are also known as dictionaries or hashes in other languages. You saw how to create key value elements and also how to remove a key and the associated value from a map. Although this hour was more theoretical than practical, arrays, slices, and maps represent fundamental building blocks for programming in Go.

Q&A

Q. Should I use an array or a slice?

A. Unless you know that you should specifically use an array, use a slice. Slices provide a convenient way to add and remove items and abstract any need to work directly with memory allocation.

Q. Is there no builtin function to remove an item from a slice?

A. You cannot use `delete` on a slice. Although it may seem strange that there is no dedicated function for removing an element from a slice, this is possible using the `append` builtin function or creating a subslice.

Q. Do I need to specify the length of a slice?

A. No. It is possible to add a second argument when initializing a map with the `make` builtin function, but this is a capacity hint rather than a hard limit. Maps can grow to accommodate the number of items stored in them, and there is no need to specify the length.

Workshop

The workshop contains quiz questions and exercises to help you solidify your understanding of the material covered. Try to answer all questions before looking at the "Answers" section that follows.

Quiz

1. Can you resize an array in Go?

2. Which index number is used to access the fourth element of an array?

3. Which builtin function can be used to resize a slice?

Answers

1. Without creating a new array from an existing one, it is not possible to resize an array. If you want to have a dynamically resizable array, use a slice instead.

2. To access the fourth element of an array, the index is 3. Remember that an index in an array starts from 0!

3. The `append` builtin function can be used to add elements to a slice.

Exercises

1. Modify example01.go in this book's code examples to include (a) cheese(s) that you like. Make sure that the initial array is initialized to a size that is big enough to take your cheese!

2. Create a slice with four elements. Create a new slice and copy the third and fourth elements only into it.

3. Create a map from the following list of HTML elements. Think about the types that need to be initialized for the keys and values.

   ▶ p - Paragraph

   ▶ img - Image

   ▶ h1 - Heading One

   ▶ h2 - Heading Two

Using Structs and Pointers

What You'll Learn in This Hour:

- ► What a struct is
- ► Initializing a struct
- ► Nesting structs
- ► Creating default values for structs
- ► Comparing structs
- ► Understanding public and private values
- ► Differentiating between pointers and value references

As its name suggests, a *struct* is a structure of data elements that is a useful programming construct. This hour introduces you to structs and the various ways to initialize them. You will understand how default values are assigned and how to assign a custom default value to data fields. You will see how to compare structs and learn about exported values. Finally, you will learn the subtle difference between using pointers and values in relation to underlying memory. By the end of this hour, you will have a good understanding of structs and how to create and use them.

What Is a Struct?

A *struct* is a collection of data fields with declared data types. Structs provide a way to reference a series of grouped values through a single variable name. This allows many different data fields of possibly different types to be stored and accessed under a single variable. Values stored within structs can be easily accessed and changed, providing a rich way to create data structures. Structs can improve modularity and allow complex data structures to be created and passed around. Structs can also be thought of as a template for creating a data record, like an employee record or an airline booking.

Listing 7.1 shows a simple struct being declared and initialized.

LISTING 7.1   Declaring and Initializing a Struct

```
1:   package main
2:
3:   import (
4:       "fmt"
5:   )
6:
7:   type Movie struct {
8:       Name    string
9:       Rating float32
11:  }
12:
13:  func main() {
14:      m := Movie{
15:          Name:  "Citizen Kane",
16:          Rating: 10,
17:      }
18:      fmt.Println(m.Name, m.Rating)
19:  }
```

Listing 7.1 can be explained as follows:

▶ The `type` keyword specifies a new type.

▶ The variable name of the type is specified as `Movie`.

▶ To the right of the name of the type is the data type. Here this is specified as a struct.

▶ Within the curly brackets, a series of data fields are specified with a name and a type. Note that no values are assigned at this point. Think of it like a template.

▶ In the `main` function, a variable `m` is initialized through shorthand variable assignment, and values are assigned to the data fields according to their types.

▶ The data fields are accessed using dot notation and printed to the console.

To access data types within a struct, dot notation can be used meaning the struct variable name, followed by a period, followed by the name of the data element to be accessed.

Initializing a Struct and Accessing Values

In this example, you will understand how to initialize a struct and access values.

1. Open hour07/example01.go from the code examples for this book.

2. Read the code and try to understand what it is doing.

3. From the terminal, run the program with `go run example01.go`.

4. You should see the following text printed to the terminal:

   ```
   Citizen Kane 10
   ```

Initializing a Struct

Once a struct has been declared, it can be initialized in a number of ways. Assuming that a struct has been declared, it can be simply assigned to a variable.

```
type Movie struct {
    Name    string
    Rating float32
}

var m Movie
```

This creates an instance of the struct with default values assigned to the specified data types. A useful tip for debugging and viewing the values of structs is to use the `fmt` package to print out the field names and values for a struct. This can be achieved using the `%+v` verb and passing a struct.

```
fmt.Printf("%+v\n", m)
```

This will print the field names and values to the terminal. Go will assign zero values for each type if a struct is initialized without values.

```
{Name: Rating:0}
```

After an instance of a struct is created in this way, values may be assigned directly to the fields as expected, using dot notation.

```
var m Movie
m.Name = "Metropolis"
m.Rating = 0.99
```

Values of struct fields are mutable, meaning they can be changed dynamically. If, for example, you want to change the name of the movie, this is allowed. It is not possible, however, to change the types in a struct after it has been declared or an instance has been created. This will result in a compile time error. Listing 7.2 shows an example of a struct being created and being assigned to a variable, and then values being assigned to data fields.

LISTING 7.2   Initializing a Struct Using a Variable

```
 1:  package main
 2:
 3:  import (
 4:      "fmt"
 5:  )
 6:
 7:  type Movie struct {
 8:      Name    string
 9:      Rating float32
10:  }
11:
12:  func main() {
13:      var m Movie
14:      fmt.Printf("%+v\n", m)
15:      m.Name = "Metropolis"
16:      m.Rating = 0.9918:
17:      fmt.Printf("%+v\n", m)
18:  }
```

Listing 7.2 can be explained as follows:

▶ The `var` keyword initializes a variable m.

▶ The zero values for the fields are set, as no values are given. For a string, this is an empty string "", and for a float32 this is 0.

▶ These values are printed to the terminal.

▶ Using dot notation, values are assigned to the struct fields.

▶ The struct is again printed to the terminal, showing the values have been assigned.

Initializing a Struct Using a Variable

In this example, you will understand how to initialize a struct using a variable.

1. Open hour07/example02.go from the code examples for this book.

2. Read the code and try to understand what it is doing. If necessary, refer to Listing 7.2.

3. From the terminal, run the program with `go run example02.go`.

4. You should see the following text printed to the terminal:

   ```
   {Name: Rating:0}
   ```

An instance of a struct can also be created with the `new` keyword, as shown in Listing 7.3. The `new` keyword allocates memory storage for a variable of a type `Movie` and assigns it to `m`. It is then possible to assign data values to the data fields as before, using dot notation.

```
m := new(Movie)
m.Name = "Metropolis"
m.Rating = 0.99
```

LISTING 7.3 Initializing a Struct Using **new**

```
 1:  package main
 2:
 3:  import (
 4:      "fmt"
 5:  )
 6:
 7:  type Movie struct {
 8:      Name    string
 9:      Rating float32
10:  }
11:
12:  func main() {
13:      m := new(Movie)
14:      m.Name = "Metropolis"
15:      m.Rating = 0.99
16:      fmt.Printf("%+v\n", m)
17:  }
```

It is also possible to create a struct using short variable assignment. This omits the `new` keyword. Values can also be assigned to fields in structs when an instance is created using the element name, followed by a colon and then the value.

```
c := Movie{Name: "Citizen Kane", Rating: 10}
```

It is possible to omit the field names and assign values in the order they are declared, although for maintainability this is not recommended.

```
c := Movie{"Citizen Kane", 10}
```

As field lists grow, it can also help maintenance and readability to put fields on a new line. Note that if you choose to do this, the line of the last data field must end in a comma.

```
c := Movie {
    Name: "Citizen Kane",
    Rating: 10,
}
```

Using short variable assignment is the most common—and recommended—way of creating a struct (see Listing 7.4).

LISTING 7.4   Initializing a Struct Using Short Variable Assignment

```
 1:   package main
 2:
 3:   import (
 4:       "fmt"
 5:   )
 6:
 7:   type Movie struct {
 8:       Name    string
 9:       Rating float32
10:   }
11:
12:   func main() {
13:       m := Movie{
14:           Name: "Metropolis",
15:           Rating: 0.99,
16:       }
17:       fmt.Printf("%+v\n", m)
18:   }
```

TRY IT YOURSELF ▼

Initializing a Struct Using Shorthand Variable Assignment

In this example, you will understand how to initialize a struct using shorthand variable assignment.

1. Open hour07/example05.go from the code examples for this book.

2. Read the code and try to understand what it is doing.

3. From the terminal, run the program with `go run example05.go`.

4. You should see the following text printed to the terminal:

   ```
   {Name:Metropolis Rating:0.99}
   ```

DID YOU KNOW?

Structs Are a Feature of C-like Languages

Structs are commonly used in C and C++ and, as a C-family language, Golang also has structs. Structs are not a way to create classes or object-oriented code. Structs are a way to create data structures that are relevant to the data you are trying to model.

Nesting Structs

Sometimes, data structures need more than one level of elements. Although you might choose to use a data type, like a slice, there are times when a data structure is more complex. Nesting one struct within another can be a useful way to model more complex structures. One example of this is a list of superheroes where an address needs to be stored for each superhero. An address can be considered its own data structure, and maps well to a struct.

```
type Superhero struct {
    Name    string
    Age     int
    Address Address
}

type Address struct {
    Number int
    Street string
    City   string
}
```

When initializing a `Superhero` struct, the `Address` struct will be embedded and assigned default values. This can improve flexibility and modularity in that the `Address` struct can also be used elsewhere.

The address can be initialized and assigned values before the Superhero struct, but initializing inline is also supported. Listing 7.5 shows a nested struct being initialized inline using short variable assignment.

LISTING 7.5 Initializing a Nested Struct Using Shorthand Variable Assignment

```
1:  package main
2:
3:  import (
4:      "fmt"
5:  )
6:
7:  type Superhero struct {
8:      Name    string
9:      Age     int
10:     Address Address
11: }
12:
13: type Address struct {
14:     Number int
15:     Street string
16:     City   string
17: }
18:
19: func main() {
20:     e := Superhero{
21:         Name: "Batman",
22:         Age:  32,
23:         Address: Address{
24:             Number: 1007,
25:             Street: "Mountain Drive",
26:             City:   "Gotham",
27:         },
28:     }
29:     fmt.Printf("%+v\n", m)
30: }
```

To access data elements of nested structs, dot notation can be used. This means the accessing data through variable name of the struct followed by a period, followed by the name of the data element, another period, and then the name of the nested data element, as shown here:

```
fmt.Println(e.Address.Street)
```

Using Nested Structs

In this example, you will understand how to use nested structs.

1. Open hour07/example06.go from the code examples for this book.

2. Read the code and try to understand what it is doing.

3. From the terminal, run the program with `go run example06.go`.

4. You should see the following text printed to the terminal:

   ```
   {Name:Batman Age:32 Address:{Number:1007 Street:Mountain Drive City:Gotham}}
   ```

Creating Default Values for Structs

When creating data structures, it can be useful to create default values for data elements. By default, Go assigns the zero value for a type. Table 7.1 lists zero values.

TABLE 7.1 Zero Values in Go

Type	Value
Boolean	false
Integer	0
Float	0.0
String	""
Pointer	nil
Function	nil
Interface	nil
Slice	nil
Channel	nil
Maps	nil

If a struct element is initialized without a value, the relevant default value from Table 7.1 is assigned. Although Go has no native method of assigning a custom default value, this can be achieved through a constructor function. This wraps the creation of the struct and assigns a default value if none is provided.

```
type Alarm struct {
    Time string
    Sound string
}

func NewAlarm(time string) Alarm {
    a := Alarm{
        Time:  time,
        Sound: "Klaxon",
    }
    return a
}
```

Instead of creating a struct directly, the `NewAlarm` function can be used to create an `Alarm` struct with a custom default value for the `Sound` field. Note that this is a technique rather than something that is part of the Golang specification. If an instance of the `Alarm` struct is created directly without a value being assigned for the `Sound` element, a default value of `""` would have been assigned. By wrapping the creation of the struct in a constructor function, the value of `Klaxon` is assigned. Note that the value of the `Sound` element can easily be overridden, so this method should be considered a way to create an initial default value rather than a constant value. Listing 7.6 shows an example of initializing a constant with a custom default value.

LISTING 7.6   Setting Default Values Using a Constructor Function

```
 1:  package main
 2:
 3:  import (
 4:      "fmt"
 5:  )
 6:
 7:  type Alarm struct {
 8:      Time    string
 9:      Sound    bool
10:  }
11:
12:  func NewAlarm(time string) Alarm {
13:      a := Alarm{
14:          Time:  time,
15:          Sound: "Klaxon",
16:      }
17:      return a
18:  }
19:
20:  func main() {
21:      fmt.Printf("%+v\n", NewAlarm("07:00"))
22:  }
```

Setting Default Values Using a Constructor Function

In this example, you will understand how to set default values on a struct using a constructor function.

1. Open hour07/example07.go from the code examples for this book.

2. Read the code and try to understand what it is doing.

3. From the terminal, run the program with `go run example07.go`.

4. You should see the following text printed to the terminal:

   `{Time:07:00 Sound:Klaxon}`

Comparing Structs

It can be useful to compare structs to see if they are the same type and whether they have the same values. Structs of the same type can be compared using Go's equality operators. To assess whether structs are the same, == can be used to test for equality and != to test for inequality. Listing 7.7 shows two structs being created that have the same values assigned to data elements. As they are equivalent, the comparison operator evaluates to true.

LISTING 7.7   Comparing Structs with the Same Values Assigned to Data Elements

```
 1:  package main
 2:
 3:  import (
 4:      "fmt"
 5:  )
 6:
 7:  type Drink struct {
 8:      Name     string
 9:      Ice      bool
10:  }
11:
12:  func main() {
13:      a := Drink{
14:          Name: "Lemonade",
15:          Ice:  true,
16:      }
17:      b := Drink{
18:          Name: "Lemonade",
19:          Ice:  true,
20:      }
```

```
21:        if a == b {
22:            fmt.Println("a and b are the same")
23:        }
24:        fmt.Printf("%+v\n", a)
25:        fmt.Printf("%+v\n", b)
26:    }
```

▼ TRY IT YOURSELF

Testing Structs for Equivalence

In this example, you will understand how to test structs for equivalence.

1. Open hour07/example08.go from the code examples for this book.

2. Read the code and try to understand what it is doing.

3. From the terminal, run the program with `go run example08.go`.

4. You should see the following text printed to the terminal:

   ```
   a and b are the same
   {Name:Lemonade Ice:true}
   {Name:Lemonade Ice:true}
   ```

It is not possible to compare structs of different types, and attempting to do so will result in a compile time error. As such, it can be necessary to check that structs are of the same type before attempting a comparison. Go's `reflect` package supports this and allows the underlying type of a struct to be interrogated. Listing 7.8 shows the `reflect` package being used to show the underlying type of a struct being shown.

LISTING 7.8   Checking the Type of Struct

```
 1:    package main
 2:
 3:    import (
 4:        "fmt"
 5:        "reflect"
 6:    )
 7:
 8:    type Drink struct {
 9:        Name     string
10:        Ice      bool
11:    }
12:
```

```
13:   func main() {
14:       a := Drink{
15:           Name: "Lemonade",
16:           Ice:  true,
17:       }
18:       b := Drink{
19:           Name: "Lemonade",
20:           Ice:  true,
21:       }
22:       fmt.Printf(reflect.TypeOf(a))
23:       fmt.Printf(reflect.TypeOf(b))
24:   }
```

Checking the Type of a Struct

In this example, you will check the type of a struct.

1. Open hour07/example09.go from the code examples for this book.

2. Read the code and try to understand what it is doing.

3. From the terminal, run the program with `go run example09.go`.

4. You should see the following text printed to the terminal:

   ```
   main.Drink
   main.Drink
   ```

Understanding Public and Private Values

If you are familiar with other programming languages, you may understand the idea of public and private values. This is where a value is public if it is exported and is available outside of a function, method, or package. If a value is private, it is only available within its context. You learn more about packaging and exporting values in Hour 13, "Using Packages to Reuse Code."

Both structs and elements within structs can be exported or not exported according to the Go convention. This is so that identifiers that start with an uppercase letter are exported, and those without are not.

For the struct and elements within it to be exported, the struct name and the elements within it must begin with an uppercase letter.

Differentiating Between Pointer and Value References

When working with structs, it is important to understand the difference between pointer and value references. This is also relevant in Hour 8, where you add methods to a struct.

You may remember from Hour 3 that data values are stored in the computer's memory. A pointer holds the memory address of a value, meaning that when it is referenced, it is possible to read or write the value that has been stored. When a struct is initialized, memory is allocated for the data elements and their default values in the struct. A pointer to this memory is returned, and this is assigned to a variable name. Using shorthand variable assignment, memory is allocated, and default values are assigned.

```
a := Drink{}
```

If you want to copy the struct, there is an important distinction to understand in terms of memory. When the variable that references the struct is assigned to another value, it is known as value assignment.

```
a := b
```

At the point that it is assigned, b will be the same as a, but notably it is a copy of a rather than a reference to it. Any changes made to b will not be applied to a and vice versa. This behavior is shown in Listing 7.9.

LISTING 7.9   Copying a Struct Using a Value Reference

```
 1: package main
 2:
 3: import (
 4:     "fmt"
 5:     "reflect"
 6: )
 7:
 8: type Drink struct {
 9:     Name    string
10:     Ice     bool
11: }
12:
13: func main() {
14:     a := Drink{
15:         Name: "Lemonade",
16:         Ice:  true,
17:     }
18:     b := a
```

```
19:        b.Ice = false
20:        fmt.Printf("%+v\n", b)
21:        fmt.Printf("%+v\n", a)
22:        fmt.Printf("%p\n", &a)
23:        fmt.Printf("%p\n", &b)
24:    }
```

Listing 7.9 can be explained as follows:

▶ A `Drink struct` type is declared.

▶ An instance of the `Drink struct` is created and assigned to the variable a.

▶ A new variable b is created and has a assigned to it.

▶ The `Ice` data field on b is changed.

▶ The values of b are printed to the terminal.

▶ The values of a are printed to the terminal, showing that the change to b has not affected a.

▶ Using `fmt.Printf`, the underlying memory addresses of a and b are printed to the terminal. These show that each variable has a separate memory address.

TRY IT YOURSELF ▼

Copying a Struct Using a Value Reference

In this example, you will understand how to copy a struct using a value reference.

1. Open hour07/example10.go from the code examples for this book.

2. Read the code and try to understand what it is doing.

3. From the terminal, run the program with `go run example10.go`.

4. You should see the following text printed to the terminal:

```
{Name:Lemonade Ice:false}
{Name:Lemonade Ice:true}
0xc42000a1e0
0xc42000a200
```

To be able to modify values contained in the original instantiation of a struct, a pointer should be used. A pointer is a reference to the memory address, so rather than operating on a copy of the struct, modifications will update any variable referencing the underlying memory. To reference a pointer, the variable name is preceded with an ampersand. Listing 7.9 can be updated to reference a pointer rather than a value, as shown in Listing 7.10.

LISTING 7.10   Copying a Struct Using a Pointer Reference

```
 1:   package main
 2:
 3:   import (
 4:        "fmt"
 5:        "reflect"
 6:   )
 7:
 8:   type Drink struct {
 9:        Name     string
10:        Ice      bool
11:   }
12:
13:   func main() {
14:        a := Drink{
15:            Name: "Lemonade",
16:            Ice:   true,
17:        }
18:        b := &a
19:        b.Ice = false
20:        fmt.Printf("%+v\n", *b)
21:        fmt.Printf("%+v\n", a)
22:        fmt.Printf("%p\n", b)
23:        fmt.Printf("%p\n", &a)
24:   }
```

The modifications made to Listing 7.9 in Listing 7.10 can be explained as follows:

▶ Instead of assigning a by value by reference, it is assigned by referencing a pointer. This is denoted by the ampersand character.

▶ When b is updated, the underlying memory that is assigned to a is updated. As both a and b both reference the same underlying memory, their values are the same.

▶ Printing the values of b and a shows that the values are the same. Note that as b is now a pointer, it must be dereferenced using the asterisk character.

▶ The underlying memory addresses of b and a are printed to the console, showing that they are the same.

Copying a Struct Using a Pointer Reference

In this example, you will understand how to copy a struct using a pointer reference.

1. Open hour07/example11.go from the code examples for this book.

2. Read the code and try to understand what it is doing.

3. From the terminal, run the program with `go run example11.go`.

4. You should see the following text printed to the terminal:

```
{Name:Lemonade Ice:false}
{Name:Lemonade Ice:false}
0xc42000a1e0
0xc42000a1e0
```

The difference between pointers and values is a subtle one, but choosing whether to use a pointer or a value is simple. If you need to modify (or mutate) the original initialization of a struct, use a pointer. If you need to operate on a struct, but do not want to modify the original initialization of a struct, use a value.

Summary

In this hour, you were introduced to structs. You learned how they can be useful for representing things like movies, superheroes, and drinks. You understood how to create a struct and how default values are assigned upon creation. You saw how to define a custom value on creation through a constructor function. You learned about exported values and the difference between pointers and values in relation to structs. When you look at the world now, you will be able to think of things in structs. How, for example, would you represent a bird in a struct? Or a star in the sky? Or a sports player? Structs provide a way to begin to reason programmatically and are a powerful fundamental construct.

Q&A

Q. I have seen three different ways of creating a struct. Which one should I use?

A. The recommended way of creating an instance of a struct is to use the shorthand variable assignment method `:=`. Using `new` and a variable is also valid, but less commonly used.

Q. I understand how to nest one struct in another. How many levels can I nest structs?

A. There is no limit as to how many levels of structs can be nested. Modeling data in deeply nested structures is probably a sign, though, that another data structure would be better suited.

Q. Can I use any data type in a struct?

A. Yes, any data type may be used in a struct, including any custom types.

Workshop

The workshop contains quiz questions and exercises to help you solidify your understanding of the material covered. Try to answer all questions before looking at the "Answers" section that follows.

Quiz

1. How do default values work in structs?

2. How do you declare whether a struct and data elements within it should be exported?

3. When should you use a pointer, and when should you use a value?

Answers

1. Default values are assigned according to Go's zero values. Depending on the type, a value will be assigned. To see a full list of zero values, refer to Table 7.1.

2. Names that begin with an uppercase letter are exported, and those that begin with a lowercase letter are not. For example, "Age" is exported, but "age" is not.

3. If you want to make a copy of a struct and do not want changes to be reflected in the original struct, a value should be used. If you wish to operate on a copy of a struct and want changes to be reflected in the original, a pointer should be used.

Exercises

1. Create a struct to represent a console game that you have enjoyed playing. Think about things like name, release date, and platform, and choose relevant data types. In a `main` function, initialize your struct and print the struct elements to the terminal.

2. Think of a data structure that can be represented using a nested struct. Some examples are a component of a larger construction, an item on a CV, or a living room within a house.

3. Explain the difference between passing a pointer and a value to yourself and what this means for memory.

Creating Methods and Interfaces

What You'll Learn in This Hour:

▶ Using methods

▶ Creating method sets

▶ Working with methods and pointers

▶ Using interfaces

In Hour 7, "Using Structs and Pointers," you learned about structs and understood that structs are a way to create data structures. You understood that it is possible to access data within structs using dot notation. Once operations get beyond being trivial, however, it can become more complex to reason about and to manipulate data. Go provides another way to operate on data through methods. In this hour, you are introduced to methods and how to create and use method sets that are associated with a data type. You are then introduced to interfaces, a way to describe method sets that offers powerful modularity.

Using Methods

A method is similar to a function with one simple addition. A method augments a function by adding an extra parameter section immediately after the `func` keyword that accepts a single argument. The following example uses the `Movie` struct that you were introduced to in Hour 7 and adds a method to it.

```
type Movie struct {
    Name string
    Rating float32
}

func (m *Movie) summary() string {
    //code
}
```

Notice that the method takes an additional parameter immediately after the `func` keyword that is called a receiver. Technically, a method receiver is a type, and in this case it is a pointer to the `Movie` struct. Next comes the method name and any arguments for the method, followed by the return value types. A method is directly equivalent to a function that you learned about in Hour 4, other than the addition of the extra parameter section containing the receiver. You can think of a receiver as something the method will be associated with. By declaring a `summary` method, any instance of the `Movie` struct will have a `summary` method available. Why then use a method instead of simply using a function? For example, the following uses a function and is equivalent to the method declaration.

```
type Movie struct {
    Name string
    Rating float64
}

func summary(m *Movie) string {
    //code
}
```

The summary function depends on the `Movie` struct and vice versa, and there is a direct relationship between the two. It is not possible, for example, to declare the `summary` function without the function being able to access the struct definition. Using a function results in code duplication in adding the struct or function definition each time one or the other was used. Furthermore, if there was a change to the function, it would need to be edited in multiple places. Where there is a strong relationship between a function and a struct, it makes sense to use a method.

The implementation of the `summary` method includes some code to convert the `float64` rating value to a `string` and format it. The benefit of using a method is that this only needs to be written once and can then be used on any instance of a struct.

```
func (m *Movie) summary() string {
    r := strconv.FormatFloat(m.Rating, 'f', 1, 64)
    return m.Name + ", " + r
}
```

Listing 8.1 shows the summary method being declared and then called on an instance of the `Movie` struct.

LISTING 8.1   Declaring and Calling a Method

```
1:  package main
2:
3:  import (
4:      "fmt"
5:      "strconv"
```

```
 6:   )
 7:
 8:   type Movie struct {
 9:       Name    string
10:       Rating float64
11:   }
12:
13:   func (m *Movie) summary() string {
14:       r := strconv.FormatFloat(m.Rating, 'f', 1, 64)
15:       return m.Name + ", " + r
16:   }
17:
18:   func main() {
19:       m := Movie{
20:       Name:    "Spiderman",
21:           Rating: 3.2,
22:       }
23:
24:       fmt.Println(m.summary())
25:   }
```

TRY IT YOURSELF ▼

Declaring and Calling a Method

In this example, you will understand how to declare and use a method on a struct.

1. Open hour08/example01.go from the code examples for this book.

2. Read the code and try to understand what it is doing.

3. From the terminal, run the program with `go run example01.go`.

4. You should see the following text printed to the terminal:

   ```
   Spiderman, 3.2
   ```

Creating Method Sets

A method set is a set of methods that are available to a data type. Any data type in Go can have a method set associated with it. This allows a data type to have a relationship with methods, as you saw in the `Movie` struct example. There is no limit to the number of methods in a method set, and it can become a useful way to encapsulate functionality and to create library code.

Suppose that you are working with spheres, and that you need to be able to calculate the surface area and volume of a sphere. This is a perfect scenario to use a struct and a method set. Using a method set allows calculations to be created once and then reused on any instance of a sphere. To create a method set, a `Sphere` struct is declared, followed by two methods that take the struct as the receiver.

```
type Sphere struct {
    Radius float64
}

func (s *Sphere) SurfaceArea() float64 {
    return float64(4) * math.Pi * (s.Radius * s.Radius)
}

func (s *Sphere) Volume() float64 {
    radiusCubed := s.Radius * s.Radius * s.Radius
    return (float64(4) / float64(3)) * math.Pi * radiusCubed
}
```

Methods for computing the surface area and volume of a sphere are declared, and they specify the function signature in the normal way. The only difference here is the addition of the receiver argument that is a pointer to an instance of a sphere. For the purposes of this hour, the formulae within the method are not particularly important. These are standard mathematical formulae. It is worth noting, however, that the `Radius` value from the struct is available within the method and is accessible through dot notation. Listing 8.2 shows an example of a method set associated with a struct being used.

LISTING 8.2   Creating and Using a Method Set

```
 1:  package main
 2:
 3:  import (
 4:      "fmt"
 5:      "math"
 6:  )
 7:
 8:  type Sphere struct {
 9:      Radius float64
10:  }
11:
12:  func (s *Sphere) SurfaceArea() float64 {
13:      return float64(4) * math.Pi * (s.Radius * s.Radius)
14:  }
15:
16:  func (s *Sphere) Volume() float64 {
17:      radiusCubed := s.Radius * s.Radius * s.Radius
18:      return (float64(4) / float64(3)) * math.Pi * radiusCubed
```

```
19:  }
20:
21:  func main() {
22:
23:      s := Sphere{
24:          Radius: 5,
25:      }
26:      fmt.Println(s.SurfaceArea())
27:      fmt.Println(s.Volume())
28:  }
```

The benefit of using a method set over just using a function is that the `SurfaceArea` and `Volume` methods only need to be written once. If, for example, a bug was found in one of these methods, it would only need to be changed in one place.

Creating and Using a Method Set

In this example, you will understand how to create and use a method set.

1. Open hour08/example02.go from the code examples for this book.

2. Read the code and try to understand what it is doing.

3. From the terminal, run the program with `go run example02.go`.

4. You should see the following text printed to the terminal as the methods are executed:

   ```
   314.1592653589793
   523.5987755982989
   ```

Working with Methods and Pointers

As with structs, it is important to understand how to work with methods and pointers. You have seen how methods are a function with a special argument known as a receiver. The receiver can either be a pointer or a value, and the difference here is quite subtle. Suppose that a struct exists to hold data for a triangle.

```
type Triangle struct {
    width  float64
    height float64
}
```

To calculate the area of a triangle, a simple equation one half of base times height be used. Although this could be calculated using the elements of the struct directly, it is much cleaner to use a method. The `area` method takes a number and returns the results of the formula. Note that the receiver expects a `Triangle` struct, and the asterisk specifies that it should be a pointer.

```
func (t *Triangle) area() float64 {
    return 0.5 * (t.width * t.height)
}
```

Listing 8.3 demonstrates a pointer reference being passed to a method.

LISTING 8.3   Passing a Pointer Reference to a Method

```
 1:   package main
 2:
 3:   import (
 4:       "fmt"
 5:   )
 6:
 7:   type Triangle struct {
 8:       base   float64
 9:       height float64
10:   }
11:
12:   func (t *Triangle) area() float64 {
13:       return 0.5 * (t.base * t.height)
14:   }
15:
16:   func main() {
17:       t := Triangle{base: 3, height: 1}
18:       fmt.Println(t.area())
19:   }
```

As you might expect, executing this example returns the area of the triangle.

```
go run example03.go
1.5
```

The difference between using a pointer reference and a value reference in the receiver argument can be demonstrated by a simple example to change the base value of a triangle where values have been assigned to data fields of an initialized struct. Suppose that there is a requirement to be able to change the base value of a triangle. This could be implemented with a `changeBase` method.

```
func (t Triangle) changeBase(f float64) {
    t.base = f
    return
}
```

In this example, note that there is no asterisk before the `Triangle` struct in the receiver argument. This signifies that the receiver is a value rather than a pointer. Listing 8.4 shows a full example of the `changeBase` method being added to the `Triangle` struct method set.

LISTING 8.4   Passing a Value Reference to a Method

```
 1:    package main
 2:
 3:    import (
 4:        "fmt"
 5:    )
 6:
 7:    type Triangle struct {
 8:        base    float64
 9:        height  float64
10:    }
11:
12:    func (t Triangle) changeBase(f float64) {
13:        t.base = f
14:        return
15:    }
16:
17:    func main() {
18:        t := Triangle{base: 3, height: 1}
19:        t.changeBase(4)
20:        fmt.Println(t.base)
21:    }
```

What do you think the value of `t.base` is after running this program?

TRY IT YOURSELF ▼

Passing a Value Reference to a Method

In this example, you will understand the implications of passing a value reference to a method.

1. Open hour08/example04.go from the code examples for this book.

2. Read the code and try to understand what it is doing. Note that a value reference is passed to the method.

3. From the terminal, run the program with `go run example04.go`.

4. You should see the following text printed to the terminal. Is it what you expected?

3

The value is 3 because the changeBase method takes a value reference. This means that the method operates on a copy of the Triangle struct and the original declaration is not modified. Within the changeBase method, the value of t.base is modified on a copy of the original triangle value.

Methods that take a pointer receiver are able to modify data elements declared within the original declaration of a struct. This is because, rather than operating on a copy of the struct, methods that take a pointer receiver have a reference to the same memory location as the original definition. Listing 8.5 can be modified so that the receiver is a pointer to a struct. This means that the data fields within the original declaration will be modified upon calling the methods.

LISTING 8.5   Passing a Value Reference to a Method

```
1:   package main
2:
3:   import (
4:       "fmt"
5:   )
6:
7:   type Triangle struct {
8:       base    float64
9:       height float64
10:  }
11:
12:  func (t *Triangle) changeBase(f float64) {
13:      t.base = f
14:      return
15:  }
16:
17:  func main() {
18:      t := Triangle{base: 3, height: 1}
19:      t.changeBase(4)
20:      fmt.Println(t.base)
21:  }
```

What do you think the value of t.base is after running this program this time?

Passing a Pointer Reference to a Method

In this example, you will understand the implications of passing a pointer reference to a method.

1. Open hour08/example05.go from the code examples for this book.

2. Read the code and try to understand what it is doing. Note that a pointer reference is passed to the method.

3. From the terminal, run the program with `go run example05.go`.

4. You should see the following text printed to the terminal. Is it what you expected?

   4

The difference between pointers and values is a subtle one, but choosing whether to use a pointer or a value is simple. If you need to modify (or mutate) the original initialization of a struct, use a pointer. If you need to operate on a struct, but do not want to modify the original initialization of a struct, use a value.

Using Interfaces

An *interface* specifies a method set and is a powerful way to introduce modularity in Go. You can think of interfaces as a blueprint for a method set, in that an interface describes all the methods in a set but does not implement them. Interfaces are powerful since they act as a specification for a method set, meaning that implementations can be swapped, providing they conform to the expectations of an interface.

An interface describes all the methods of a method set and provides the function signatures for each method. The following example supposes that some code needs to be written to control a Robot. At a high level, it can be supposed that there may be more than one type of Robot, and that they may have slightly different ways of controlling their behavior. Given this programming task, you may think that you might need a different code for each Robot. Interfaces provide a way to promote code reuse across entities that share the same behavior. For this example of the Robot, the interface describes a way to turn a Robot on and off.

```
type Robot interface {
    PowerOn() err
}
```

The `Robot` interface contains a single method, `PowerOn`. The interface also describes the function signature for the `PowerOn` methods that takes no arguments and returns an error type. From a high level, interfaces can also help to reason about code design. It is easy to see without being concerned about an implementation what the surface layer of the design looks like.

So, how is an interface used? As interfaces act as a blueprint for method sets, they must be implemented before being used. Code that satisfies an interface is said to *implement* it. The Robot interface can be implemented by declaring a method set that satisfies the interface.

```
type T850 struct {
    Name string
}

func (a *T850) PowerOn() err {
    return nil
}
```

Although this is a bare-bones implementation, it satisfies the Robot interface as it contains a PowerOn method, and the function signature matches the expectations of the interface. The powerful thing about interfaces is that they support multiple implementations. The Robot interface can also be satisfied as follows:

```
type R2D2 struct {
    Broken bool
}

func (r *R2D2) PowerOn() err {
    if r.Broken {
        return errors.New("R2D2 is broken")
    } else {
        return nil
    }
}
```

This also satisfies the Robot interface, as it conforms to the method set definition of requiring a PowerOn method. It also conforms to the function signature. Note that the R2D2 struct that the method set is attached to has a different set of data fields to the T850 implementation. The PowerOn method is also completely different, although it conforms to the function signature. For the interface, all that matters is that it conforms with implementing the method set with the correct function signatures.

At this stage there are two implementations of the Robot interface, and although it is useful to have a common definition for a Robot, there is no code that can be used for both the T850 and R2D2 instances. As an interface is a type, it can be passed to a function as an argument. This allows functions to be written that can be reused for multiple implementations of an interface.

For the `Robot` interface, a function can be written to boot any Robot.

```
func Boot(r Robot) error {
    return r.PowerOn()
}
```

This function accepts any implementation of the `Robot` interface as an argument and returns the result of calling the `PowerOn` method. This function can be used to boot any `Robot`, regardless of how the code inside the `PowerOn` method is actually implemented. Both the T850 and R2D2 Robots can make use of this method.

Listing 8.6 shows a full example of using the `Robot` interface.

LISTING 8.6   Using the Robot Interface

```
 1:  package main
 2:
 3:  import (
 4:      "errors"
 4:      "fmt"
 5:  )
 6:
 7:  type Robot interface {
 8:      PowerOn() error
 9:  }
10:
11:  type T850 struct {
12:      Name string
13:  }
14:
15:  func (a *T850) PowerOn() error {
16:      return nil
17:  }
18:
19:  type R2D2 struct {
20:      Broken bool
21:  }
22:
23:  func (r *R2D2) PowerOn() error {
24:      if r.Broken {
25:          return errors.New("R2D2 is broken")
26:      } else {
27:          return nil
28:      }
29:  }
30:
31:  func Boot(r Robot) error {
```

```
32:     return r.PowerOn()
33:   }
34:
35:   func main() {
36:       t := T850{
37:           Name: "The Terminator",
38:       }
39:
40:       r := R2D2{
41:           Broken: true,
42:       }
43:
44:       err := Boot(&r)
45:
46:       if err != nil {
47:           fmt.Println(err)
48:       } else {
49:           fmt.Println("Robot is powered on!")
50:       }
51:
52:       err = Boot(&t)
53:
54:       if err != nil {
55:           fmt.Println(err)
56:       } else {
57:           fmt.Println("Robot is powered on!")
58:       }
59:   }
```

NOTE

Is Golang Object-Oriented?

After gaining a basic understanding of structs and methods, if you have any familiarity with other languages, you may ask yourself whether Go is an object-oriented language. Object-oriented programming refers to a programming paradigm where data is modeling in terms of objects that behave in certain ways. Typically, object-oriented languages offer the ability to inherit one object from another.

Although Golang does not have formal features of object orientation like classes and class inheritance, the functionality of structs and method sets offers some element of object orientation. Although this is still the topic of ongoing debate, it can be said that Go offers functionality similar to object-oriented programming without formal objects or inheritance.

The layer of abstraction provided by interfaces may initially seem complex, but it promotes code reuse and the ability to swap out implementations entirely. Consider a scenario where a computer program has been written to use a MySQL database. Without using an interface, it is likely that the code will be quite specific to MySQL. In the scenario of having to swap the MySQL database to another one, like PostgreSQL, it is probable that a large amount of code will need to be rewritten.

By defining a database interface, the implementation of the interface becomes more important than the database used. If the implementation satisfies the interface, theoretically any database could be used and can easily be swapped out. The idea that a database interface can include one or more implementations introduces the idea of polymorphism.

The word *polymorphic* means many forms, and supports the idea that an interface can have more than one implementation. Interfaces in Go offer polymorphism in a declarative way, since the interface describes the expected method set and the function signatures of these methods. If a method set implements an interface, it can be said to be behaviorally polymorphic with another method set that implements the same interface. A compiler can also verify an interface through checking the method set and ensuring that it really is polymorphic. By formalizing an interface, there can be no doubt that two implementations of an interface are polymorphic. This certainty leads to verifiable, testable, and flexible code.

Summary

During this hour, you learned about methods and interfaces. You should now understand how to declare a method and how methods can promote code reuse and consistency over simply using functions. You saw how a method set can group together operations on a data type. You then saw the difference between value and pointer references and understood the difference between operating on a copy of a struct or the original declaration. Finally, you were introduced to interfaces, which are a powerful way to create polymorphic implementations that can share methods, or be swapped out entirely.

Q&A

Q. **What is the difference between a function and a method?**

A. Technically, the only difference between a method and a function is that a method has an additional argument to specify a receiver. This allows methods to be called on a type, promoting code reuse and modularization.

Q. **When should I use a pointer reference, and when should I use a value reference?**

A. If you need to modify data within the original declaration of a struct, use a pointer. If you want to operate on a copy of the original data, use a value reference.

Q. **Can an interface implementation include methods not in the interface?**

A. Yes. Additional methods can be added to an implementation of an interface, although these are only available within the context of the struct and not the interface.

Workshop

The workshop contains quiz questions and exercises to help you solidify your understanding of the material covered. Try to answer all questions before looking at the "Answers" section that follows.

Quiz

1. What are some of the benefits of using a method?

2. Can methods be associated to a slice?

3. What does polymorphism mean?

Answers

1. Methods mean that code only needs to be written once. Methods can enhance usability, consistency, and reliability.

2. Yes. Method sets can be associated with any type in Go.

3. Polymorphism is the condition of occurring in several different forms. Interfaces in Go support multiple implementations allowing code to be shared or swapped out.

Exercises

1. Write an interface for a taxi. You can include any methods you like, but you may think of things like whether the taxi is hired, how many passengers there are, and whether the taxi is available for hire.

2. Extend the `Robot` interface to add a method called `Talk`. Modify Listing 8.6 so that both the T850 and R2D2 structs implement the talk method.

3. Read the source code for the errors package at https://golang.org/src/errors/errors.go. Can you see how a method is associated with a struct?

HOUR 9
Working with Strings

What You'll Learn in This Hour:

▶ Creating String Literals

▶ Understanding Rune Literals

▶ Concatenating Strings

▶ Encoding

Strings are a fundamental building block of programming. During this hour, you will learn how to work with strings in Go. You will understand how to initialize strings and the idea of runes in Go. You will learn how to manipulate strings and explore encoding systems behind strings.

Creating String Literals

Go supports two ways of creating string literals. Interpreted string literals are characters within double quotes, as in "hello". A simple example of creating a string using interpreted string literals is shown in Listing 9.1.

LISTING 9.1 Creating a String Literal

```
1:  package main
2:
3:  import (
4:      "fmt"
5:  )
6:
7:  func main() {
8:      s := "I am an interpreted string literal"
9:      fmt.Println(s)
10: }
```

Creating an Interpreted String Literal

In this example, you will understand how to create an interpreted string literal.

1. Open the file hour09/example01.go in a text editor and try to understand what the example is doing.

2. From the terminal, run the program with `go run example01.go`.

3. You will see the string literal printed in the console:

```
I am an interpreted string literal
```

Interpreted string literals can contain any character other than a newline character or an unescaped double quote. Characters preceded by a backslash \ are interpreted as they are in rune literals. Table 9.1, taken from the Golang Language Specification, details single character escapes that map to Unicode characters.

TABLE 9.1   English-Language Special Characters

Rune Literal	Unicode Character
\a	U+0007 alert or bell
\b	U+0008 backspace
\f	U+000C form feed
\n	U+000A line feed or newline
\r	U+000D carriage return
\t	U+0009 horizontal tab
\v	U+000b vertical tab
\\	U+005c backslash
\'	U+0027 single quote (valid escape only within rune literals)
\\"	U+0022 double quote (valid escape only within string literals)

Understanding Rune Literals

Rune literals allow an interpreted string literal to be formatted into multiple lines and for tabs and other formatting options to be added. In Listing 9.2, rune literals are used to add a new line and a tab character even though the string declaration is on a single line.

LISTING 9.2   Using Rune Literals

```
 1:  package main
 2:
 3:  import (
 4:      "fmt"
 5:  )
 6:
 7:  func main() {
 8:      s := "After a backslash, certain single character escapes represent
    special values\nn is a line feed or new line \n\t t is a tab"
 9:      fmt.Println(s)
10:  }
```

Running this example produces a formatted string:

```
go run example02.go
After a backslash, certain single character escapes represent special values
n is a line feed or new line
t is a tab
```

Raw string literals are created between back quotes (or backticks), as in 'hello'. Unlike interpreted strings, backslashes have no special meaning, and Go will interpret the string as it is presented. Using a raw string literal, the same output from the previous example can be achieved without using backslash characters, as shown in Listing 9.3.

LISTING 9.3   Raw String Literals

```
 1:  package main
 2:
 3:  import (
 4:      "fmt"
 6:  )
 7:
 8:  func main() {
 9:      s := `After a backslash, certain single character escapes represent
    special values
10:  n is a line feed or new line
11:    t is a tab`
12:      fmt.Println(s)
13:  }
```

Using Raw String Literals

In this example, you will understand how to create a raw string literal.

1. Open the file hour09/example03.go in a text editor and try to understand what the example is doing.

2. From the terminal, run the program with `go run example03.go`.

3. You will see the raw string literal printed in the console.

4. Edit the file and add some spaces and formatting of your own. Do you understand the difference between interpreted and string literals?

Concatenating Strings

To concatenate (or combine) strings in Go, the + operator may be used to combine variables with a string type. It does not matter whether the string was created using an interpreted or raw string literal. The + operator combines strings to the left and right of it into a single string, as shown in Listing 9.4.

LISTING 9.4   Combining Strings into a Single String

```
 1:  package main
 2:
 3:  import (
 4:      "fmt"
 5:  )
 6:
 7:  func main() {
 8:      s := "Oh sweet ignition" + " be my fuse"
 9:      fmt.Println(s)
10:  }
```

Strings may also be concatenated using the += assignment operator, as shown in Listing 9.5. This takes any string to the right and combines it with a string to the left of it. This may be repeated to build up a string in a loop, for example.

LISTING 9.5   Concatenation with an Assignment Operator

```
1:  package main
2:
3:  import (
4:      "fmt"
5:  )
6:
7:  func main() {
8:      s := "Can you hear me?"
9:      s += "\nHear me screamin'?"
10: }
```

Using the Assignment Operator

This example shows you how to use the assignment operator to concatenate strings.

1. Open the file hour09/example05.go in a text editor and try to understand what the example is doing.

2. From the terminal, run the program with `go run example05.go`.

3. You will see the concatenated string printed in the console.

Only variables of the string type may be concatenated. Attempting to concatenate an `int` with a `string` results in a compiler error, as shown in Listing 9.6.

LISTING 9.6   Concatenation and Types

```
1:  package main
2:
3:  import (
4:      "fmt"
7:  )
8:
9:  func main() {
10:     var i int = 1
11:     var s string = " egg"
12:     var breakfast string = i + s
13:     fmt.Println(breakfast)
14: }
```

Listing 9.6 can be explained as follows:

1. A variable i of explicit type int is initialized and assigned the value of '1'.

2. A variable s of explicit type string is initialized and assigned the value of 'egg'.

3. A variable breakfast of explicit type string is assigned the concatenated value of i and s.

4. The value of breakfast is printed.

What do you think this code will do? Running this code results in a compile time error.

```
go run types.go
# command-line-arguments
./types.go:8: invalid operation: i + s (mismatched types int and string)
```

The error says that the int type cannot be combined with a string. So how do we combine these values? Go offers the strconv package in the standard library and the Itoa method to accomplish this: it converts an int to a string, as shown in Listing 9.7.

LISTING 9.7   Converting Types to a String

```
 1:    package main
 2:
 3:    import (
 4:        "fmt"
 6:    )
 7:
 8:    func main() {
 9:        var i int = 1
10:        var s string = " egg"
11:        intToString := strconv.Itoa(i)
12:        var breakfast string = intToString + s
13:        fmt.Println(breakfast)
14:    }
```

Running this example now outputs a correctly concatenated string:

```
go run strconv.go
1 egg
```

Concatenating Strings with a Buffer

For simple (and small) concatenations, the + and += assignment operators work well. As the number of operations to be concatenated grows, this becomes less efficient. If a string needs to be created from within a loop, using a buffer of empty bytes is a more efficient way to build a string. In Listing 9.8, a string is created with a loop that runs 500 times. Although this could be created with the += operator, using a buffer is much faster.

LISTING 9.8   Using a Buffer for Concatenation

```
 1:  package main
 2:
 3:  import (
 4:      "fmt"
 6:  )
 7:
 8:  func main() {
 9:      var buffer bytes.Buffer
10:
11:      for i := 0; i < 500; i++ {
12:          buffer.WriteString("z")
13:      }
14:
15:      fmt.Println(buffer.String())
16:  }
```

Listing 9.8 can be explained as follows:

1. An empty bytes buffer is initialized and assigned to the variable `buffer`.

2. A loop runs 500 times and writes the string `"z"` into the buffer.

3. Once the loop has completed the value, the `String()` function is called on the buffer to output the result as a string.

TRY IT YOURSELF ▼

Using a Bytes Buffer to Create a String

In this example, you will understand how to use the bytes buffer to create a string.

1. Open the file hour09/example08.go in a text editor and try to understand what the example is doing.

2. From the terminal, run the program with `go run example08.go`.

3. You will see a long string of z's in your console.

Understanding What a String Is

To understand what a string is, you must first understand how characters are displayed and stored on a computer. Computers interpret data as numbers rather than text, and although humans never see it, computers store characters as numbers.

Historically, a number of encoding standards arose so that an agreed set of numbers could map to an agreed set of characters. One of the most important encoding standards was ASCII, or the American Standard Code for Information Interchange. This standardized the numbers to be used to represent characters within the English alphabet.

The ASCII encoding standard defines how 128 characters should be represented through 7-bit integers, or, more colloquially, numbers. Table 9.2 lists a few characters from the ASCII encoding standard. Do not worry if you do not understand everything. It is enough to understand that numbers map to characters.

TABLE 9.2 English-Language Special Characters

Binary	Octal	Decimal	Hexadecimal	Character
1000001	101	65	41	A
1000001	102	66	42	B
1000001	164	116	74	t

Although ASCII was an important step in standardizing English language characters, it offered nothing for other language character sets. In short, it was possible to say "hello" in English, but not こんにちは in Japanese.

To respond to this, the Unicode encoding scheme was created in 1987, and it offered support for most character sets on the planet. The latest version supports 128,000 characters covering 135 modern and historic scripts. Conveniently, Unicode incorporated ASCII into the standard as the first 128 characters.

A number of character-encoding schemes implement Unicode, most notably UTF-8. It is a happy coincidence that Rob Pike and Ken Thompson, two of the co-creators of Go, are also the co-creators of UTF-8. As you may imagine, the result is that Go has fantastic support for UTF-8 and international character sets, and Go source code is always UTF-8.

To understand strings in more detail and know how to manipulate them, it is important to understand that a string in Go is in effect a read-only slice of bytes. Using Go's len built-in method, it is possible to see the number of bytes in a string:

```
s := "hello"
fmt.Printf(len(s))
// outputs 5
```

Western characters (e.g., a, b, c) generally map to a single byte. The word "hello" has 5 bytes, and because Go strings are a slice of bytes, it is possible to output byte values at a specific position in a string. In the following example, the first byte of the string is returned:

```
s := "hello"
fmt.Printf(s[0])
//outputs 104
```

You might think that the character "h" should be the result. But because indexing the string accesses the bytes rather than the character, the byte value is shown in base 10 (or decimal) format. Table 9.3 shows the decimal and binary representations of several letters.

TABLE 9.3   English-Language Special Characters

	h	e	l	l	o
Decimal	104	101	108	108	108
Binary	1101000	1100101	1101100	1101100	1101111

Go can format a base 10 value back to a character literal and show the underlining binary format:

```
s := "hello"
fmt.Println("%q", s[0])
// outputs 'h'
fmt.Println("%b", s[0])
// outputs 1101000
```

For international characters, many are longer than 1 byte. Each character here is 3 bytes long:

```
s := "こんにちは"
fmt.Println(len(s))
// outputs 15
```

It does not matter if you do not understand the full complexity of binary, bytes, and character literals. Note that strings are really just a slice of bytes, and that this means they can be manipulated as you would any other slice of bytes in Go.

Working with Strings

Once a string variable has been assigned, it is possible to use any of the methods provided by the strings package in the standard library. This provides a comprehensive set of functions for working with strings. The documentation for this package is very good, and can be found at https://golang.org/pkg/strings. A few examples are showcased here, but you are encouraged to read the documentation to fully understand what the package provides.

Converting a String to Lowercase

The `ToLower` function takes a string and converts all uppercase characters to lowercase, as shown in Listing 9.9.

LISTING 9.9   Lowercasing a String

```
 1:  package main
 2:
 3:  import (
 4:      "fmt"
 5:      "strings"
 6:  )
 7:
 8:  func main() {
 9:      fmt.Println(strings.ToLower("VERY IMPORTANT MESSAGE"))
10:  }
```

▼ TRY IT YOURSELF

Converting a String to Lowercase

In this example, you will understand how to convert a string to lowercase.

1. Open the file hour09/example09.go in a text editor and try to understand what the example is doing.

2. From the terminal, run the program with `go run example09.go`.

3. You will see the lowercased string in your console:

   ```
   very important message
   ```

Searching for a Substring in a String

Another common task when working with strings is to search for a substring within a string. The INDEX method provides this, and takes a second argument of a string to search for. If a match is found, the index number of the first match is returned. If no match is found, the value –1 is returned. Remember that the index starts from 0!

LISTING 9.10   Searching for Substrings

```
 1:   package main
 2:
 3:   import (
 4:       "fmt"
 5:       "strings"
 6:   )
 7:
 8:   func main() {
 9:       fmt.Println(strings.Index("surface", "face"))
10:       fmt.Println(strings.Index("moon", "aer"))
11:   }
```

TRY IT YOURSELF ▼

Looking for a Substring in a String

In this example, you will understand how to search a string for another string.

1. Open the file hour09/example10.go in a text editor and try to understand what the example is doing.

2. From the terminal, run the program with `go run example10.go`.

3. You will see that the first search was found at position 3, and that the second was not found:

   ```
   3
   -1
   ```

Trimming Space from a String

The `strings` package provides many methods for trimming parts of a string. A common task when dealing with input from users or data sources is to ensure there are no leading or trailing spaces. The `TrimSpace` method provides this, as shown in Listing 9.11.

LISTING 9.11   Trimming Leading and Trailing Whitespace

```
 1:   package main
 2:
 3:   import (
 4:       "fmt"
 5:       "strings"
 6:   )
 7:
 8:   func main() {
 9:       fmt.Println(strings.TrimSpace("   I don't need all this space    ")
10:   }
```

▼ TRY IT YOURSELF

Trimming White Space

In this example, you will understand how to trim leading and trailing white space from a string.

1. Open the file hour09/example11.go in a text editor and try to understand what the example is doing.

2. From the terminal, run the program with `go run example11.go`.

3. You will see the string with all leading and trailing space removed printed to your console:

   ```
   I don't need all this space
   ```

Summary

During this hour, you were introduced to strings in Go. You learned the difference between an interpreted string literal and a raw string literal. You became familiar with rune literals and how they may be used to format a line of text. You learned how to concatenate strings with the + and += operators before understanding how to concatenate strings using a buffer. You were introduced to some of the underlying principles of strings, and to UTF-8 and how it works in Go. Finally, you learned how to work with strings using the `strings` package from the standard library.

Q&A

Q. **Why is a string called a string?**

A. Although there is no definitive answer, a string is named a string as it is a sequence, or string, of bytes that represent a character or set of characters.

Q. **If Go supports UTF-8, can I code in a language other than English?**

A. Yes. Go code is interpreted as UTF-8, meaning function and method names can comprise any character supported by UTF-8. Go wild.

Q. **Can I change a string after it is created?**

A. A string is immutable in Go, meaning you cannot change it after it has been assigned. If you try to redeclare a variable, a compilation error will occur. You are permitted to concatenate strings using the += assignment operator.

Workshop

This workshop contains quiz questions and exercises to help you solidify your understanding of the material covered. Try to answer all questions before looking at the "Answers" section that follows.

Quiz

1. What is the difference between an interpreted string literal and a raw string literal?

2. What is the rune literal character for a tab, and how can you use it in an interpreted string literal?

3. What is the most efficient way to create a string with a large number of concatenations?

4. Why was UTF-8 created?

Answers

1. An interpreted string literal uses double quotes (") and supports the expansion of rune literals within it. This means special characters may be used to add formatting. A raw string literal uses back quotes (`). Anything between the back quotes will be formatted as it is, including spaces, tabs, and carriage returns.

2. A tab is represented as \t. When used in an interpreted string literal (double quotes), it will add a tab to the string.

3. The most efficient way to create a string with a large number of concatenation operations is to use a bytes buffer. Herman Schaaf conducted a series of benchmarks that outline the different approaches and performance of string concatenations in Go.

4. UTF-8 was created to provide a standard way to represent almost every character set on the planet.

Exercises

Write a short program that takes the string, "Oh I do like to be beside the seaside," and prints the following information:

▶ A line that converts the string to uppercase

▶ A line that replaces "seaside" with "bar"

▶ A line that shows the index of the word "the"

Hint: All the methods you will need are in the `strings` package in the standard library.

HOUR 10
Handling Errors

What You'll Learn in This Hour:

▶ Handling Errors and Idiomatic Go
▶ Understanding the Error Type
▶ Creating Errors
▶ Formatting Errors
▶ Returning an Error from a Function
▶ Errors and Usability
▶ Don't `panic`

It is a fact of life that software will contain errors and scenarios that are not accounted for. Many languages choose to throw exceptions when errors occur that must be caught or trapped. Go offers an interesting approach to errors in that they are a type in the language. This means that they may be passed around functions and methods. During this hour, you will be introduced to error handling in Go and how you can use error handling to your advantage.

DID YOU KNOW?

Start Thinking About Disasters!

Good programmers look at seemingly safe situations, think about how they could go wrong, and write code to handle disasters! If you find yourself preparing for an interview by imagining all the things that could go wrong, you are in good company. You will make the interview if the bus does not turn up, because you already have a plan B.

Error handling is an important part of programming robust, reliable, and maintainable code. If you are writing code for yourself, it can help account for unexpected scenarios. If you are writing libraries or packages that others will use, handling errors is part of creating robust, reliable, and trustworthy code.

Handling Errors and Idiomatic Go

When calling a method or function that could fail, one of Go's conventions is to return an error type as its final value. This means that generally no exception will be thrown within a function if something goes wrong. Instead, it is up to the caller to decide what to do with the error. Listing 10.1 shows this convention where the `ioutil.Readfile` function returns an error if something goes wrong.

LISTING 10.1   Error Handling when Reading a File

```
1:   package main
2:
3:   import (
4:       "fmt"
5:       "io/ioutil"
6:   )
7:
8:   func main() {
9:       file, err := ioutil.ReadFile("foo.txt")
10:      if err != nil {
11:          fmt.Println(err)
12:          return
13:      }
14:      fmt.Println("%s", file)
15:  }
```

Running this example on a filesystem where `foo.txt` does not exist triggers the error:

```
go run example01.go
open foo.txt: no such file or directory
```

Although this example has a little amount of code, it expresses many of the opinions within Go about errors, such as:

- A file is read using the `ReadFile` function from the `io/ioutil` standard library package.

- If an error is returned, this will mean the error type is not `nil`.

- The error is printed, and the program exists.

- If there is no error, the contents of the file are printed.

The important part in understanding Go's approach to errors is that the `ReadFile` function takes an argument of a string and returns a slice of bytes and an error. Here is the function definition:

```
func ReadFile(filename string) ([]byte, error)
```

This means calling the ReadFile function will always return an error value that can be checked. In the first line of the main function in the example, the return values of the ReadFile method are read into two variables, file and err. This is a common pattern in Go code, and you will see the following pattern frequently:

```
file, err := ioutil.ReadFile("foo.txt")
```

The := syntax is a short assignment statement in Go that may be used within a function. The Go compiler will infer the types of the variables automatically without needing to explicitly declare them. So in this case, there is no need to tell the compiler that file is a byte slice and err is an error type. This is a handy convenience, and the same code is equivalent.

```
var file []byte
var err error
file, err = ioutil.Readfile("foo.txt")
```

The convention in Go is that the error type will be nil if there is no error in execution. This allows programmers to check whether the execution is completed as expected when they call a method or function.

```
if err != nil {
    // something went wrong
}
```

This idiom is common within the Go programs. Some developers have written about how this approach is tedious in that it requires each method or function to call to check an error, leading to code repetition.

Although this may be true, Go's approach to errors offers more flexibility than some languages in that errors may be passed around functions just like any other type. This can often mean that code can be significantly shortened. If you are interested in exploring this more, read Rob Pike's blog post "Errors are Values" (https://blog.golang.org/errors-are-values).

TRY IT YOURSELF ▼

Error Handling in Go

In this example, you will run a program that returns an error.

1. Open the file hour10/example01.go in a text editor and try to understand what the example is doing. If you need to, refer to the bullet points.

2. From the terminal, run the program with go run example01.go.

3. You should see a message:

```
open foo.txt: no such file or directory
```

Understanding the Error Type

In Go, an error is a value. The standard library declares the `error` interface as follows:

```
type error interface {
    Error() string
}
```

This features a single method called `Error` that returns a string.

Creating Errors

You have seen how to work with errors, but what if you want to create and return errors? The standard library `errors` package supports creating and manipulating errors.

Listing 10.2 shows an error being created and then printed.

LISTING 10.2　Creating and Printing an Error

```
 1:  package main
 2:
 3:  import (
 4:      "fmt"
 5:  )
 6:
 7:  func main() {
 8:      err := errors.New("Something went wrong")
 9:      if err != nil {
10:          fmt.Println(err)
11:      }
12:  }
```

Running the example prints the error:

```
go run example02.go
Something went wrong
```

The example shows how an error may be created and then checked. The code can be explained as follows:

- An error is created using the `New` method from the `errors` package.

- An `if` statement checks whether the error value was not `nil`.

- If the value is found to not be `nil`, it is printed.

Creating Errors

In this example, you will learn how to create an error.

1. Open the file hour10/example02.go in a text editor and try to understand what the example is doing. If you need to, refer to the bullet points above and step through the code.

2. From the terminal, run the program with `go run example02.go`.

3. You should see a message as follows:

   ```
   Something went wrong
   ```

Formatting Errors

In addition to the `errors` package, the `fmt` standard library package offers a `Errorf` method that supports formatting the string returned (see Listing 10.3). This allows multiple values to be combined into a more meaningful error string and for dynamic error strings to be created.

LISTING 10.3   Using the `fmt` Package to Format Errors

```
 1:  package main
 2:
 3:  import (
 4:      "fmt"
 5:  )
 6:
 7:  func main() {
 8:      name, role := "Richard Jupp", "Drummer"
 9:      err := fmt.Errorf("The %v %v quit", role, name)
10:      if err != nil {
11:          fmt.Println(err)
12:      }
13:  }
```

Running the example prints the error.

```
go run example03.go
The Drummer Richard Jupp quit
```

▼ TRY IT YOURSELF

Formatting Errors in Go

In this example, you will learn how to format an error.

1. Open hour10/example03 in the code examples for this book.

2. Open the file example03.go in a text editor and try to understand what the example is doing.

3. From the terminal, run the program with `go run example03.go`.

4. You should see a message:

   ```
   The Drummer Richard Jupp quit
   ```

5. Change the return values and run the script again. Can you see how using variables would be useful to make the message dynamic?

Returning an Error from a Function

The beginning of this chapter explored how the convention in Go is to return an error type as the last return value of functions and methods. With an understanding of how errors are created and returned, Listing 10.4 shows an example.

LISTING 10.4   Errors as Return Values

```go
 1: package main
 2:
 3: import (
 4:     "fmt"
 5: )
 6:
 7: func Half(numberToHalf int) (int, error) {
 8:     if numberToHalf%2 != 0 {
 9:         return -1, fmt.Errorf("Cannot half %v", numberToHalf)
10:     }
11:     return numberToHalf / 2, nil
12: }
13:
14: func main() {
15:     n, err := Half(19)
16:     if err != nil {
17:         fmt.Println(err)
18:         return
19:     }
20:     fmt.Println(n)
21: }
```

The example shows a function returning an error and the caller handling the error. The code may be explained as follows:

- An integer value of 19 is passed to the `Half` function.

- The `Half` function checks to see if the value is even. This uses Go's modulus arithmetic operator that returns the remainder after the division. If it is not zero, it cannot be an even number. In this case, it is not zero.

- The `Half` function returns -1 and an error value.

- The caller checks for an error and finds one.

- The error is printed and the execution returns.

Running this example returns an error:

```
go run function.go
Cannot half 19
```

The example illustrates a strength of Go's error handling in that error handling does not happen in the function but rather where the function is called. This allows for greater flexibility in handling errors rather than a one-size-fits-all approach.

Errors and Usability

Aside from the technical side of error generation and Go conventions, it is worth considering errors from a user-centered perspective for a moment. If you are tasked with coding a library or package that will be used by others, how you choose to write and use errors greatly affects the usability, or ease of use, of your library. Users of your library will likely encounter errors and will look to recover from them. Consider the following error. Do you think this would allow you to handle or recover from an error easily?

```
You broke something! Good luck!!
```

This is a bad error message, as it offers no clues as to what went wrong, nor does it offer advice about how to recover. The following is an example of a better error message.

```
No config file found. Please create one at ~/.foorc.
```

This is a better error message, because:

- It is specific about the problem.

- It offers a resolution to the problem.

- It is respectful to the user.

If users of your library can be confident that errors are returned in a consistent way with helpful error messages, there is a far higher probability they can recover from errors. It is likely they will also consider your library more trustworthy and usable.

Don't `panic`

`panic` is a built-in function in Go that stops the ordinary flow of control and begins panicking, halting the execution of the program. For normal errors this is usually a bad idea, since execution will stop and it does not offer any alternative. Listing 10.5 demonstrates how `panic` is a hard stop on execution.

LISTING 10.5   Using `panic` to Halt Execution

```
 1:  package main
 2:
 3:  import (
 4:      "fmt"
 5:  )
 6:
 7:  func main() {
 8:      fmt.Println("This is executed")
 9:      panic("Oh no. I can do no more. Goodbye.")
10:      fmt.Println("This is not executed")
11:  }
```

Running the example results in `panic` and a crash.

```
go run panic.go
This is executed
panic: Oh no. I can do no more. Goodbye.

goroutine 1 [running]:
panic(0x48a560, 0xc42000a320)
    /usr/lib/go/src/runtime/panic.go:500 +0x1a1
    main.main()
    /home/go/golang-book-examples/hour10 /example05.go:7 +0xef
    exit status 2
```

Execution is halted after `panic` is called, so the line "This is not executed" is never reached.

The following example is often overused in Go code, and is really saying, "this is probably the end, my friend, crash the program." There are times when this is appropriate, but in general avoid doing this:

```
if err != nil {
    panic(err)
}
```

There are some scenarios where using panic may be the correct thing to do, however:

▶ The program reaches a state that is unrecoverable. This may mean that the state is lost or that continuing to execute the program will cause even more problems. In this scenario, the best thing to do is to crash the program.

▶ A scenario where the error cannot be handled.

Using panic

In this example, you will learn how to use panic.

1. Open the file hour10/example05.go in a text editor and try to understand what the example is doing.

2. From the terminal, run the program with `go run example05.go`.

3. Note that the program panics and halts execution.

Summary

This hour introduced Go's approach to errors. You were introduced to how to work with errors, then moved on to understand how to create errors. You then walked through Go's idiomatic approach to errors where the caller is responsible for handling errors. You learned that beyond a technical understanding of how errors work, it is worth thinking about how errors will be used and how they can support recovery. You learned that `panic` is a hard stop to execution, and should be used sparingly.

Q&A

Q. I see the `if err != nil` pattern everywhere in Go code. This seems like a lot of repetition. Is this the best way?

A. Although this may seem like a lot of repetition, being able to check errors is actually a feature of Go, and offers a lot of power to programmers. Although there are techniques and third-party packages that can reduce repetition, most Go programmers learn to enjoy being able to handle errors as they want to.

Q. Should I really care about errors?

A. Absolutely! Handling errors is a core part of writing resilient and stable software. The more you can think about how your program *could* go wrong and how you can recover from it, the better your code will be.

Q. Does Go have exceptions?

A. If you are coming from a language such as Java, Go does not have the traditional `try-catch-finally` control structure. Instead, errors are reported to callers of functions or methods. Go's approach to errors is not without controversy, but it is a design decision of the language to make errors a return value.

Workshop

This workshop contains quiz questions and exercises to help you solidify your understanding of the material covered. Try to answer all questions before looking at the "Answers" section that follows.

Quiz

1. What is different about Go's approach to error handling?

2. Can you use variables in Go errors?

3. When should you use `panic`?

Answers

1. Go functions support multiple return values, and the convention is to return errors as the last return value. This allows errors to be customized and returned to the caller. After that, it is up to the caller what happens with the error. Other languages take a view that all errors should crash the application immediately. Go is more flexible, and leaves it to the caller of a method or function to decide what to do with an error.

2. Yes. In fact, any code may be used to generate an error before it is returned. In his post "Errors are Values", Rob Pike outlines this idea:

"Values can be programmed, and since errors are values, errors can be programmed. Errors are not like exceptions. There's nothing special about them, whereas an unhandled exception can crash your program."

3. `Panic` should be used in situations where a program cannot recover from an error. It should be a last resort, and used if a program has reached a state where crashing is the most responsible thing to do.

Exercises

1. Think through your programming experience or your general computer usage, and think of a time when you found errors frustrating. What was bad about it?

2. Search for a third-party package on the Internet to read and parse files in "toml" format. From the project page, are you able to understand what the package does and how to use it? Install the package, and create a basic example to show that you understand it.

3. Extend the temperature package created in this hour to offer a function to convert degrees Celsius to kelvins. Add a table test to test a range of values.

HOUR 11
Working with Goroutines

What You'll Learn in This Hour:

▶ Understanding concurrency
▶ Concurrency versus parallelism
▶ Understanding concurrency through a web browser
▶ Blocking and non-blocking code
▶ Handling concurrent operations with Goroutines
▶ Using Goroutines to manage latency
▶ Defining Goroutines

In this hour, you will be introduced to the idea of concurrency and Goroutines. You will understand the difference between sequential execution and concurrent execution. You will see how Goroutines can be one way to deal with network latency. You will be introduced to the difference between concurrency and parallelism and see how Goroutines make programs run faster. Goroutines are one of Go's most elegant features, so if at any stage you feel this looks complicated, read on. Go solves it all with one keyword!

Understanding Concurrency

To understand Goroutines, it is first necessary to understand concurrency. In most simple computer programs, things happen sequentially and are executed in the order they appear. In a simplistic way, think of the lines of code in a script. Lines are executed in the order they appear. Until one line has finished executing, the next line will not be executed. For many programs this is the desired behavior, and allows a programmer to reason about the logic of a script safe in the knowledge that one line will not be executed until the next one has finished.

A simple representation of this is a restaurant server taking an order from a customer. A server cannot give an order to a chef before a customer has read the menu or before the server has given a menu to the customer. A sequence of events can be defined for a waiter to give a customer food:

1. Give customer menu.

2. Take customer order.

3. Give order to chef.

4. Get food from chef.

5. Give food to customer.

If a programmer were given the task to encode this process, it would seem reasonable to consider that one task cannot be completed without the previous one finishing. This process maps well to the idea of code executing in the order that it appears in a script, where one thing happens after another.

For many programming tasks, the idea of things executing in order is desired, and works well. Some examples of this are:

▶ Simple turn-based terminal game

▶ Temperature converter

▶ Random number generator

As programming and programming environments became more complicated, the idea of not having to wait for operations to complete before executing another became more important. This was driven by the need for programs to respond to more complex scenarios, but also for programs to be able to execute quickly without the need to wait for each line to finish executing. If a program is executed entirely in the sequence, the entire program can halt temporarily if a line takes a long time to complete. This may cause an end user to wait a long time for an event to happen.

Modern programming must account for many variables where time is unpredictable. It is not known, for example, how long it will take for a network call to complete, or how long it will take for a file to be read from a disk.

Suppose a program needs to call out to a weather service to get the current weather for a location. Some code is written to complete this request and handle the response from the web server. Once the request leaves the application, many things could affect how quickly the response returns, such as:

▶ Speed of the DNS lookup to find the address of the weather service

▶ Speed of the Internet connection between the application and the weather service servers

▶ Speed of establishing a connection with the weather service's servers

▶ Speed that the weather service application responds

Given that all these factors are beyond the control of the initiating application, it is entirely reasonable to assume that the speed of the response cannot be predicted. Furthermore, it is likely that each request will take a different amount of time to respond. Faced with this scenario, a programmer can either choose to wait for the response and block the program until the response returns or get on with other work that might be useful. The approach of most modern programming languages is to provide a way to wait for the response but allow a programmer to get on with other things.

Returning to the idea of a server in a restaurant, each step in the process has a number of unknowns in terms of the time that things will take to complete:

- How long will it take for the customer to sit down?
- How long will it take for customers to choose what they want?
- How quickly can the order be taken?
- How quickly can the chef take the order?
- How quickly can the chef cook the food?

If a server were to operate in a sequential way, he would be able to serve one customer effectively, but would have no ability to serve anyone else! It would be an expensive restaurant if one server was allocated to each customer. Instead, servers complete tasks concurrently. This means they can take other orders while a chef cooks the food, and they can deliver food while other customers choose their meals.

In the real world, most things happen concurrently. Humans can listen to music while getting on a bus, or read a book while waiting in line. As such, it makes sense for programming languages to provide a way to model this.

As the Internet has grown, programming within the context of a network has become far more prevalent. An application might now call out to multiple web services for pieces of information, or a database might be located on an entirely different network. With all things network-based, it is difficult to predict reliably when things will complete.

Concurrency Versus Parallelism

Now that we understand concurrency, before we discuss Goroutines it is important to understand the difference between concurrency and parallelism. For this, we will use a task of having to bake 100 cupcakes for a birthday party. Let's assume that there is an unending supply of cake mix and baking trays, and that we are interested in baking cakes quickly.

A sequential approach would entail baking a single cupcake in an oven one at a time. This is clearly inefficient, since it will take a long time. It would be necessary to wait until one cupcake had finished baking before another could be put in the oven. Furthermore, it would be unpredictable, since a cupcake may bake faster or slower, and may need a little less or extra time in the oven.

A concurrent approach would be to use a baking tray and bake more than one cupcake at once. This is vastly more efficient, but it still does not mean that all cupcakes will be ready at the same time. It is likely, for example, that some cakes will need more or less baking based on where they are in the oven or how much mix there is. Compared to a sequential approach, the baking will be exponentially quicker based on the number of cupcakes that can be baked at the same time.

The concurrency is limited by a number of factors, one of them being the size of the oven. If a friend also has an oven, the efficiency can be further improved by dividing the work between two ovens in different locations. The cupcakes can be baked at the same time, taking advantage of concurrency before they were taken to the party. The cupcakes are baked in parallel by splitting the work down into smaller parts before they are joined at the end. Parallelism can choose to take advantage of concurrency or not; it is more the idea of dividing up work and joining a result at the end.

Although this can seem complex (and includes some intricate computer science), Rob Pike, one of the creators of Go, came up with an excellent statement for the difference between the two: *"Concurrency is about dealing with lots of things at once. Parallelism is about doing lots of things at once."*

Especially in a modern programming context, concurrency is a regular part of programming. Some applications where concurrency is important, particularly in relation to performance, are:

- ► Chat
- ► Multiplayer games
- ► Web browsers
- ► Reading data from a disk

Responding to these requirements in the context of what Google does on a daily basis partly prompted Go's design, as traditional systems languages make it difficult to write efficient, concurrent code.

Understanding Concurrency Through a Web Browser

Using a web browser has become an everyday occurrence, and websites generally load extremely quickly. Yet the technology behind a browser has to do a large amount of concurrent work to assemble a web page and display it to a user. Often, pages are made up of images and scripts from many different servers around the Internet.

To help understand concurrency, you will open the hood on a browser and watch a web page being assembled. This can be achieved using the Developer Tools in your preferred browser. In Google Chrome, the Developer Tools can be found by opening the menu and choosing

'Developer', then selecting 'Network'. If you prefer to use another browser and do not know how to open the Developer Tools, enter 'Developer Tools' into Google along with the name of your preferred browser.

With Developer Tools open, type 'https://www.bbc.co.uk' into the address bar and hit return. As the page loads, watch as the requests are sent. You will be able to watch the requests complete. For each request, it is possible to dive into how long a request took and where the time was spent. Although the Developer Tools involve a little too much detail for the purposes of this hour, the point is that rather than make requests sequentially, a web browser makes concurrent requests and renders a page, or portions of it, as fast as possible. This results in a page loading quickly for the user of the browser. Although a page is not considered loaded until all the requests are complete, a browser can still do useful things with requests that have completed. If an image has been loaded, for example, it can be rendered on the page, as shown in Figure 11.1.

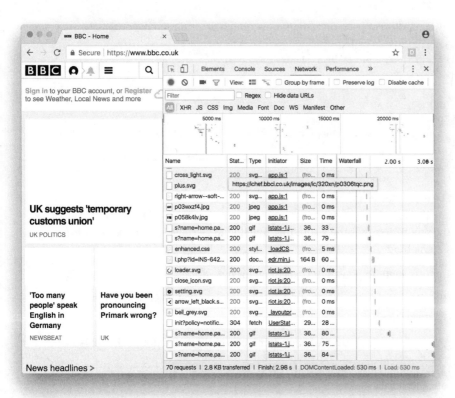

FIGURE 11.1
Loading the BBC Homepage. (Source: BBC News Online)

Blocking and Non-Blocking Code

Based on a high-level understanding of concurrency, the following example simulates a program where a function call blocks the execution of a program until an operation completes. A slow function call can be simulated using `time.Sleep`, which pauses the execution of a program for a particular duration. In reality, this might be a slow network call or a long-running function. Listing 11.1 shows a program that simulates a blocking function call.

LISTING 11.1   Simulating a Blocking Function Call

```
 1:  package main
 2:
 3:  import (
 4:      "fmt"
 5:      "time"
 6:  )
 7:
 8:  func slowFunc() {
 9:      time.Sleep(time.Second * 2)
10:      fmt.Println("sleeper() finished")
11:  }
12:
13:  func main() {
14:      slowFunc()
15:      fmt.Println("I am not shown until slowFunc() completes")
16:  }
```

Listing 11.1 can be explained as follows:

▶ Running the program causes the `slowFunc` function to be called that executes the `time.Sleep` method.

▶ The `time.Sleep` method pauses the execution for two seconds.

▶ Although the execution is paused, nothing else happens, so the second line in the `main` function is not executed.

▶ After two seconds, the `slowFunc` function completes and prints a line to that effect.

▶ Execution is returned to the main function and the second line is executed, printing a message to the terminal.

This code can be said to be blocking, as no other execution can occur while the program waits for `slowFunc()` to return.

Blocking Code

In this example, you will understand blocking code.

1. Open hour11/example01.go from the code examples for this book.

2. Read the code and try to understand what it is doing. If you need to, refer to the explanation of Listing 11.1.

3. From the terminal, run the program with `go run example01.go`.

4. After a pause, you will see the following text printed to the terminal:

```
sleeper() finished
I am not shown until slowFunc() completes
```

Handling Concurrent Operations with Goroutines

Go provides Goroutines as a way to handle operations concurrently. In the case of Listing 11.1, a Goroutine can allow for the `slowFunc` function to be called and for the second line in the `main` function to be executed immediately after it is called. The `slowFunc` function will still execute, but it will no longer block the execution of other lines in the program.

Using Goroutines is incredibly simple, and is just a case of putting the `go` keyword before any function or method that should be executed by a Goroutine. Returning to Listing 11.1, this can be amended to use a Goroutine, as shown in Listing 11.2.

LISTING 11.2   Using a Goroutine

```
 1:  package main
 2:
 3:  import (
 4:      "fmt"
 5:      "time"
 6:  )
 7:
 8:  func slowFunc() {
 9:      time.Sleep(time.Second * 2)
10:      fmt.Println("sleeper() finished")
11:  }
12:
13:  func main() {
14:      go slowFunc()
15:      fmt.Println("I am now shown straightaway!")
16:  }
```

Executing this code, however, yields an unexpected result.

▼ TRY IT YOURSELF

Understanding how Goroutines Return

In this example, you will understand how Goroutines return.

1. Open hour11/example02.go from the code examples for this book.

2. Read the code and try to understand what it is doing.

3. From the terminal, run the program with `go run example02.go`.

4. Immediately, you will see the following text printed to the terminal:

   ```
   I am now shown straightaway!
   ```

The result of the call to `slowFunc` is never seen, because Goroutines return immediately, meaning execution continues, and the program exits. If there is nothing else to prevent a program exiting, even before a Goroutine has returned, it will do so. In Hour 12, you will understand how to use Channels to manage Goroutines, but for now we can prevent the example exiting by adding another call to `time.Sleep`. Listing 11.3 shows a Goroutine being used to execute code concurrently.

LISTING 11.3   Showing Goroutine Concurrent Execution

```
 1:  package main
 2:
 3:  import (
 4:      "fmt"
 5:      "time"
 6:  )
 7:
 8:  func slowFunc() {
 9:      time.Sleep(time.Second * 2)
10:      fmt.Println("sleeper() finished")
11:  }
12:
13:  func main() {
14:      go slowFunc()
15:      fmt.Println("I am not shown until slowFunc() completes")
16:      time.Sleep(time.Second * 3)
17:  }
```

Running Listing 11.3 gives the expected behavior of allowing the program to continue execution before `slowFunc` completes.

Understanding how Goroutines Support Non-Blocking Code

In this example, you will learn how Goroutines support non-blocking code.

1. Open hour11/example03.go from the code examples for this book.

2. Read the code and try to understand what it is doing.

3. From the terminal, run the program with `go run example03.go`.

4. Immediately, you will see the following text printed to the terminal:

   ```
   I am now shown straightaway!
   ```

5. After a pause, you see the following text printed to the terminal:

   ```
   slowFunc() finished
   ```

Using Goroutines to Manage Latency

Dealing with network latency is a good example of where Goroutines can be useful—especially when working with third-party websites or services, which can be unpredictable.

As an example of a program that will be more efficient through the use of Goroutines, consider a website that takes an average of 1 second to respond. If this program uses sequential execution, it is likely to take around 3 seconds to complete. By using Goroutines, requests can be made concurrently, meaning the program may only take 1 second to complete. Furthermore, the order of responses in sequential execution will be the order in which they are declared in a script, since a request will not be made until the previous request has finished executing. In reality, one web service may respond more quickly than another. By using Goroutines, a response can be used as soon as it is received, regardless of the order that it appears in the script.

Suppose that three websites need to be tested. As you learned in Hour 6, a slice can be created to hold these addresses:

```
urls := make([]string, 3)
urls[0] = "https://www.usa.gov/"
urls[1] = "https://www.gov.uk/"
urls[2] = http://www.gouvernement.fr/
```

The slice can then be iterated over to make a request to the website and print the response time.

```
for _, u := range urls {
    responseTime(u)
}
```

The code to make a request and record the response is as follows. Do not be overly concerned with this function, as you will learn more about creating HTTP clients in Hour 19, "Using HTTP Clients in Go."

```
func responseTime(url string) {
    start := time.Now()

    res, err := http.Get(url)

    if err != nil {
        log.Fatal(err)
    }

    defer res.Body.Close()

    elapsed := time.Since(start).Seconds()

    fmt.Printf("%s took %v seconds \n", url, elapsed)
}
```

Using `range`, the `responseTime` function is called repeatedly for the slice of URLs. Provided you have an Internet connection, running Listing 11.4 yields a list of response times for this website. Depending on where you are in the world, you are likely to experience different timings.

LISTING 11.4   **Demonstrating Network Latency**

```
 1:  package main
 2:
 3:  import (
 4:      "fmt"
 5:      "log"
 6:      "net/http"
 7:      "time"
 8:  )
 9:
10:  func responseTime(url string) {
11:      start := time.Now()
12:
13:      res, err := http.Get(url)
14:
15:      if err != nil {
16:          log.Fatal(err)
17:      }
18:
19:      defer res.Body.Close()
20:
21:      elapsed := time.Since(start).Seconds()
```

```
22:
23:        fmt.Printf("%s took %v seconds \n", url, elapsed)
24:    }
25:
26:    func main() {
27:        urls := make([]string, 3)
28:        urls[0] = "https://www.usa.gov/"
29:        urls[1] = "https://www.gov.uk/"
30:        urls[2] = "http://www.gouvernement.fr/"
31:
32:        for _, u := range urls {
33:            responseTime(u)
34:        }
35:    }
```

TRY IT YOURSELF ▼

Understanding Network Latency

In this example, you will understand network latency. You need the Internet to run this example.

1. Open hour11/example04.go from the code examples for this book.

2. Read the code and try to understand what it is doing.

3. From the terminal, run the program with `go run example04.go`.

4. You will see the following text printed to the terminal. Note that depending on where you are, your Internet connection timings will vary.

   ```
   go run example04.go
   https://www.usa.gov/ took 0.14065427 seconds
   https://www.gov.uk/ took 0.083158559 seconds
   http://www.gouvernement.fr/ took 0.094341583 seconds
   ```

It is interesting to look at the response times. The network connection for running the "Try It Yourself" example was in the UK. It is possible to see that the fastest response came from the UK government website, probably because the servers are closest to the request. Running the example from a server in North America gives very different results.

```
go run example04.go
https://www.usa.gov/ took 0.86816862 seconds
https://www.gov.uk/ took 1.099022534 seconds
http://www.gouvernement.fr/ took 0.937821075 seconds
```

Now the example is run closer to servers in North America, so the connection to the United States government is quicker. Finally, running the example from a server in France shows that the French government website is quicker.

```
go run example04.go
https://www.usa.gov/ took 0.154239614 seconds
https://www.gov.uk/ took 0.15066432 seconds
http://www.gouvernement.fr/ took 0.068570371 seconds
```

The example shows that even though the difference in timing is relatively small, response times will vary depending on where you are in the world. This is known as network latency, and expresses how much time it takes for a packet of data to get from one point to another. If you are in Washington, for example, it will take longer for a packet to reach Paris than if you were in Lille.

The example also demonstrates how network latency introduces a problem. The order of execution is decided by the order that the URLs are declared in the script. Note that responses always come in the same order. This is because requests are executed in sequence, so requests can only be completed one at a time. There can be times when network latency is very important, like in a financial or gambling system, where a request needs to complete as soon as possible. It seems inefficient that someone in France should have to wait for requests to complete from the United States and UK before getting a response from the French website. This is where Goroutines can be used, and Go makes it incredibly easy to make code concurrent. All that needs to be changed in the previous example is to add the go keyword before the call to the responseTime function. Listing 11.5 shows the full example using Goroutines. This is identical to Listing 11.4 other than the addition of the go keyword and a sleep to stop the script from exiting.

LISTING 11.5   Using Goroutines to Manage Latency

```
 1:  package main
 2:
 3:  import (
 4:       "fmt"
 5:       "log"
 6:       "net/http"
 7:       "time"
 8:  )
 9:
10:  func responseTime(url string) {
11:       start := time.Now()
12:
13:       res, err := http.Get(url)
14:
15:       if err != nil {
16:           log.Fatal(err)
17:       }
18:
```

```
19:        defer res.Body.Close()
20:
21:        elapsed := time.Since(start).Seconds()
22:
23:        fmt.Printf("%s took %v seconds \n", url, elapsed)
24:    }
25:
26:    func main() {
27:        urls := make([]string, 3)
28:        urls[0] = "https://www.usa.gov/"
29:        urls[1] = "https://www.gov.uk/"
30:        urls[2] = "http://www.gouvernement.fr/"
31:
32:        for _, u := range urls {
33:            go responseTime(u)
34:        }
35:
36:        time.Sleep(time.Second * 5)
37:    }
```

TRY IT YOURSELF ▼

Managing Network Latency with Goroutines

In this example, you will understand how Goroutines can manage network latency. You will need an Internet connection to run this example.

1. Open hour11/example05.go from the code examples for this book.

2. Read the code and try to understand what it is doing.

3. From the terminal, run the program with `go run example05.go`.

4. You will see the following text printed to the terminal. Note that depending on where you are and your Internet connection, timing will vary.

```
go run example05.go
https://www.gov.uk/ took 0.11060096 seconds
http://www.gouvernement.fr/ took 0.175455318 seconds
https://www.usa.gov/ took 0.194380501 seconds
```

When running this example, something interesting happens. The order of the responses has changed, and they are ordered by the response time. Why is this? The `go` keyword has caused the function to be called concurrently. This means requests to the websites are made at the same time rather than one after another. When each request completes, it prints the response time to the console. Using Goroutines has many advantages for this scenario:

▶ The time it takes to execute the three requests is shorter, as they are executed concurrently. There is no need to make the requests one after the other.

▶ As soon as a response is received, it can be used immediately. There is no need for a previous request to complete.

▶ It does not matter in which order the URLs appear in a script. Data is available as soon as a response is received.

Although Goroutines do not remove network latency, they provide a way to make programming more efficient through a single keyword. Running the example from a server in France also shows that responses are handled in the order they are received.

```
go run example05.go
http://www.gouvernement.fr/ took 0.086887192 seconds
https://www.usa.gov/ took 0.167663493 seconds
https://www.gov.uk/ took 0.174901876 seconds
```

Although it is impossible to understand which website will respond the most quickly, Goroutines provide a way to manage network latency more efficiently and make code faster. If you have any exposure to using threads and locking, you will know that managing concurrency can be a complex and painful task. Go offers a single keyword to programmers to deliver this, and it is one of the language's most powerful and elegant features.

Defining Goroutines

If you have some exposure to other programming languages, you may know that concurrency is a common feature of programming languages. Node.js, for example, uses an event loop to manage concurrency, while Java uses threads. Web servers such as Apache and Nginx also have different approaches to concurrency, with Apache favoring threads and processes, and Nginx using an event loop. Do not worry if you do not understand all these terms. The point is that there are many approaches to solving concurrency, and they use the resources on a computer in different ways and make it easier or harder to write reliable software.

Like Java, Go uses threads behind the scenes to manage concurrency. There is no requirement, however, for a programmer to manage threads directly, and the Goroutine abstraction removes the pain of working with threads directly. The creation of a Goroutine uses only a few kilobytes of memory, so many thousands of Goroutines can be created without running out of memory. Goroutines can also be created and destroyed very efficiently.

Goroutines is a concurrency abstraction, so generally there is no requirement for a developer to understand precisely what is happening with the operating system.

Summary

During this hour, you were introduced to the idea of concurrency and one of Go's most elegant features. You saw how in the real world, most things happen concurrently. You understood that increasingly, modern programming has many challenges to deal with regarding concurrency. You learned how Goroutines make it incredibly easy to make code concurrent, and saw an example of how network latency can be managed using Goroutines.

Q&A

Q. Goroutines seem like magic! Do I need to understand more than just a single keyword?

A. To use Goroutines, just use a single keyword. What's more difficult to understand is what concurrency is and how it affects programming. In terms of the technical implementation of Goroutines, you can learn more about this, but in essence the language designers have taken care of this.

Q. Why does a Goroutine return immediately?

A. Goroutines return immediately because this is in line with the idea of not blocking execution. During Hour 12, you will learn about Channels, a way to connect and manage concurrent Goroutines.

Q. What can I use Goroutines for?

A. In any scenario where the order of events is unknown, Goroutines can be a good option. This includes network calls, reading files from a disk, and creating event-driven programs such as chat applications and games.

Workshop

This workshop contains quiz questions and exercises to help you solidify your understanding of the material covered. Try to answer all questions before looking at the "Answers" section that follows.

Quiz

1. What are some of the benefits of concurrent execution over sequential execution?

2. What is blocking code?

3. What are some scenarios other than network latency where concurrent programming may be useful?

Answers

1. Executing code concurrently means that a program may be able to complete more quickly and return data when it is ready rather than waiting for other parts of a program to complete.

2. Blocking code halts the execution of a program. In the examples in this hour, `Time.Sleep` was used to halt the execution of a program. Without programming concurrently, slow functions and poorly performing code can block the execution of a program, making it slow. Goroutines are one way to avoid blocking code, since a Goroutine will return a result when it is ready rather than blocking the entire execution of a program.

3. Some other scenarios where concurrent programming is useful include reading or writing data from a file on disk, reading or writing data from a network, and reading or writing data from a database.

Exercises

1. If you have time, watch "Concurrency Is Not Parallelism" by Rob Pike, one of the creators of Golang (https://www.youtube.com/watch?v=cN_DpYBzKso). The talk is about 30 minutes in duration, but is an excellent introduction to concurrency and how Go approaches it.

HOUR 12
Introducing Channels

What You'll Learn in This Hour:

- ▶ Using Channels
- ▶ Using buffered Channels
- ▶ Blocking and flow control
- ▶ Using Channels as function arguments
- ▶ Employing the select statement
- ▶ Quitting Channels

Hour 11 introduced you to Goroutines as a way to handle concurrent operations. You saw how it is possible to program tasks to run concurrently and handle responses when they return. You also saw that it was necessary to create timers to manage Goroutines. During this hour, you will be introduced to *Channels*, a way to manage communication between Goroutines. ~When combined, Channels and Goroutines offer a carefully curated environment in which to develop concurrent software.

Using Channels

If you consider that Goroutines are a way to support concurrent programming, Channels are a way to communicate with Goroutines. Channels allow data to flow in and out of Goroutines and facilitate communication between Goroutines themselves. Go's approach to concurrency is neatly encapsulated in a slogan defined in Effective Go.

Don't communicate by sharing memory; share memory by communicating.

This is an important differentiation in terms of Go's approach to concurrency, so it is worth some exploration. In other programming languages, concurrent programming is often achieved by using a shared piece of memory between multiple processes or threads. The shared memory allows programs to synchronize and ensure that execution happens in a logical way. At various stages of execution, one process or thread may lock this memory to prevent other processes or threads from modifying it. This is reasonable in that if shared memory is changed in the middle of an operation by another process, it can have catastrophic results and cause bugs or crashes. Where memory is locked in this way, it can be said to be mutually exclusive—only one process or thread can access it.

If this seems too theoretical, consider two holders of a joint account who are trying to spend money at the same time. The combined amount of the two transactions is greater than the total amount in their account. If both transactions are initiated at the same time and no locking is used, a balance check could show that funds are available even though there are insufficient funds. If, however, the first transaction initiates a lock on the balance value until it is completed, a double-spending scenario can be avoided. This may seem a reasonable way to manage a simple concurrent scenario, but consider a similar scenario where there are 20 account holders all making transactions frequently. Managing locks can quickly become complex.

Managing shared memory and locks is not an easy task, and many programming languages expect an in-depth knowledge of memory and memory management. Most seasoned program-mers will tell of scenarios where they spent days trying to track down a bug caused by a race condition between processes or threads using shared memory. In a concurrent environment where it is not always clear which part of a program will update a piece of data first, it can become extremely complex to reason about things using shared memory.

Although using shared memory certainly has its place, Go proposes Channels as a way to avoid using shared memory, instead favoring using messages between Goroutines. Although Goroutines are not technically threads, they can be considered threads in that they can execute code without blocking. Returning to the example of two holders of a joint account, taking the Goroutine approach means the account holders have a communication Channel open between them and choose to act accordingly. A transaction might initiate a message being sent to a Channel that could change the ability to make further transactions, or to change the way in which the other account holder will act. Messaging allows a push approach to orchestrating concurrent events. When an event happens, a message can be triggered and pushed to a receiver. In a shared memory approach, a program must check the shared memory (pulling). For highly dynamic concurrent programming environments, many feel that using messaging is a better way to model communication flows.

In Hour 11, you saw Listing 12.1, an example where a Goroutine was used to account for a slow-running function so that the execution of the program was not blocked (see Listing 12.1).

LISTING 12.1   Simple Goroutine Example

```
1:   package main
2:
3:   import (
4:       "fmt"
5:       "time"
6:   )
7:
```

```
 8:  func slowFunc() {
 9:       time.Sleep(time.Second * 2)
10:       fmt.Println("sleeper() finished")
11:  }
12:
13:  func main() {
14:       go slowFunc()
15:       fmt.Println("I am not shown until slowFunc() completes")
16:       time.Sleep(time.Second * 3)
17:
```

On line 9 of Listing 12.1, a timer is used to prevent the program from exiting before the Goroutine has returned. While this is fine for an example to introduce Goroutines, using timers in more complex concurrent programs is not a good option. In Channels, Golang offers a way to manage Goroutines and concurrency in general. In Listing 12.1, it would be useful if there were a way to communicate between the Goroutine and the program so that the Goroutine could let the main Goroutine know it has finished. Channels can do just that.

Initializing a Channel is as follows:

```
c := make(chan string)
```

This can be explained as follows:

▶ A variable c is initialized using shorthand variable assignment and is assigned the value to the right of :=.

▶ The builtin function make is used to initialize a Channel that is denoted by the chan keyword.

▶ After the declaration of chan comes string. This denotes that the Channel will hold data of the string type. This also means that only string type values can be sent and received on the Channel.

To send a message to a Channel is as follows:

```
c <- "Hello World"
```

Note the <- syntax. This denotes that the string to the right should be sent to the Channel to the left. If a Channel is initialized to expect strings, only strings may be sent as messages to the Channel. Trying to send a message of another type will result in an error.

Receiving a message on a Channel is as follows:

```
msg := <-c
```

DID YOU KNOW?

The syntax for receiving messages on a Channel is <- followed by the Channel name. A message can be assigned directly to a variable using shorthand variable assignment. If at any time you are unsure at the direction of the arrow in relation to the Channel, an arrow to the left indicates that data is going out of a Channel (receiving), and an arrow to the right indicates that data is going into a Channel (sending).

The basic syntax of creating a Channel, sending a message, and receiving a message comprises a large part of how Channels work. Revisiting Listing 12.1, this can now be reworked to use Channels, as shown in Listing 12.2.

LISTING 12.2   Using Channels to Communicate

```
 1: package main
 2:
 3: import (
 4:     "fmt"
 5:     "time"
 6: )
 7:
 8: func slowFunc() {
 9:     time.Sleep(time.Second * 2)
10:     c <- "slowFunc() finished"
11: }
12:
13: func main() {
14:     c := make(chan string)
15:     go slowFunc()
16:
17:     msg := <-c
18:     fmt.Println(msg)
19: }
```

The changes to Listing 12.1, as shown in Listing 12.2, can be explained as follows:

- ▶ A Channel c is initialized to take data of the string type.
- ▶ As in Listing 12.1, a Goroutine is started to execute the slowFunc function.
- ▶ The slowFunc method takes the Channel as an argument.
- ▶ The single argument to the slowFunc function specifies a Channel and the data type that is a string.

▶ A variable `msg` is initialized to receive a message from the `c` Channel. This blocks the process until a message has been received, preventing the process from exiting.

▶ When the `slowFunc` method completes a message, it is sent to the `c` Channel.

▶ The message is received and printed.

▶ As there is no more execution to complete, the program exits.

TRY IT YOURSELF

Using Channels to Communicate with Goroutines

In this example, you will understand how to use Channels to communicate with a Goroutine.

1. Open hour12/example01.go from the code examples for this book.

2. Read the code and try to understand what it is doing.

3. From the terminal, run the program with `go run example01.go`.

4. After two seconds, a message will be printed to the terminal:

```
slowFunc() finished
```

Using Buffered Channels

Often, a receiver will be available to receive messages once they are sent. But sometimes, no receiver is available to receive a message. In this scenario, a buffered Channel can be used. Buffering means that data is held in the Channel until a receiver is ready. Once a receiver is available, the message will be delivered. To create a buffered rather than an unbuffered Channel, the builtin `make` can take an additional argument of a buffer length.

```
messages := make(chan string, 2)
```

This creates a buffered Channel that can buffer up to two messages. Now two messages can be added to the Channel—even if there is no receiver. Note that a buffered Channel can only hold as many messages as specified; sending more will result in an error.

```
messages <- "hello"
messages <- "world"
```

Messages will be held in the Channel until a receiver is available. Listing 12.3 shows an example of a buffered Channel receiving two messages and the messages being received once a receiver is available.

LISTING 12.3 Receiving Two Messages in a Buffered Channel

```
 1:  package main
 2:
 3:  import (
 4:      "fmt"
 5:      "time"
 6:  )
 7:
 8:  func slowFunc(c chan string) {
 9:      for msg := range c {
10:          fmt.Println(msg)
11:      }
12:  }
13:
14:  func main() {
15:      messages := make(chan string, 2)
16:      messages <- "hello"
17:      messages <- "world"
18:      close(messages)
19:      fmt.Println("Pushed two messages onto Channel with no receivers")
20:      time.Sleep(time.Second * 1)
21:      receiver(messages)
22:  }
```

Something new in this example is the usage of `close`. This denotes that the message Channel is closed and no more messages can be sent to it.

```
close(messages)
```

Listing 12.3 can be explained as follows:

- A buffered Channel with a length of two is initialized.

- Two messages are sent to the Channel. There is no receiver at this point of execution, and the messages are buffered.

- The Channel is closed, meaning no more messages can be sent to it.

- The program prints a message to say the Channel contains two messages, and sleeps for a second.

- The Channel is passed as an argument to a function called `receiver`.

- The `receiver` function iterates over the Channel using `range`, and prints the buffered messages in the Channel to the console.

Buffered Channels are useful when you know the number of Goroutines that you need to start or want to be able to limit the amount of work that is scheduled.

Understanding Buffered Channels

In this example, you will understand how to use buffered Channels.

1. Open hour12/example02.go from the code examples for this book.

2. Read the code and try to understand what it is doing.

3. From the terminal, run the program with `go run example02.go`.

4. You will see the following printed to the terminal:

```
Pushed two messages onto Channel with no receivers
hello
world
```

Blocking and Flow Control

In Hour 11, "Working with Goroutines," you learned that Goroutines are a way to program concurrently in Go. You were introduced to the idea of a program blocking execution via a slow network call or function, and how Goroutines are a way to manage this. Although blocking operations are generally to be avoided in concurrent programming, there are times when code should block. A program that needs to run in the background, for example, needs to block execution so it should not exit.

Goroutines are designed to return immediately (not block), so using some control flow techniques are required if you want a process to block. For example, a program that receives messages from a Channel and prints them to a terminal needs to block the process so that it does not terminate.

Setting up a receiver on a Channel is a blocking operation in that it will prevent a function from returning until a message has been received. Listing 12.4 demonstrates some of the subtlety of blocking and Channels. What do you think this program will print?

LISTING 12.4 Channels and Flow Control

```
1:  package main
2:
3:  import (
4:      "fmt"
5:      "time"
6:  )
7:
8:  func slowFunc(c chan string) {
9:      t := time.NewTicker(1 * time.Second)
```

```
10:        for {
11:            c <- "ping"
12:            <-t.C
13:        }
14:    }
15:
16:    func main() {
17:        messages := make(chan string)
18:        go pinger(messages)
19:        msg := <-messages
20:        fmt.Println(msg)
21:    }
```

▼ TRY IT YOURSELF

Understanding Channels and Flow Control

In this example, you will understand some subtleties of Channels and flow control.

1. Open hour12/example03.go from the code examples for this book.

2. Read the code and try to understand what it is doing. What do you think it will print?

3. From the terminal, run the program with `go run example03.go`.

4. You will see the following printed to the terminal:

   ```
   ping
   ```

If you thought that this program will print a single ping message and exit, you are correct. Once a single message has been received, the blocking operation returns and the program exits. So how do you create a listener that will listen forever for messages on a Channel? Achieving this is not so much part of Channels, but more about the Go runtime and execution flow. During Hour 5, "Using Control Flow," you were introduced to control flow in Go, and understood the `for` statement. A `for` statement can be used to block a process indefinitely or to block for a certain number of iterations.

By adding a `for` statement to Listing 12.4, the process will run indefinitely and print messages to the console as they are sent to the Channel, as shown in Listing 12.5.

LISTING 12.5   Running a Process Indefinitely

```
1:    package main
2:
3:    import (
4:        "fmt"
5:        "time"
6:    )
```

```
 7:
 8:  func slowFunc(c chan string) {
 9:      t := time.NewTicker(1 * time.Second)
10:      for {
11:          c <- "ping"
12:          <-t.C
13:      }
14:  }
15:
16:  func main() {
17:      messages := make(chan string)
18:      go pinger(messages)
19:      for {
20:          msg := <-messages
21:          fmt.Println(msg)
22:      }
23:  }
```

TRY IT YOURSELF ▼

Preventing a Process from Exiting

In this example, you will understand how to prevent a process from exiting.

1. Open hour12/example04.go from the code examples for this book.

2. Read the code and try to understand what it is doing.

3. From the terminal, run the program with `go run example04.go`.

4. You will see the following printed to the terminal repeatedly:

   ```
   ping
   ping
   ping
   ```

If a process should receive a certain number of messages before exiting, a `for` statement including an iterator can be used. Once the iterations are complete, the process will exit.

```
for i := 0; i < 5; i++ {
    msg := <-messages
    fmt.Println(msg)
}
```

It is important to understand that Goroutines are non-blocking by design, so if a program needs to block for the purposes of receiving a number of messages or to run a process in perpetuity, other flow control techniques need to be employed.

Using Channels as Function Arguments

You saw how Channels can be passed to functions as arguments and messages sent to the Channels within the function. To further specify how Channels can be used within a function, it is possible to specify whether a Channel should be read-only, write-only, or read-write when passing it to a function. The syntax for specifying whether a Channel is read-only, write-only, or read-write is subtly different.

```
func channelReader(messages <-chan string) {
    msg := <-messages
    fmt.Println(msg)
}

func channelWriter(messages chan<- string) {
    messages <- "Hello world"
}

func channelReaderAndWriter(messages chan string) {
    msg := <-messages
    fmt.Println(msg)
    messages <- "Hello world"
}
```

If the <- syntax is to the left of the chan keyword, it signifies that the Channel is read-only within the function. If the <- is to the right of the chan keyword, it signifies that the Channel is write-only within the function. If no <- exists, the Channel will be read-write.

Specifying permissions on a Channel can be useful for ensuring the integrity of data within a Channel and specifying which parts of a program can send and receive data from a Channel.

Employing the select Statement

Suppose there is a scenario where multiple Goroutines and a program should only operate on the one that returns first. For this scenario, the select statement can be employed. A select statement can be thought of as the switch statement you learned about in Hour 5. A select statement creates a series of receivers for Channels and executes whichever one receives a message first. A select statement looks similar to a switch statement.

```
channel1 := make(chan string)
channel2 := make(chan string)

select {
    case msg1 := <-channel1:
        fmt.Println("received", msg1)
    case msg2 := <-channel2:
        fmt.Println("received", msg2)
}
```

If a message is received on `channel1`, the first case will be executed. If a message is received on `channel2`, the second case will be executed. The execution is determined by the timing of the message, with the first message determining which case is executed. Generically, any other messages received after that will be discarded. Once a message has been received, `select` stops blocking.

Listing 12.6 demonstrates a `select` statement.

LISTING 12.6 `select` Statement

```
 1:  package main
 2:
 3:  import (
 4:      "fmt"
 5:      "time"
 6:  )
 7:
 8:  func ping1(c chan string) {
 9:      time.Sleep(time.Second * 1)
10:      c <- "ping on channel1"
11:  }
12:
13:  func ping2(c chan string) {
14:      time.Sleep(time.Second * 2)
15:      c <- "ping on channel2"
16:  }
17:
18:  func main() {
19:      channel1 := make(chan string)
20:      channel2 := make(chan string)
21:
22:      go ping1(channel1)
23:      go ping2(channel2)
24:
25:      select {
26:      case msg1 := <-channel1:
27:          fmt.Println("received", msg1)
28:      case msg2 := <-channel2:
29:          fmt.Println("received", msg2)
30:      }
31:  }
```

Listing 12.6 is as follows:

▶ Two Channels are created that will hold string type data.

▶ Two functions are created to send messages to these Channels. To simulate the speed of the function, the first sleeps for one second and the second for two seconds.

▶ Two Goroutines are started for each of these functions.

▶ The `select` statement creates two receivers for messages from `channel1` and `channel2`.

▶ After one second, the ping1 function returns, sending a message to `channel1`.

▶ As a message has been received on `channel1`, the `msg1` case is executed, and a message is printed to the terminal.

▶ A `select` statement completes and no longer blocks the process, so the program exits.

▼ TRY IT YOURSELF

Using `select` with Channels

In this example, you will understand how to use a `select` statement.

1. Open hour12/example05.go from the code examples for this book.

2. Read the code and try to understand what it is doing.

3. From the terminal, run the program with `go run example05.go`.

4. You will see the following printed to the terminal:

   ```
   received ping on channel1
   ```

Listing 12.5 can be modified to show that `select` statements choose the first case that returns. The `ping2` function is made to return first by changing the sleep in the `ping1` function to 3 seconds. Now, because a message is sent to `channel2` first, the `msg2` case is executed.

▼ TRY IT YOURSELF

Understanding how `select` Executes a Case

In this example, you will understand how the `select` statement executes the case that receives a message first.

1. Open hour12/example06.go from the code examples for this book.

2. Read the code and try to understand what it is doing.

3. From the terminal, run the program with `go run example06.go`.

4. You will see the following printed to the terminal:

   ```
   received ping on channel2
   ```

You saw how the `select` statement is a useful way to respond to the first message that is received. But what if no messages are received? For this, a timeout can be used. This allows the `select` statement to stop blocking after a certain amount of time and for execution to continue. Returning to Listing 12.6, a timeout case can be added that will be executed if no other cases are executed within half a second.

```
select {
    case msg1 := <-channel1:
        fmt.Println("received", msg1)
    case msg2 := <-channel2:
        fmt.Println("received", msg2)
    case <-time.After(500 * time.Millisecond):
        fmt.Println("no messages received. giving up.")
}
```

TRY IT YOURSELF ▼

Using a Timeout with `select`

In this example, you will understand how to use a timeout with the `select` statement.

1. Open hour12/example07.go from the code examples for this book.

2. Read the code and try to understand what it is doing.

3. From the terminal, run the program with `go run example07.go`.

4. You will see the following printed to the terminal:

   ```
   no messages received. giving up.
   ```

Quitting Channels

Using a timeout is great for scenarios where execution should stop after a known amount of time. Sometimes, however, the time at which a `select` statement should return is not known, and a timer cannot be used. For this scenario, a quit Channel can be used. This is a technique rather than part of the language specification, but it can send a message to a Channel and immediately exit a `select` blocking statement.

Consider a scenario where a program needs a `select` statement to block indefinitely but then be able to make it return at will. By adding a quit Channel to a select block, a message can be sent to a quit Channel to terminate the statement and end blocking. Think of a quit Channel as a kill switch for blocking `select` statements. A quit Channel can be called anything, but is typically named "stop" or "quit." In the following example, a `select` statement is declared in a `for` loop, meaning it will block forever and receive messages indefinitely. By sending a message to the stop Channel, the `select` statement can be triggered to stop blocking, return from the loop, and continue execution.

```
messages := make(chan string)
stop := make(chan bool)

for {
    select {
    case <-stop:
        return
    case msg := <-messages:
        fmt.Println(msg)
    }
}
```

A scenario where this might be useful is where a part of an application is sending messages to a Channel, and this should be terminated at some unknown point in the future.

For the purposes of this example, a function will be created in a Goroutine that will send a message to the messages Channel every second.

```
func sender(c chan string) {
    t := time.NewTicker(1 * time.Second)
    for {
        c <- "I'm sending a message"
        <-t.C
    }
}

messages := make(chan string)
go sender(messages)
```

A `select` statement within a `for` loop allows messages to be printed as they are received. As this is a blocking operation, these messages will continue to be printed until the process is manually terminated.

```
for {
    select {
    case msg := <-messages:
        fmt.Println(msg)
    }
}
```

If you want to execute this example, it is available as `example08.go` in this hour's examples.

In this example, there is no way to exit this program without killing the process, and it will run indefinitely. A quit Channel allows execution to return from the blocking operation and for the program to terminate. By creating a stop Channel, the program can send a message to the stop Channel and break out of the `for` loop.

```
stop := make(chan bool)

for {
    select {
    case <- stop:
        return
    case msg := <-messages:
        fmt.Println(msg)
    }
}
```

Listing 12.7 shows a full example of using a quit Channel. For the purposes of the example, a message is sent to the quit Channel after a certain amount of time. In reality, this might be determined by an unknown event happening elsewhere in an application.

LISTING 12.7   Using a Quit Channel

```
 1:  package main
 2:
 3:  import (
 4:      "fmt"
 5:      "time"
 6:  )
 7:
 8:  func sender(c chan string) {
 9:      t := time.NewTicker(1 * time.Second)
10:          for {
11:              c <- "I'm sending a message"
12:              <-t.C
13:          }
14:  }
15:
16:  func main() {
17:      messages := make(chan string)
18:      stop := make(chan bool)
19:      go sender(messages)
20:      go func() {
21:          time.Sleep(time.Second * 2)
22:          fmt.Println("Time's up!")
23:          stop <- true
24:      }()
25:
```

```
26:        for {
27:            select {
28:            case <-stop:
29:                return
30:            case msg := <-messages:
31:                fmt.Println(msg)
32:            }
33:        }
34:    }
```

▼ **TRY IT YOURSELF**

Using a Stop Channel

In this example, you will understand how to use a stop Channel.

1. Open hour12/example09.go from the code examples for this book.

2. Read the code and try to understand what it is doing.

3. From the terminal, run the program with `go run example09.go`.

4. You will see the following printed to the terminal:

   ```
   I'm sending a message
   I'm sending a message
   Time's up!
   ```

Summary

This hour introduced you to Channels. Combined with Goroutines, Channels offer a powerful way to manage concurrency. You saw how to create a Channel and use it to send a message between Goroutines. You learned how to create a buffered Channel and pass Channels as arguments to a function. You learned how `select` can be used to wait for messages on several Channels and then operate on the first one that receives a message. Concurrent programming is a large and complex topic, but if you have grasped how Channels support communication with Goroutines, you have achieved a lot!

Q&A

Q. Can Channels have more than one data type?

A. No. Channels can only have one data type. Channels can be created with any type, so it is possible to use a struct to hold more complex data structures.

Q. **What happens if two Channels within a `select` statement receive a message at the same time?**

A. One Channel will be chosen at random and executed. Only the selected one is executed.

Q. **If I close a Channel, are buffered messages lost?**

A. Closing a buffer means that no more messages may be sent to a Channel. Buffered messages are retained so they can be read by a receiver.

Workshop

The workshop contains quiz questions and exercises to help you solidify your understanding of the material covered. Try to answer all questions before looking at the "Answers" section that follows.

Quiz

1. What do Channels offer over Goroutines?

2. What does a timeout do in a select statement?

3. How could you write a program to receive ten messages from a Channel and then exit?

Answers

1. Channels complement Goroutines and offer the ability to communicate between them. This offers programmers a carefully curated environment in which to conduct concurrent programming.

2. A timeout will return from a `select` statement after a certain amount of time, halting the blocking operation. A `select` statement will execute the first message it receives. If no messages are received, a timeout can be used to return from the `select` statement after a certain amount of time.

3. To receive ten messages from a Channel and then exit, a `select` statement can be used inside a `for` loop that iterates ten times.

Exercises

1. Revisit example05.go in Hour 11 where you were introduced to Goroutines. Modify the example to use Channels. Use a `for` loop with a `select` statement and introduce a timeout that will cancel the execution if responses are not received after a certain amount of time. A solution is given as example10.go in the code examples for this hour.

HOUR 13
Using Packages for Code Reuse

What You'll Learn in This Hour:

- ▶ Importing packages
- ▶ Using third-party packages
- ▶ Installing a third-party package
- ▶ Managing dependencies
- ▶ Creating a package

A Go package is used to group code so it may be imported and used in a Go program. During this hour, you will be introduced to packages and how they can be used to create Go programs. You will also be introduced to dependency management in Go before creating and sharing your own package.

Importing Packages

The basic Go "Hello World!" program is useful for understanding how a package may be imported and used (see Listing 13.1).

LISTING 13.1 Importing a Package

```
 1:  package main
 2:
 3:  import (
 4:      "fmt"
 6:  )
 7:
 8:  func main() {
 9:      fmt.Println("Hello World!")
10:  }
```

Go programs start with a package clause. The main package is a special type of package in that it is unimported. The only requirement for a main package is that it must declare a function main that takes no arguments and returns no value. In short, the main package is the root of your program.

A main package is free to import other packages using the import declaration. After importing a package, the exported (or public) identifiers are available. Identifiers in Go, among other things, can be variables, constants, types, functions, or methods. This allows packages to provide rich and varied functionality through a scoped interface. The math package, for example, provides access to a Pi constant (see Listing 13.2).

LISTING 13.2   Accessing Pi Through the Math Package

```
 1:  package main
 2:
 3:  import (
 4:      "fmt"
 5:      "math"
 6:  )
 7:
 8:  func main() {
 9:      fmt.Println(math.Pi)
10:  }
```

An example of a package exporting a function is the strings package that exports a ToLower function for making a string lowercase, as shown in Listing 13.3.

LISTING 13.3   Converting Types to a String

```
 1:  package main
 2:
 3:  import (
 4:      "fmt"
 6:  )
 7:
 8:  func main() {
 9:      fmt.Println(strings.ToLower("STOP SHOUTING!"))
10:  }
```

The pattern of importing a package and using the exported identifiers is fundamental to how code reuse works in the standard library and with third-party code. Although it is a simple pattern, it is worth understanding, as it supports a great deal of flexibility and code reuse.

Understanding Package Usage

Before understanding how to use a package, how do you know what is the correct package to use? In the standard library, at least, the Go authors have taken a consistent approach to naming to help programmers understand how packages are organized. Go package names are short, concise, and evocative. The `strings` package contains functions for working with strings; the `bytes` package contains functions for working with `bytes`. The more you work with Go, the more you will memorize which package to use for a specific task; if you cannot remember, there is intuitive, well-organized documentation available.

Suppose a particular program needs to manipulate some strings. By reading through the list of standard library packages at https://golang.org/pkg/, it is possible to see that the `strings` package exists. Great! This can be imported and used to build the program. But how do you know what it can do? Go has a strong approach toward documentation, and the packages in the standard library offer excellent documentation. The `strings` package documentation is available at https://golang.org/pkg/strings/.

This documentation features a list of exported identifiers available for use. Suppose that in the program there is a requirement to lowercase a string. The documentation shows that there is a method available called `ToLower`. It also documents that the function takes a string and returns a string:

```
func ToLower(s string) string
```

There is also a short description describing what the function does and some example code demonstrating usage. The example can be executed in the browser. If you are interested in understanding the function in more detail, it is possible to jump to the source code for the package.

Using Third-Party Packages

The standard library provides a huge amount of functionality, but Go's design keeps the core standard library small and stable. As such, standard libraries are not provided for connecting to specific databases, parsing specific file formats, or working with authentication protocols. Before long, a program will reach the limit of the standard library. At this point, a programmer is faced with two choices:

- ▶ Write some code to solve the problem.
- ▶ Find a package (or library code) that solves the problem.

By nature, programmers are lazy, and will most likely opt for the second option. However, adding additional dependencies into a program should be considered carefully, as it has implications for the stability and maintainability of a program. There are a few questions to ask when considering using a third-party library:

▶ Do I understand what the code does?

▶ Is the code trustworthy?

▶ How well maintained is the code?

▶ Do I need this library?

When answering these questions, consider these points:

▶ It is important to understand what a package does. Good third-party packages have excellent documentation, and often follow the Go Documentation conventions of offering documentation for exported identifiers. Reading the documentation can establish whether a package offers the required functionality.

▶ Establishing a level of trust with a third-party package is important. Remember that packages imported into a program have access to an underlying operating system. Depending on the level of paranoia, trust may be established by looking at the number of other people using the package, through a recommendation from a colleague, or by reading the source code.

▶ The nature of software means that third-party packages will have bugs. Picking an actively maintained third-party package over one that has seen no updates for years means the package is likely to be more stable over time.

▶ Importing a third-party package increases complexity. Often, an entire package will be imported for a single function. In this case, it is acceptable to copy the function rather than use a third-party package.

Installing a Third-Party Package

To use a third-party package, the same `import` statement is used as for the standard library. In the following example, the `stringutil` package from the Go team will be used. This simple package demonstrates third-party packages and contains one exported function, `Reverse`. This takes a string, reverses it, and returns a string.

To use a third-party package, it must first be installed using the `go get` command. This is installed by default with Go, and it takes a path to a remote server and installs it locally:

```
go get github.com/golang/example/stringutil
```

The package is installed with your `$GOPATH` so is available to use within programs. The source code may be reviewed by opening the files within your `src` directory. The folder pattern follows the download path:

```
// OSX and Linux
$GOPATH/src/github/golang/example/stringutil
// Windows
%GOPATH%\src\github\golang\example\stringutil
```

Now that the package is installed, it may be imported.

LISTING 13.4   Using a Third-Party Package

```
 1:  package main
 2:
 3:  import (
 4:      "fmt"
 5:      "github.com/golang/example/stringutil"
 6:  )
 7:
 8:  func main() {
 9:      s := "ti esrever dna ti pilf nwod gniht ym tup I"
10:      fmt.Println(stringutil.Reverse(s))
11:  }
```

Running the program uses the third-party package and reverses the string:

```
go run example01.go
I put my thing down flip it and reverse it
```

Often, a third-party package will depend on other third-party packages. The `go get` command is smart enough to also download these dependencies, so there is no need to do this manually for each package.

▼ TRY IT YOURSELF

Installing and Using a Third-Party Package

In this example, you will understand how to install and use a third-party package.

1. Open the file hour13/example01.go in a text editor and try to understand what the example is doing.

2. Install the stringutil library by running `go get github.com/golang/example/stringutil`

3. Run the example `go run example01.go`.

4. You should see that text is reversed:

   ```
   I put my thing down flip it and reverse it
   ```

Managing Third-Party Dependencies

Many languages have package managers that simplify working with third-party packages. Python has pip, .NET has Nuget, Ruby has RubyGems, Node.js has npm. At the time of this writing, Go had no official package manager, although dep https://github.com/golang/dep is being actively developed.

This hour has shown you how to install a remote package, but in working with third-party packages and moving beyond trivial usage, there are numerous considerations:

▶ How do you update a package when a bug fix is available?

▶ How do you specify a version of a package?

▶ How do you share a dependency manifest with other developers?

▶ How do you install dependencies on a build server?

The `go get` command supports updating individual or all packages on a filesystem. To update dependencies for a project, the following may be run from within a project folder:

```
go get -u
```

Specific packages may also be updated:

```
go get -u github.com/spf13/hugo
```

All packages on a filesystem may also be updated:

```
go get -u all
```

The behavior of `go get` is to pull source code from a remote branch that matches the local branch. For example, if the local branch is `master`, it will pull the latest from `master`.

Although the simplicity of the updating package is great, complexity can quickly arise if, for example, a third-party library is being used across multiple projects. Suppose that Project A relies on version 1.2 of a third-party library, but Project B relies on version 1.3.

As a response to this from version 1.5 of Go, the `vendor` folder was introduced. This supports adding third-party modules to a `vendor` folder within the project root and moving all package files to this folder. Rather than installing a package globally across a machine, it is installed directly into the project. The `stringutil` package installed earlier may be moved into a vendor folder. As such, the directory structure to use the `stringutil` package from `github .com/golang/example/stringutil` is as follows:

```
example02/
├── example02.go
└── vendor
    └── github.com
        └── golang
            └── example
                └── stringutil
                    ├── reverse.go
                    └── reverse_test.go
```

Note that the `stringutil` package will now only be available within this project, rather than across a machine. This approach has some advantages:

- ▶ Packages may be locked to a specific version by simply copying a version into a project directory.

- ▶ There is no requirement for build servers to download dependencies, since they are in the project.

If you are used to package managers, you may see some disadvantages:

- ▶ Dependencies must be included in a repository.

- ▶ It is not immediately apparent which version of a package is being used.

- ▶ Dependencies within a package are not handled.

- ▶ It is not possible to specify the exact commit or branch in a manifest.

Currently, the responsibility for more complex dependency management is pushed onto programmers; there are a number of third-party tools that use the `vendor` folder to allow precise versions of packages to be installed.

▼ TRY IT YOURSELF

Using the Vendor Folder

In this example, you will understand how to use the `vendor` folder to manage dependencies.

1. This example relies on the book's code examples being in the GOPATH. If you did not install them using `go get`, do so now: `go get github.com/shapeshed/golang-book-examples`

2. Open hour13/example02 in the code examples for this book.

3. Examine the `vendor` folder and understand that this acts as a local copy of the package.

4. For this example, there is no need to run `go get`.

5. Run the example `go run example02.go`.

6. You should see that text is reversed:

   ```
   I put my thing down flip it and reverse it
   ```

Creating a Package

As well as using third-party packages, at some point you may wish to create a package. In this example, an example package will be created and published to Github to allow it to be shared with others. The package will deal with temperatures and provide functions for converting one temperature format to another. Create a file called `temperature.go`, with the content shown in Listing 13.5.

LISTING 13.5   Simple Package

```
1:  package temperature
2:
3:  func CtoF(c float64) float64 {
4:      return (c * (9 / 5)) + 32
5:  }
6:
7:  func FtoC(c float64) float64 {
8:      return (f - 32) * (9 / 5)
9:  }
```

Remember that any identifier starting with an uppercase letter will be available when importing the package. To create private identifiers (variables, functions, etc.), start the name with a lowercase letter.

To test the package, a test file can be created as temperature_test.go, as shown in Listing 13.6. You will learn about testing in Hour 15. For now, it is enough to know that this file adds tests for the package.

LISTING 13.6   Testing the Package

```
 1:  package temperature
 2:
 3:  import (
 4:      "testing"
 5:  )
 6:
 7:  type temperatureTest struct {
 8:      i  float64
 9:      expected Temperature
10:  }
11:
12:  var CtoFTests = []temperatureTest{
13:      {4.1, 39.38},
14:      {10, 50},
15:      {-10, 14},
16:  }
17:
18:  var FtoCTests = []temperatureTest{
19:      {32, 0},
20:      {50, 10},
21:      {5, -15},
22:  }
23:
24:  func TestCtoF(t *testing.T) {
25:      for _, tt := range CtoFTests {
26:          actual := CtoF(tt.i)
27:          if actual != tt.expected {
28:              t.Errorf("expected %v, actual %v", tt.expected, actual)
29:          }
30:      }
31:  }
32:
33:  func TestFtoC(t *testing.T) {
34:      for _, tt := range FtoCTests {
35:          actual := FtoC(tt.i)
36:          if actual != tt.expected {
37:              t.Errorf("expected %v, actual %v", tt.expected, actual)
38:          }
39:      }
40:  }
```

Running the tests, you see that they pass correctly:

```
go test
PASS
ok      github.com/shapeshed/temperature        0.001s
```

It is important to think about the users of your package if you are going to make it available on the Internet. As such, include these three recommended files with your package:

- A LICENSE file describing how people may use the code

- A README file containing information on the package

- A Changelog file detailing changes made to the package

As the creator of the code, it is your choice how you license it. There are many open source licenses available, with some being permissive and others restricted. A list of Open Source Licenses is available for review at https://opensource.org/licenses.

The README file should contain information on the package, how to install it, and how to use it. You may wish to include information on how to submit contributions to the project. If you are publishing your package to Github, consider writing in Markdown format. Github automatically formats markdown files.

The Changelog file should list changes to the package. This might include the addition of features or the removal of an API. Often, git tags are used to denote releases so that users of a library can easily check out a specific version.

The example package from this hour is available at https://github.com/shapeshed/temperature.

Summary

This hour introduced you to packages as a way to encapsulate, reuse, and share Go code. You learned how to install packages and use them within Go programs. You saw how to use the vendor folder to manage dependencies. You understood how to write your own packages. Finally, you understood how you can share the packages you create on the Internet.

Q&A

Q. When should I write code, and when should I use a third-party package?

A. This is a difficult question! Especially when you are starting out, it is tempting and often efficient to use a third-party package. Over time, as you become more proficient, you may find you rely on third-party libraries less. For particular packages such as database drivers, it makes sense to use a third-party package. For other scenarios, it may make sense to write code or simply copy parts of third-party packages into your code.

Q. How much should I be worried about security?

A. Introducing any third-party code into your project introduces a security risk. Go does not offer package signing, so it is quite possible for a Github account to be compromised and for an attacker to replace a popular package with some malicious code. In reality, it is unlikely that this will happen, and how paranoid you are depends on the level of security you need. The level of security you will need for a college project will differ from a military project, for example.

Q. How can I copy a third-party package's dependencies into the `vendor` folder?

A. At the time of this writing, Go does not provide an official tool to move a third-party package's dependencies into the vendor folder. This needs to be done manually or via a third-party dependency management tool.

Workshop

The workshop contains quiz questions and exercises to help you solidify your understanding of the material covered. Try to answer all questions before looking at the "Answers" section that follows.

Quiz

1. In a package file, what is the difference between identifiers starting with an uppercase letter and identifiers starting with a lowercase letter?

2. How do you install a third-party package?

3. How does the vendor folder work?

Answers

1. Identifiers beginning with an uppercase letter are exported, meaning they are available when importing a package. Identifiers beginning with a lowercase letter are not exported, meaning they are not available when importing a package. In short, identifiers starting with an uppercase letter are public, and identifiers with a lowercase letter are private.

2. Third-party packages can be installed using the `go get` command and passing a domain name and path to the command. Packages are installed into your $GOPATH and are available to programs within your $GOPATH.

3. The vendor folder allows Go to link any packages that are in the vendor folder to a program rather than using a globally installed version. This means an exact version of a package may be used. Several third-party tools add further functionality.

Exercises

1. Read through the `strings` package source code at https://golang.org/src/strings/strings.go. Try to identify exported identifiers. Do not worry if you do not understand all of the code, just try to understand how a package works.

2. Search for a third-party package on the Internet to read and parse files in "toml" format. You should find a package at https://github.com/toml-lang/toml. From the project page, are you able to understand what the package does and how to use it? Install the package and create a basic example to show that you understand it.

3. Extend the temperature package created in this hour to offer a function to convert degrees Celsius to kelvins. Add a table test to test a range of values.

HOUR 14
Naming Conventions in Go

What You'll Learn in This Hour:

- ▶ Formatting code in Go
- ▶ Using `gofmt`
- ▶ Configuring text editors
- ▶ Naming conventions
- ▶ Using `golint`
- ▶ Using `godoc`
- ▶ Automating workflow

In exploring the Go ecosystem, you will find the phrase *Idiomatic Go* used regularly as a reference to the accepted way of doing things. There is no enforced standard or compiler checking for what Idiomatic Go means, and at times Idiomatic Go can seem mysterious and unclear. This hour explores Go conventions and tools that can help promote writing Idiomatic Go. In reality, Idiomatic Go means following the standard conventions. After reading this hour, you will understand many of the conventions used within the Go community.

Formatting Code in Go

The formatting of code refers to the way that code is formatted in a file. In particular, it refers to the way that code is indented and how carriage returns are used. Go does not enforce specific conventions around code formatting, but does have a de facto standard that is widely used and adopted in the community. Consider Listing 14.1, which is legal Go code and will compile and execute. Do you find this easy to read?

LISTING 14.1   Formatting in Go

```
1:  package main        ; import "fmt";
2:  func main() { fmt.Println("Hello World") }
```

Code formatting styles are a topic of frequent debate among programmers and, for the majority of the time, these debates detract from the code behind the formatting. Furthermore, maintaining a code base where developers use different styles can lead to confusing code, arguments around pull requests, and, at worst, errors. JavaScript, for example, offers a rich and permissive syntax and is frequently the source of debate around how code is written. The following are valid ways of importing a module in Node.js.

```
var http = require("http");
var crypto = require("crypto");

var http = require("http")
  , crypto = require("crypto")

var http = require("http"),
    crypto = require("crypto");
```

Although there is some standardization within the Node.js community, it is common to see all three styles used in projects. Frequently, code contributions to Open Source projects need to be reformatted, as they do not conform with the prevailing convention. It may be difficult to believe, but this can be a source of friction on projects without even getting down to the code.

Go takes a pragmatic but strong approach to code formatting. Although it is not enforced, there is a formatting convention for Go, and this is encapsulated in the gofmt command. The compiler does not enforce that code is formatted per the gofmt command, but almost all the Go community use gofmt and expect code to be formatted in this way.

Although some programmers are initially unhappy with the default choices around formatting, the fact that a choice has been made and that it is encapsulated in official code is liberating. There is no longer any need to have lengthy discussions around the correct approach or to produce style guidelines for a team. It is strongly recommended that you format your code according to the Go conventions.

Using gofmt

Go provides the gofmt tool to help ensure that Go code is formatted in line with expected conventions. The beauty of this tool is that you do not even need to learn the conventions. Over time, as you learn how code is formatted, adhering to the conventions will become second nature. Returning to Listing 14.1, the gofmt tool may be used to format the file in line with the conventions. Running `gofmt` on a file prints the results to standard output without modifying the original file.

```
gofmt example01.go
package main

import "fmt"

func main() {
    fmt.Println("Hello World")
}
```

Notice that the file has been reformatted and is now more readable, with consistent spacing. To see the difference between a file and the expected conventions, the –d option may be used to show a `diff`. This shows the difference between the current file and what `gofmt` expects.

```
diff example01.go gofmt/example01.go
--- /tmp/gofmt062251244 2017-08-26 14:38:12.554082827 +0100
+++ /tmp/gofmt593374555 2017-08-26 14:38:12.554082827 +0100
@@ -1,4 +1,7 @@
-package main; import "fmt";
+package main

-func main() {
-fmt.Println("Hello World") }
+import "fmt"
+
+func main() {
+        fmt.Println("Hello World")
+}
```

If you are happy for the `gofmt` tool to rewrite the file, the –w flag can be used. This overwrites the current file with formatting applied.

```
gofmt -w example01.go
```

Using `gofmt`

In this example, you learn how to use the `gofmt` tool.

1. Open hour14/example01.go from the code examples for this book.

2. Notice that the code is poorly formatted.

3. From the terminal, run the program with `gofmt -w example01.go`.

4. Open the file example01.go. You should see that it has been reformatted by the `gofmt` tool.

Configuring Text Editors

When writing Go code, many text editors have third-party Go plugins that automatically run `gofmt` when a file is saved and correct the formatting before a file is saved. Many of these tools also ensure that your text editor is correctly configured to use tabs for indentation rather than spaces, as the Go convention expects. Using a plugin in your text editor can be an excellent way of using tooling like `gofmt` without even thinking about it. Most text editors have a plugin available for Go.

- ▶ Vim (vim-go): https://github.com/fatih/vim-go

- ▶ Emacs (go.mode.el): https://github.com/dominikh/go-mode.el.

- ▶ Sublime (GoSublime): https://github.com/DisposaBoy/GoSublime

- ▶ Atom (go-plus): https://github.com/joefitzgerald/go-plus

- ▶ Eclipse (goclipse): https://goclipse.github.io/

- ▶ Visual Studio (vscode-go): https://github.com/Microsoft/vscode-go

Many of these plugins also go beyond simple formatting; they allow developers to build, test, and run code from within the text editor. Although these plugins are not required to develop Go code, they improve productivity, so it's recommended that you review which Go plugins are available for your text editor.

Naming Conventions

It is said that the two hardest things in computer science are caching and naming things. Although this is slightly tongue-in-cheek, expressive and clear naming helps with readability and maintainability of code. There are some conventions in Go that are enforced by the compiler, and others that are more at the whim of a programmer. Being sensitive to other programmers and the conventions used within Go will help you to become a good citizen of the Go community. In terms of naming elements, you learned in Hour 13, "Using Packages for Code Reuse," that element names that begin with an uppercase letter are intended to be exported, and ones that begin with a lowercase letter are not.

```
var Foo := "bar" // Exported
var foo := "bar" // Not Exported
```

Many other languages have conventions for public and private variables, including using underscores to represent private variables. These should not be used in Go, and the convention of uppercase and lowercase should be followed.

It is unlikely that every programmer will agree on how to name a variable, but providing they take a consistent approach, it matters less. The convention in Go is to use Camel Case or Pascal Case for variable names where two words need to be compounded. Depending on whether a value should be exported or not, Camel or Pascal case is chosen.

```
var fileName // Camel Case
var FileName // Pascal Case
```

It is common in Go programs to see short variable names that reference a data type. This is favored to allow a programmer to focus on logic rather than the variable. In this case, i represents an Integer data type, s a String data type, and so on. Initially, it may seem that variables get lost in logic, but using the ubiquitous use of this convention quickly means that you become accustomed to it.

```
var i int = 3
var s string = "hello"
var b bool = true
```

Good naming can also help code become more readable. During Hour 4 you learned about function signatures, and later in Hour 8 you learned about methods. Once you are familiar with how function signatures work, a good approach to naming can become self-documenting code for functions and methods. Consider the two following function signatures:

```
func a(f float64) float64
func (t *Triangle) Area() float64
```

The first example favors brevity in the function and variable name, but without looking at the function signature in context, it is difficult to understand what this function does. The second example is a method that uses both a good name for a receiver argument. It is clear that the method is working with a triangle! The function name is also clear in what it is going to do. Given the receiver and function name, it is immediately clear from the function signature that it computes the area of a triangle.

During Hour 8, "Creating Methods and Interfaces," you learned about interfaces, which are named collections of method signatures. Typically, in the Go source code interfaces are named with verbs and an "er" suffix to form a noun. The "er" suffix generally signifies an action, so the naming indicates an action. Some examples are Reader, Writer, and ByteWriter. Sometimes, names created this way are not even in the English language. Search the Go source code and you will find interface names like "Twoer".

For exported functions, the convention is to respect the fact that when a package is imported, it will be accessed through the package name and then the exported function. For example, in the standard library the math package follows this convention by naming the function to compute a square root Sqrt rather than MathSqrt. This makes sense when the function is used, because the code reads `math.Sqrt` rather than `math.MathSqrt`, and it is immediately clear what the function does. Without reading the implementation of a function, a programmer can easily understand what it does. Listing 14.2 shows the `math` package being used to compute a square root. The conventions followed by the Go authors make the code easy to understand.

LISTING 14.2   `math` Package Computing a Square Root

```
 1:  package main
 2:
 3:  import (
 4:      "fmt"
 5:      "math"
 6:  )
 7:
 8:  func main() {
 9:      var f float64 = 9
10:      fmt.Println(math.Sqrt(f))
11:  }
```

Naming will always be a somewhat subjective exercise, but it is worth spending some time considering how you will name things. Some things to consider when naming variables, functions, and interfaces include:

▶ Who will be using this code? Is it just me or a wider team?

▶ Are there any conventions established in the project?

▶ Could someone who is new to the code read it and understand roughly what it is doing?

It is important to maintain some conventions around naming, but being dogmatic about naming can also be a hindrance. Consider the context in which you are writing the code, the other people, and the dynamics of a team. For the majority of cases, it should be possible to satisfy your own conventions and the context in which the code is being used.

Using `golint`

`golint` is provided as part of the official tooling around Go. Whereas `gofmt` formats code into expected conventions, the `golint` command looks for style mistakes in terms of the conventions of the Go project itself. The `golint` executable is not installed by default but can be installed as follows:

```
go get -u github.com/golang/lint/golint
```

To check that the tool was installed correctly, type `golint --help` at the terminal. You should see some help text printed to the terminal. The `golint` tool provides useful hints on style and can also help with learning the accepted conventions of the Go ecosystem. Listing 14.3 shows code with Go style that could be improved.

LISTING 14.3   Go Code with Style that Needs Improvement

```
 1:   package main
 2:
 3:   import "fmt"
 4:
 5:   const Foo string = "constant string"
 6:
 7:   func main() {
 8:       fmt.Println(Foo)
 9:       a_string := "hello"
10:       fmt.Println(a_string)
11:   }
```

This code compiles and passes `gofmt`. According to the compiler the code is correct, and according to `gofmt` it is correctly formatted. But, as you are probably aware, there are some style problems with this code. You may notice that a variable name uses an underscore, for example. These types of style errors can be found using the `golint` tool. Running the code against `golint` gives some advice on how the code style could be improved.

```
go lint example02.go
example02.go:5:7: exported const Foo should have comment or be unexported
example02.go:9:2: don't use underscores in Go names; var a_string should be aString
```

The linter helpfully shows the lines and positions within the code that need attention. If you are using Vim as your text editor, this also integrates with the Quickfix menu. These recommendations are not mandatory, as the code will compile, but given that the Go project itself uses this tool, it is a good idea to try and fix the warnings and learn the conventions. Using the `golint` tool can also be a great way to learn to learn how to write Idiomatic Go. The tool covers many conventions, including naming, styles, and general conventions. It is recommended to use `golint` in your Go projects. Many of the text editor plugins provide a way to run `golint` in a project on save, and you may want to consider using this when you run tests on your project or just to run this periodically to improve your learning.

▼ TRY IT YOURSELF

Understanding `golint`

In this example, you will understand how to use the `golint` tool.

1. Open hour14/example02.go from the code examples for this book.

2. See that there are some examples of Go style that could be improved.

3. From the terminal, run `golint example02.go`.

4. You will see the following printed to the terminal:

```
go lint example02.go
example02.go:5:7: exported const Foo should have comment or be unexported
example02.go:9:2: don't use underscores in Go names; var a_string should be
aString
```

Using `godoc`

As you develop more complex programs, documenting code becomes an important part of writing good software. Even if you are working on your own, comments in code can quickly help to understand what a piece of code is doing. Go has excellent support for writing documentation, and the authors of Golang have thought carefully about making documentation as easy as possible. The `godoc` tool is an official tool that can parse Go source code and produce documentation from both the code and comments within it. As the code itself creates the documentation, it is unlikely that documentation will get out of synchronization, a common problem for software projects.

Although the `godoc` tool is an official tool, it must be installed. Provided your Go environment is set up, this is just a case of installing the package.

```
go get golang.org/x/tools/cmd/godoc
```

To check that it installed correctly, type `godoc --help` at the terminal. You should see some help text for the tool.

If you have exposure to other programming languages, you might have some familiarity with code commenting protocols. Sometimes these enforce a particular way of writing comments in order that documentation may be generated. Java has `javadoc` for writing comments, and Listing 14.4 shows `javadoc` being used to document some code.

LISTING 14.4   `javadoc`

```
1:  /**
2:  * The HelloWorld program just says hello
3:  *
4:  * @author George Ornbo
```

```
 5:    * @version 1.0
 6:    * @since    2017-08-17
 7:    */
 8:   public class HelloWorld {
 9:       public static void main(String[] args) {
10:           System.out.println("Hello World!");
11:       }
12:   }
```

In this Java code, some fields require a @ before them so that `javadoc` knows where to look for specific pieces of data like the author and version. The `godoc` tool has no such requirements, and commenting code is just a case of using standard comments and adhering to a few simple conventions. To add a comment about a section of code, simply begin the line with the name of the element that you are commenting on. Listing 14.5 shows an example package with comments applied using the `godoc` conventions.

LISTING 14.5   Using godoc

```
 1:   // Package example03 shows how to use the godoc tool.
 2:   package example03
 3:
 4:   import (
 5:       "errors"
 6:   )
 7:
 8:   // Animal specifies an animal
 9:   type Animal struct {
10:       Name string // Name holds the name of a thing.
11:
12:       // Age holds the name of a thing.
13:       Age int
14:   }
15:
16:   // ErrNotAnAnimal is returned if the name field of the Animal struct is Human.
17:   var ErrNotAnAnimal = errors.New("Name is not an animal")
18:
19:   // Hello sends a greeting to the animal.
20:   func (a Animal) Hello() (string, error) {
21:       if a.Name == "Human" {
22:           return "", ErrNotAnAnimal
23:       }
24:       s := "Hello " + a.Name
25:       return s, nil
26:   }
```

For the purposes of this hour, the code contained in the example is less important than the way it is documented. Note how each line starts with the name of the type it is documenting. Comments are full sentences beginning with a capital letter and ending in a period. Running the `godoc` tool on this code produces instant documentation for the package.

```
godoc ./example03
PACKAGE DOCUMENTATION

package example03
    import "./example03"

    Package example03 shows how to use the godoc tool.

VARIABLES

var ErrNotAnAnimal = errors.New("Name is not an animal")
    ErrNotAnAnimal is returned if the name field of the Animal struct is
    Human.

TYPES

type Animal struct {
    Name string // Name holds the name of an Animal.

    // Age holds the name of an Animal.
    Age int
}
Animal specifies an animal

func (a Animal) Hello() (string, error)
    Hello sends a greeting to the animal.
```

▼ TRY IT YOURSELF

Using godoc

In this example, you will understand how to use the `godoc` tool.

1. Open hour14/example03.go from the code examples for this book.

2. Notice how comments have been added to the code.

3. From the terminal, run `godoc example03.go`.

4. You will see documentation printed to the terminal.

The godoc tool can produce a number of different outputs, including html. The documentation for the standard libraries available at https://golang.org/doc/ is driven from godoc, and a number of third-party sites provide documentation in HTML format for Open Source projects. Using godoc conventions means that code has a standard approach to documentation and that producing and maintaining documentation for code becomes something that happens by default.

Documentation practices for the standard libraries are a great way to learn how to write documentation. Once you have installed godoc, the documentation for any of the standard libraries is available from the terminal. To view documentation for the strings package, for example, the following command can be run.

```
godoc strings
```

This outputs documentation for the strings standard library to standard output. If you are on a UNIX type system, you can use this to quickly find the function signature on a method that you want to use by combining it with grep.

```
godoc string | grep "func Replace"
func Replace(s, old, new string, n int) string
```

Furthermore, you can even launch a web server to review standard library documentation. This can be useful if you are offline or have limited connectivity.

```
godoc -http=":6060"
```

After running this command, documentation for standard libraries is available via a browser at http://localhost:6060/pkg/.

TRY IT YOURSELF ▼

Using godoc to Read Documentation

In this example, you will understand how to use godoc to read documentation.

1. At the terminal, run godoc -http=":6060".
2. Open a web browser and type http://localhost:6060/pkg/.
3. You should see the Go documentation and be able to browse around it.

The power of writing documentation in the way that godoc expects is immediately obvious for the standard library, and this also applies to third-party packages. There are a number of third-party sites that provide hosted HTML versions of documentation derived from the godoc tool. If you are offline, you can also use the godoc tool to view documentation on a third-party project. In the following example, the godoc tool is used to view documentation on the `github.com/BurntSushi/toml` package, a widely used package for parsing data in TOML format (https://github.com/toml-lang/toml).

```
godoc $GOPATH/src/github.com/BurntSushi/toml
```

Although developers are free to use their own conventions, `godoc` is a de facto standard, and it provides a standardized, low-friction way for writing and reading documentation.

Automating Workflow

During this hour, you learned about using `gofmt`, `golint`, and `godoc`. These are all excellent tools, but remembering to run them can be a problem. Even if you know the tools and how to use them, you sometimes might forget to use them. As such, it is recommended that where possible, you automate tooling to check code.

Depending on your text editor, there may be a plugin or tooling available to run tools on demand or on save. If you are on a UNIX-type system, another option is to use a `Makefile`. A `Makefile` is a tool to simplify compiling, testing, and linting of source code. `Makefiles` are useful in that they can combine a number of commands in sequence. Furthermore, they can be used in Continuous Integration environments to automatically run tests, lint code, and compile code.

Listing 14.6 shows a `Makefile` that runs `gofmt` on all files in a folder. If any files are found to not be formatted correctly, the path is printed to the terminal.

LISTING 14.6   Using `Makefile`

```
1:  all: check-gofmt
2:
3:  check-gofmt:
4:  @if [ -n "$(shell gofmt -l .)" ]; then \
5:      echo 1>&2 'The following files need to be formatted:'; \
6:      gofmt -l .; \
7:      exit 1; \
8:  fi
```

To run this script, simply type `make`. If any of the files in the directory are incorrectly formatted, these will be printed to the terminal. Listing 14.1 showed code that was poorly formatted. Using a `Makefile`, this file can be checked for compliance with `gofmt` conventions. Using a `Makefile` can support professional development workflows in that it can be used to automate checks in scenarios like pushing code into repositories. In this example, running `make` discovers that the file is not formatted correctly and reports it accordingly.

```
Make
The following files need to be formatted:
example04.go
make: *** [Makefile:4: check-gofmt] Error 1
```

Using a Makefile to Automate Workflow

In this example, you will understand how to use a Makefile to automate workflow.

1. Open the folder hour14/example04 from the code examples for this book.

2. At the terminal, type `make`.

3. You should see a message printed to the terminal noting that the file is incorrectly formatted.

```
go lint example02.go
example02.go:5:7: exported const Foo should have comment or be unexported
example02.go:9:2: don't use underscores in Go names; var a_string should be
aString
```

Summary

This hour introduced you to Go conventions and official Go tooling. Although these are not necessary for writing Go, they provide an excellent environment for writing and sharing code. It is recommended that you adhere to the conventions expressed in official tooling. This includes the `gofmt` tool, a tool for formatting Go files, the `golint` tool that offers advice on style and conventions, and `godoc`, a tool for creating and reading documentation. By adhering to Go conventions, you do not need to worry about style and different opinions, and you just get on with the important bit—writing code.

Q&A

Q. I do not like the large indentation that `gofmt` gives to my code. Can I change it?

A. Although you may not like some of the choices that have been made, the benefits of the conventions mean that everyone agrees. In time, you will forget about it.

Q. I am used to using all uppercase letters for a constant variable (e.g., **CONSTANT**). Should I use this in Go?

A. Constants in Go are treated the same way as any other data element, so all-uppercase letters should not be used.

Q. Where can I host documentation for my Open Source Go project?

A. There are several third-party sites that can parse Go code and provide an HTML version of the documentation. One popular site is GoDoc (https://godoc.org/). Information about how to add your package is available on the About page (https://godoc.org/-/about).

Workshop

The workshop contains quiz questions and exercises to help you solidify your understanding of the material covered. Try to answer all questions before looking at the "Answers" section that follows.

Quiz

1. If code is not formatted according to `gofmt`, will it run?

2. Why is writing documentation a good thing?

3. What is the idiomatic way of naming interfaces in Go?

Answers

1. Providing the code compiles, it does not need to be formatted according to `gofmt` for it to run.

2. Documentation can help with readability and maintainability of code. It allows a single developer to revisit code and quickly understand it, and for other team members to get up to speed more quickly.

3. The idiomatic way of naming interfaces is to use a verb with "er" on the end. This describes what the interface does. Examples include `Parser` and `Authorizer`.

Exercises

1. Conduct some research on whether there is a Go plugin available for your text editor. If there is one available, install it, and see what it provides.

2. Write a short "Hello World" program and some documentation for it. Use the `godoc` tool to print the documentation to a terminal.

3. Find a popular Open Source Go project on the Internet and download the source code. Run the tools that you have learned in this hour against the code.

HOUR 15
Testing and Performance

What You'll Learn in This Hour:

▶ The importance of testing
▶ Testing Package
▶ Benchmarking in Go
▶ Providing test coverage

In this hour, you will be introduced to the importance of testing in Go. You will write tests for Go programs, see why testing is important, and learn the different types of tests that you can run. You will also learn several useful patterns in Go testing to benchmark code. By the end of this hour, you will be able to test and benchmark Go code.

Testing: The Most Important Aspect of Software Development

Testing software programs is perhaps the most important thing a software developer can do. By testing the expected functionality of code, a developer can have a good level of confidence that a program works. Furthermore, a developer can run tests each time a code change occurs, and have confidence that bugs and regressions have not been introduced. Testing software also allows a software engineer to declare the expected way a program should work.

Often, software tests are derived from a User Story or Specification that outlines how a feature should work. For example, if a User Story expresses that a function should take two numbers, add them together, and return the result, a test can easily be written to test this. Some projects also mandate that new code has an accompanying test.

Well-written tests can act as documentation. Since a test describes the expected way a program should run, developers joining a project can often read tests as a way to understand how a program operates.

Several types of tests are commonly used.

- ▶ Unit Tests
- ▶ Functional Tests
- ▶ Integration Tests

Unit Tests

Unit tests cover small parts of a code base and test these in isolation. Often, this might be a single function, and the inputs and outputs of a function are tested. A typical unit test might say, "If I give function x these values, I should expect this value to be returned." These types of tests are extremely useful to confirm that the smallest building blocks of a program function in the way that is expected. As a program grows and changes, unit tests are an excellent way to catch any regressions. A regression is a bug or fault that has been introduced as a result of a change. Regressions mean that code was working before the change, but not after it. Unit tests can often catch regressions as they test the smallest parts of a program.

Integration Tests

Integration tests typically test how the various parts of an application work together. If unit tests verify the smallest parts of a program, integration tests look at how the components of an application work together. Integration tests also test things like network calls and database connections, verifying that the system as a whole works as expected. Typically, integration tests are more complex and difficult to construct than unit tests, as the tests need to assess dependent parts of an application.

Functional Tests

Functional tests are often known as end-to-end tests and outside-in tests. These tests verify that software works as expected from an end-user perspective. They assess how a program works from the outside without being concerned with how the software works internally. For users of software, functional tests are perhaps the most important tests that can be run. Examples of functional tests include:

- ▶ Testing that a command line tool responds to certain inputs with certain outputs.
- ▶ Running automated tests on a web page.
- ▶ Running outside-in tests against an API to check response codes and headers.

Test-Driven Development

Many developers advocate using test-driven development (TDD). This is the practice of thinking about a new feature in terms of a test. Before any code is written, a test is created that describes the expected functionality of a piece of code. This has many benefits.

- ▶ It can help to inform code design; thinking clearly about how a piece of code works can often improve the design.

- ▶ It can help to provide definition about how a feature should work.

- ▶ There is a test that will verify there are no regressions in the future.

- ▶ There is a test to verify that the code is correctly implemented.

Using TDD software, engineers can improve code design and confirm that the code is functional by ensuring that the test passes.

testing **Package**

Go provides support for testing through the standard library `testing` package and the supporting `go test` command. As with many things in Go, there are some well thought-out conventions to understand in relation to the `testing` package.

The first convention is that tests in Go live right next to the code they are testing. They are not placed in a separate test directory. Instead, they are placed in the same directory as the code that should be tested. Test files have the same name as the file they are testing, with the addition of a `_test` suffix. So, a file to test the `strings.go` package is called `strings_test.go`, and is placed in the same directory as the `strings.go` file.

```
Project
├─── strings.go
└─── strings_test.go
```

The second convention is that tests are functions that begin with the word "Test". Listing 15.1 shows a test to see whether a true Boolean is equivalent to another true Boolean. If this ever evaluates to false, we are in trouble!

LISTING 15.1   Running a Basic Test

```
1:  package example01
2:
3:  import "testing"
4:
5:  func TestTruth(t *testing.T) {
6:      if true != true {
7:          t.Fatal("The world is crumbling")
8:      }
9:  }
```

Listing 15.1 can be explained as follows:

▶ The `testing` package is imported.

▶ The `TestTruth` function indicates that it is a test by starting with the word "Test".

▶ The `T` type is passed to the function, which includes many functions to test code.

▶ An `if` statement evaluates whether true is not equal to true.

▶ The `if` statement evaluates to true, so the test failure is ignored.

Running Listing 15.1 shows that the test passes.

```
go test
PASS
    ok      _/home/go/src/golang-book-examples/hour15/example01      0.001s
```

If the function were changed to test whether true was equal to false, the test will fail.

```
go test
--- FAIL: TestTruth (0.00s)
    example01_test.go:7: The world is crumbling
FAIL
exit status 1
FAIL    _/home/go/src/golang-book-examples/hour15/example01      0.001s
```

The `go test` gives some helpful information about the test failure. The name of the test, the file name, and the line number where the failure occurred are all shown. This can help with recovering from test failures, as it is immediately clear where to look.

▼ TRY IT YOURSELF

Running Tests in Go

In this example, you will understand how to run test in Go.

1. In your terminal, navigate to the hour15/example01 folder.

2. At the terminal, type `go test`.

3. You will see that the test passes.

Another convention used in testing a Go package is to set up two variables: `got` and `want`. These represent the value to be tested and the expected value. Listing 15.2 shows a simple package to return a greeting.

LISTING 15.2   Returning a Greeting with a Simple Package

```
1:  package example02
2:
3:  import "testing"
4:
5:  func Greeting(s string) string {
6:      return ("Hello " + s)
7:  }
```

This package can be tested to verify that the string returned by the Greeting function is as expected. Listing 15.3 shows a test for the Greeting function.

LISTING 15.3   got want Pattern

```
1:  package example01
2:
3:  import "testing"
4:
5:  func TestGreeting(t *testing.T) {
6:      got := Greeting("George")
7:      want := "Hello George"
8:      if got != want {
9:          t.Fatalf("Expected %q, got %q", want, got)
10:     }
11: }
```

Listing 15.3 can be explained as follows:

▶ The test named TestGreeting is created, and this maps the function name to the function being tested. This can help readability because it is easy to see that TestGreeting tests the Greeting function.

▶ The got variable is assigned the return value from the Greeting function, and represents the value to test.

▶ A second variable want expresses the expected output.

▶ An if statement evaluates that got and want are the same. If they are not, an error is thrown.

Running this example shows that the test passes:

```
go test
PASS
     ok       _/home/go/src/golang-book-examples/hour15/example02      0.001s
```

If another developer were to change the greeting in the Greeting function to "Hi," the test would catch this and fail. This is a good example of declaring expected outcomes and being able to show that things have changed through tests.

```
go test
--- FAIL: TestGreeting (0.00s)
     example02_test.go:9: Expected "Hello George", got "Hi George"
FAIL
exit status 1
FAIL    _/home/go/src/golang-book-examples/hour15/example02      0.001s
```

Using the `got want` pattern is useful, as it is quickly evident why the test has failed. Furthermore, adding helpful error messages when a failure occurs can speed the ability to fix a failure.

▼ TRY IT YOURSELF

Understanding the `got want` Pattern

In this example, you understand how to use the `got want` pattern in Go tests.

1. In your terminal, navigate to the hour15/example02 folder.

2. At the terminal, type `go test`.

3. You see that the test passes.

4. Edit the file example02.go and change "Hello" to "Hi".

5. At the terminal, type `go test`.

6. Notice that the tests fail, and that output is printed to the terminal.

Running Table Tests

Often, functions and methods will respond differently depending on the input received. For this scenario, a test that takes a single value results in massive code duplication. Listing 15.4 shows an extension of Listing 15.2, allowing a locale to be passed into the Greeting function, so that a greeting can be given in a specific language.

LISTING 15.4   Switching Output Based on Input

```
 1:  package example03
 2:
 3:  func translate(s string) string {
 4:      switch s {
 5:      case "en-US":
 6:          return "Hello "
 7:      case "fr-FR":
 8:          return "Bonjour "
 9:      case "it-IT":
10:          return "Ciao "
11:      default:
12:          return "Hello "
13:      }
14:  }
15:
16:  func Greeting(name, locale string) string {
17:      salutation := translate(locale)
18:      return (salutation + name)
19:  }
```

To test this using the single test approach in Listing 15.2 results in duplicated code as each condition is tested.

```
package example03

import "testing"

func TestFrTranslation(t *testing.T) {
    got := translate("fr")
    want := "Bonjour "
    if got != want {
        t.Fatalf("Expected %q, got %q", want, got)
    }
}

func TestUSTranslation(t *testing.T) {
    got := Greeting("George", "en-US")
    want := "Hello George"
    if got != want {
        t.Fatalf("Expected %q, got %q", want, got)
    }
}
```

For this scenario, Go has a pattern of table tests that allow many conditions to be tested. Listing 15.5 shows this example reworked to use a table test.

LISTING 15.5   Using a Table Test

```
 1:  package example04
 2:
 3:  import "testing"
 4:
 5:  type GreetingTest struct {
 6:      name    string
 7:      locale  string
 8:      want    string
 9:  }
10:
11:  var greetingTests = []GreetingTest{
12:      {"George", "en-US", "Hello George"},
13:      {"Chloé", "fr-FR", "Bonjour Chloé"},
14:      {"Giuseppe", "it-IT", "Ciao Guiseppe"},
15:  }
16:
17:  func TestGreeting(t *testing.T) {
18:      for _, test := range greetingTests {
19:          got := Greeting(test.name, test.locale)
20:          if got != test.want {
21:              t.Errorf("Greeting(%s,%s) = %v; want %v", test.name, test.locale,
     actual, test.want)
22:          }
23:  }
```

Listing 15.5 can be explained as follows.

▶ A struct is created to hold the necessary data for constructing a test. This includes the inputs and the expected output.

▶ A slice of structs is created to hold all of the scenarios to test, including the expected outputs.

▶ Within the test, a range loops over all of the structs within the slice and tests each for equality.

▶ If any of the tests fail, a message is printed to the console.

Understanding Table Tests

In this example, you will understand how to use table tests.

1. In your terminal, navigate to the hour15/example04 folder.

2. At the terminal, type `go test`.

3. You will see that the test passes.

Benchmarking in Go

Hour 9, "Working with Strings," introduced you to strings and how to concatenate strings together. You understood that there were several techniques for concatenating a string, including assignment, appending through a join, and using a buffer. The advice given in Hour 9 was that the most performant method is to use buffers. Can this be proven to be true?

Go offers a powerful benchmarking framework that allows discussions over the most performant way of doing something to be resolved with a benchmark. Listing 15.6 shows three different ways of concatenating a string. Do not be overly concerned about the functions, as the performance aspect is this hour's focus.

LISTING 15.6   Three Ways of Concatenating Strings

```
 1:   package example04
 2:
 3:   import (
 4:       "bytes"
 5:       "strings"
 6:   )
 7:
 8:   func StringFromAssignment(j int) string {
 9:       var s string
10:       for i := 0; i < j; i++ {
11:           s += "a"
12:       }
13:       return s
14:   }
15:
16:   func StringFromAppendJoin(j int) string {
17:       s := []string{}
18:       for i := 0; i < j; i++ {
19:           s = append(s, "a")
20:       }
```

```
21:        return strings.Join(s, "")
22:    }
23:
24:    func StringFromBuffer(j int) string {
25:        var buffer bytes.Buffer
26:        for i := 0; i < j; i++ {
27:            buffer.WriteString("a")
28:        }
29:        return buffer.String()
30:    }
```

These functions build a string of an arbitrary length based on an integer value passed to the function. In fact, they all do the same thing. So how can the most performant way of concatenating a string be determined?

The testing package includes a powerful benchmarking framework that allows a function to be run repeatedly and a benchmark to be applied. The number of times a function is run is not set, but is adjusted by the benchmarking framework to have a reliable data set. At the end of the benchmark, a report is given on the number of operations that were complete per nanosecond.

Benchmark tests start with the Benchmark keyword and take the B type as an argument that provides functions to benchmark code. Listing 15.7 shows benchmark tests for the three different techniques.

LISTING 15.7 **Benchmarking Efficiency**

```
1:  package example05
2:
3:  import "testing"
4:
5:  func BenchmarkStringFromAssignment(b *testing.B) {
6:      for n := 0; n < b.N; n++ {
7:          StringFromAssignment(100)
8:      }
9:  }
10:
11: func BenchmarkStringFromAppendJoin(b *testing.B) {
12:     for n := 0; n < b.N; n++ {
13:         StringFromAppendJoin(100)
14:     }
15: }
16:
17: func BenchmarkStringFromBuffer(b *testing.B) {
18:     for n := 0; n < b.N; n++ {
19:         StringFromBuffer(100)
20:     }
21: }
```

The benchmark tests set up a loop and repeatedly call the functions, so that a benchmark may be recorded. To run these tests, the -bench flag must be passed to the go test command.

```
go test -bench=.
BenchmarkStringFromAssignment-4        200000           5330 ns/op
BenchmarkStringFromAppendJoin-4        500000           2719 ns/op
BenchmarkStringFromBuffer-4           1000000           1213 ns/op
PASS
ok      _/home/go/src/golang-book-examples/hour15/example05    3.752s
```

This runs through the test and shows a benchmark value. From these tests, it is possible to see that assignment is the slowest, followed by append join. The fastest method is to use a buffer. The benchmark has proven empirically that using buffers for string concatenation is the fastest!

TRY IT YOURSELF ▼

Using Benchmark Tests

In this example, you will understand how to use benchmark tests.

1. In your terminal, navigate to the hour15/example05 folder.

2. At the terminal, type go test --bench=.

3. You will see that the benchmark tests run.

Providing Test Coverage

Test coverage is a measure of how well your code is tested. It provides a percentage value of the codebase that have tests that exercise the code. Returning to Listing 15.2, suppose that a new function is added to the package, as shown in Listing 15.8.

LISTING 15.8 Extending the Simple Package

```
 1: package example02
 2:
 3: import "testing"
 4:
 5: func Greeting(s string) string {
 6:     return ("Hello " + s)
 7:
 8: func Farewell(s string) string {
 9:     return ("Goodbye " + s)
10: }
```

Running the tests on this file shows that the tests pass.

```
go test example06.go
PASS
ok      _/home/go/src/golang-book-examples/hour15/example06     0.002s
```

But there is a problem. Although the tests pass, there are no tests for the new `Farewell` function. With this approach, a developer could think that a program is functioning as expected, even though it is not. To help with this scenario, the `go test` tool provides a `-cover` flag that outputs a test coverage percentage.

```
go test -cover example06.go
PASS
coverage: 50.0% of statements
ok      _/home/go/src/golang-book-examples/hour15/example06     0.001s
```

This shows that only 50 percent of the code is covered. It is a noble goal to aim for 100 percent coverage, but in reality this is not always possible because some code is very difficult to test. It is recommended that test coverage be regularly checked.

Summary

During this hour, you were introduced to testing in Go. You learned about the importance of testing code and the difference between unit, functional, and integration tests. You were introduced to TDD, a technique that involves writing a failing test before you write code. You saw how to write tests in Go and learned about the want and got pattern. You learned how to write table tests to support testing multiple inputs. You then understood how to benchmark code before understanding how to see test coverage on a codebase. You have understood how to test Go code, an important part of being an effective Go programmer.

Q&A

Q. Do I *really* need to write tests? My codebase is small, and I don't have time.

A. In the long run, writing tests pays dividends, even on small projects. Although it might seem like an overhead, writing tests has many benefits. It helps to reason about code, ensures that code is correctly implemented, and identifies regressions.

Q. How often should I run tests?

A. Ideally, tests should be run each time you commit code. Some developers run tests each time a file is saved, but this can become noisy and a distraction. When you are ready to commit is a perfect time to run tests.

Q. **For what level of test coverage should I aim?**

A. Although 100 percent is a worthy goal for test coverage, on large projects it is rarely possible. Around 80 percent is a good level, depending on the complexity of a project. If you can get to 100 percent, do it!

Workshop

The workshop contains quiz questions and exercises to help you solidify your understanding of the material covered. Try to answer all questions before looking at the "Answers" section that follows.

Quiz

1. Where should test files be placed?

2. What is test-driven development (TDD)?

3. Why is benchmarking good?

Answers

1. Test files are placed in the same folder as the files they are testing. They are given the same file name with a `_test` suffix.

2. Test-driven development is the practice of writing a failing test to describe the expected functionality before writing any code. Many developers argue that this helps with code design and ensures that test coverage is an integral part of the development process.

3. Benchmarking takes an objective, empirical approach to understanding performance. Using benchmarks means that a repeatable test can be used to show that one function is faster than another, or that performance has increased or decreased as a result of a code change.

Exercises

1. Read the source code of the strings package here: https://golang.org/src/strings/. Look at the test files in the package. Do you recognize any of the patterns from this hour?

HOUR 16
Debugging

What You'll Learn in This Hour:

▶ Using logging to help debug
▶ Printing data
▶ Using the `fmt` package
▶ Using Delve
▶ Using `gdb`

Debugging is the process of finding out why a program is not working the way you expect it to. The definition of a program not working the way you expect it to can be a multitude of things, including compiler errors, runtime errors, problems with file permissions, or bad data. As a programmer, debugging is something you should expect to do regularly, and an understanding of the tooling available to you in Go is an important part of understanding the language. As you begin to develop more complex programs in Go, debugging will become part of your daily workflow. During this hour, you are introduced to some of the ways you can debug Go code.

Logging

Logging is the practice of recording what is happening inside a program as a program executes. This occurs regardless of whether a program needs to be debugged, and can be useful for understanding events that happen as a program executes. Many common applications provide logging capabilities. These logs can be useful to monitor the health of an application, track down issues, and identify problems.

Logging is not so much a technique for responding to a bug report, but is rather an infrastructure to use when a bug occurs. Web servers like Nginx (https://www.nginx.com/) write logs to files as they run, recording both an access log and an error log. Server administrators are able to use these logs to debug issues or just to check that everything is running smoothly. As these files are text files, it can be easy to find and understand an event or an error.

A standard access log writes a line whenever a page is requested from the server.

```
66.249.70.15 - - [27/Aug/2017:00:12:30 +0100] "GET /robots.txt HTTP/1.1" 200 12 "-"
"Mozilla/5.0 (compatible; Googlebot/2.1; +http://www.google.com/bot.html)"
```

This single line provides a huge amount of information about the request to the web server.

▶ Remote IP address

▶ Date and time

▶ Type of HTTP request

▶ Page requested

▶ HTTP protocol used

▶ HTTP response code

▶ User agent of the HTTP client

The log shows that this is a normal operation of Google requesting a `robots.txt` file from the server to see if it is allowed to index the site. In a scenario where a site is running slowly, log entries like this are useful. If an access log shows many requests from a single IP address in a short period of time, there is probably something untoward going on. Action can then be taken to ban requests from the offending IP address from using the server.

The Nginx web server also writes to a separate file when it considers that an error has occurred.

```
2017/08/27 05:33:21 [error] 26706#26706: *322079 access forbidden by rule, client:
52.57.254.218, server: shapeshed.com, request: "GET /wp-login.php HTTP/1.1", host:
"shapeshed.com"
```

In this example, an event has occurred that Nginx considers an error. The log gives information about the error, and it shows that someone has tried to access a page that is forbidden on the server. This client is trying to access the login page of a WordPress site, a popular Open Source blogging engine. Many malicious bots scan servers for WordPress login pages and then attempt to gain access to the server. The log shows that the request was forbidden by a rule on the server, so in fact everything is ok.

For the example of Nginx, logging is a proactive approach to debugging in that when an unexpected event occurs, there is already a large amount of information available to help debug an issue. Without any logging, it would be difficult to debug an issue. Furthermore, logging can help with the daily administration of an application by ensuring that a program is running as expected.

The `log` package in Go provides a way for applications to log to the terminal or a file. Listing 16.1 shows a trivial program that outputs a log message.

LISTING 16.1   Logging in Go

```
1:  package main
2:
3:  import "log"
4:
5:  func main() {
6:      log.Printf("This is a log message")
7:  }
```

Running this program prints the log message to the terminal.

```
go run example01.go
2017/08/27 07:17:46 This is a log message
```

Note that the date and time is added to the log message, which can be useful for reviewing logs at a later time. The `log` package can also log errors in scenarios where fatal errors occur. Listing 16.2 shows a fatal error occurring and a log of the error being made.

LISTING 16.2   Logging a Fatal Error

```
1:  package main
2:
3:  import (
4:      "errors"
5:      "log"
6:  }
7:
8:  func main() {
9:      var errFatal = errors.New("We only just started and we are crashing")
10:      log.Fatal(errFatal)
11:  }
```

Running this program, a log message is written to the terminal, even though the error causes the program to exit.

```
go run example02.go
2017/08/27 07:26:13 We only just started and we are crashing
exit status 1
```

Logs are useful to watch as a program executes and can be handy for debugging, but they are more useful to review after an event has occurred. This means that logs need to be written to a file so that they can be accessed at a later time. Writing logs to a file can be achieved through Go itself or through the operating system that Go is running on. Writing logs to a file is as simple as instructing the log package to write logs to a file.

```
err := os.OpenFile("example03.log", os.O_APPEND|os.O_CREATE|os.O_RDWR, 0666)
if err != nil {
        log.Fatal(err)
}

defer f.Close()

log.SetOutput(f)
```

The final line directs the log package to use the example03.log file to record the logs of an application. You will learn more about working with files in Hour 21, "Working with Files." Listing 16.3 shows a full example of log messages being written to a file.

LISTING 16.3   Writing Logs to a File

```
 1:  package main
 2:
 3:  import (
 4:      "log"
 5:      "os"
 6:  )
 7:
 8:  func main() {
 9:      f, err := os.OpenFile("example03.log", os.O_APPEND|os.O_CREATE|os.O_RDWR,
     0666)
10:      if err != nil {
11:          log.Fatal(err)
12:      }
13:
14:      defer f.Close()
15:
16:      log.SetOutput(f)
17:
18:      for i := 1; i <= 5; i++ {
19:          log.Printf("Log iteration %d", i)
20:      }
21:  }
```

Understanding how to Write Logs to a File

In this example, you will understand how to write logs to a file.

1. Open hour16/example03.go from the code examples for this book.

2. Try to understand what the code is doing.

3. From the terminal, run `go run example03.go`.

4. In the same folder, you will find a new file `example03.log`.

An equally valid approach to writing logs to a file is to use the operating system to redirect log output from a terminal to a file. This does not entail any Go code, but instead uses the capabilities of an operating system to handle the operation. Listing 16.4 shows an example of logging five messages.

LISTING 16.4   Sample Logging Program

```
 1:  package main
 2:
 3:  import (
 4:      "log"
 5:  )
 6:
 7:  func main() {
 8:      for i := 1; i <= 5; i++ {
 9:          log.Printf("Log iteration %d", i)
10:      }
11:  }
```

Running this program in the normal way outputs five messages to the terminal. Using shell redirection, however, the output can be written to a file. This works for both Linux and Windows.

```
go run example04.go > example04.log 2>&1
```

Typically, it is better to use an operating system to redirect logs to a file rather than redirect to a file through Go code. This is more flexible and allows other tools to consume logs if desired.

Printing Data

Often, a bug in code is caused by a piece of data differing from the expected value. In Listing 16.5, a simple program prompts a player for input and makes a decision as to whether the player has won a prize based on the input. If players guess the correct name, they win a prize, but if they do not, they get a message saying they did not win.

LISTING 16.5   Simple Guessing Game

```
 1:  package main
 2:
 3:  import (
 4:      "bufio"
 5:      "fmt"
 6:      "os"
 7:      "strings"
 8:  )
 9:
10:  func main() {
11:      reader := bufio.NewReader(os.Stdin)
12:      fmt.Print("Guess the name of my pet to win a prize: ")
13:      text, _ := reader.ReadString('\n')
14:      text = strings.Replace(text, "\n", "", -1)
15:
16:      if text == "John" {
17:          fmt.Println("You won! You win chocolate!")
18:      } else {
19:          fmt.Println("You didn't win. Better luck next time")
20:  }
```

As the developer of this program, you receive a report that someone who knows the name of your pet is never winning. He tells you that he is entering the name of your pet correctly. You ask him whether he is entering John as the name and he confirms that he is. It is time to debug! For this scenario, printing data is a fast and easy way to discover what is happening. Adding a line before the `if` statement that prints out the data received is a very simple way to debug this program.

```
fmt.Println("[DEBUG] text is:", text)
```

Running the program now prints the input data that is evaluated.

```
go run example06.go
Guess the name of my pet to win a prize: john
[DEBUG] text is: john
You didn't win. Better luck next time
```

Debugging the code by printing the variable to be evaluated has shown that the player has entered "john" rather than "John". Because the `if` statement expects the name to begin with a capital letter, the `if` statement evaluates to false and the player does not win. Using this technique, the bug has been discovered quickly. To fix the bug, the program can be amended to make the user input lowercase before evaluating the input against "john". This means that case sensitivity would no longer be an issue.

Printing lines like this is often seen as "quick and dirty" in that it is fast to add a line to print a value and to potentially resolve a bug. Using this technique litters code with debugging lines, however.

Using the `fmt` Package

In terms of using the technique of printing values to the terminal, it is worth exploring the `fmt` package and some techniques for using it in debugging. The `fmt` package can use verbs for formatting, and these can be used to output data as required for debugging. Using the `Printf` function, this pattern can be used to construct a string to print and reference a variable using the percent sign. The `fmt` package will parse the variables and output a string. Listing 16.6 shows a simple example of using the `Printf` function to output a debugging statement to the terminal.

LISTING 16.6   Using the `fmt` Package for Debugging

```
 1:  package main
 2:
 3:  import (
 4:      "fmt"
 5:  )
 6:
 7:  func main() {
 8:      s := "Hello World"
 9:      fmt.Printf("String is %v\n", s)
10:  }
```

TRY IT YOURSELF ▼

Using the `fmt` Package to Debug Code

In this example, you will understand how to use the `fmt` package to debug code.

1. Open hour16/example07.go from the code examples for this book.

2. Try to understand what the code is doing.

3. From the terminal, run `go run example07.go`.

4. You should see a debugging statement printed to the terminal:

   `String is Hello World`

Note at the end of the string is the \n character. This is used to denote a new line, as by default the Printf function does not add a carriage return. The %v verb is the default format of a type.

It is also possible to use multiple variables in the same line. Listing 16.7 shows two variables being used to construct a debugging statement. Variables are parsed in the order that they appear.

LISTING 16.7 Printing Multiple Variables Using the `fmt` Package

```
 1:  package main
 2:
 3:  import (
 4:      "fmt"
 5:  )
 6:
 7:  func main() {
 8:      s := "Hello World"
 9:      t := "Goodbye, Cruel World"
10:      fmt.Printf("s is %v, t is %v\n", s, t)
11:  }
```

▼ TRY IT YOURSELF

Printing Multiple Variables Using the `fmt` Package

In this example, you will understand how to print multiple variables using the `fmt` package.

1. Open hour16/example08.go from the code examples for this book.

2. Try to understand what the code is doing.

3. From the terminal, run `go run example08.go`.

4. You should see a debugging statement printed to the terminal:

   ```
   s is Hello World, t is Goodbye, Cruel World
   ```

As you saw in Hour 8, the v verb can be used with an additional + to print the field names within a struct. This is useful, as there is no need to look up field names or remember the order in which field names occur in a struct.

```
fmt.Printf("%+v\n", someStruct)
```

Listing 16.8 shows a struct being printed to the console, both with and without the field names.

LISTING 16.8 Printing the Values of a Struct Using the `fmt` Package

```go
 1:  package main
 2:
 3:  import (
 4:      "fmt"
 5:  )
 6:
 7:  type Animal struct {
 8:      Name  string
 9:      Color string
10:  }
11:
12:  func main() {
13:      a := Animal{
14:          Name:  "Cat",
15:          Color: "Black",
16:      }
17:      fmt.Printf("%v\n", a)
18:      fmt.Printf("%+v\n", a)
19:  }
```

TRY IT YOURSELF ▼

Printing the Values of a Struct Using the `fmt` Package

In this example, you will understand how to print the values of a struct.

1. Open hour16/example09.go from the code examples for this book.

2. Try to understand what the code is doing.

3. From the terminal, run `go run example09.go`.

4. You should see a debugging statement printed to the terminal:

```
{Cat Black}
{Name:Cat Color:Black}
```

Using Delve

Although Go has no official debugger, a number of community projects provide debugging for Go. Delve (https://github.com/derekparker/delve) is one such project, and provides a rich debugging environment for Go projects. Delve can be installed as follows:

```
go get github.com/derekparker/delve/cmd/dlv
```

To check that Delve was installed correctly, run `dlv --help` at the terminal. You should see some help text outputted to the terminal. Delve offers a much more sophisticated debugging environment than simply logging or printing lines. Although using the `fmt` package to debug was the "quick and dirty" approach, Delve offers a much more sophisticated environment to debug programs. Delve allows a developer to interact with a program while it is executing, attach to a running process, examine core dumps, and stack traces. Listing 16.9 shows a simple program that will be used to demonstrate Delve.

LISTING 16.9   Simple Program to Demonstrate Using Delve

```
 1:  package main
 2:
 3:  import (
 4:      "fmt"
 5:  )
 6:
 7:  func main() {
 8:      s := "Hello World"
 9:      t := "Goodbye Cruel World"
10:      echo(s)
11:      echo(t)
12:  }
```

Delve can begin execution of this program and pause execution to allow debugging.

```
dlv debug example10.go
Type 'help' for list of commands.
(dlv)
```

Effectively, this console is inside the program and has paused execution. The console is waiting for a debugging process to press play on the execution. Suppose that we are interested in the s variable that is passed to the echo function. The Delve tool allows the program to be paused each time the echo function is called. This is known as a breakpoint, meaning that the execution of the program is paused at a particular point. This is useful, as variables can be examined and altered before the execution continues. To instruct Delve to break when a function is called is as follows:

```
(dlv) break echo
Breakpoint 1 set at 0x47b7b8 for main.echo()  ./example10.go:7
```

Now each time the echo function is called, the program will pause and allow the debugger to inspect the state of the program. It is possible to add any number of breakpoints throughout the program. Once all the breakpoints have been created, the program can be executed by using `continue`.

```
(dlv) continue
> main.echo() ./example10.go:7 (hits goroutine(1):1 total:1) (PC: 0x47b7b8)
 2:
 3: import (
```

```
4:              "fmt"
5: )
6:
=>   7: func echo(s string) {
8:           fmt.Println(s)
9:           return
10: }
11:
12: func main() {
```

The program executes up to the first breakpoint and then pauses execution. The Delve tool helpfully prints out the context of the breakpoint, and it is possible to see that the echo function is being called. It is possible to examine the state of the program at this point, so the value of s can be printed using print.

```
(dlv) print s
"Hello World"
```

Because this is the first time the function was called, the value is "Hello World" as expected. The program can then be continued with another continue command.

```
(dlv) continue
Hello World
> main.echo() ./example10.go:7 (hits goroutine(1):2 total:2) (PC: 0x47b7b8)
2:
3: import (
4:              "fmt"
5: )
6:
=>   7: func echo(s string) {
8:           fmt.Println(s)
9:           return
10: }
11:
12: func main() {
```

Note that the output of the first call to the echo function is printed, as this part of the program has been executed. The program then breaks again at the same place as the echo function is called again. This time, examining the value of the s variable shows "Goodbye Cruel World".

```
(dlv) print s
"Goodbye Cruel World"
```

Running the continue command again continues the execution, and as there are no more breakpoints, the program exits.

```
(dlv) continue
Goodbye Cruel World
Process 7094 has exited with status 0}
```

▼ TRY IT YOURSELF

Using Delve to Debug Go Code

In this example, you will understand how to debug Go code using Delve.

1. Install Delve using the following command:

   ```
   go get github.com/derekparker/delve/cmd/dlv
   ```

2. Begin debugging the code from hour16/example10.go in the book's code examples:

   ```
   dlv debug example10.go
   ```

3. Step through the example, setting breakpoints and printing variable values.

4. Continue until the program exits.

Using gdb

If you are on a UNIX type system (MacOS or Linux), the GNU Debugger is available to debug Golang programs. The GNU Debugger is widely available and almost always available to install via package managers. The GNU Debugger operates on binary files, so a Go binary needs to be compiled.

```
go build example10.go
```

This creates a binary file called example10. To begin debugging with the GNU Debugger, start the debugger as follows.

```
gdb example10
```

You will see a lot of output that will eventually drop into a console that has paused execution in the program. Using the GNU Debugger, it is possible to inspect parts of the code using the list command.

```
list main.echo
(gdb) l main.echo
2
3       import (
4               "fmt"
5       )
6
7       func echo(s string) {
8               fmt.Println(s)
9               return
10      }
11
```

This shows the context of the echo function. To set a breakpoint, the break command can be used. This accepts either a line number or a function name.

```
break main.echo
```

To begin execution of the program, the run command is used. This continues execution until the first breakpoint is hit. At this point, just like the Delve tool, the s variable can be examined.

```
(gdb) print s
$1 = 0x4a5891 "Hello World"
```

At this point, gdb can continue execution with the continue command. This hits the breakpoint again when the echo function is called for the second time. Inspecting the s variable shows the value has changed as expected.

```
(gdb) print s
Goodbye Cruel World
$2 = 0x4a6831 "Goodbye Cruel World"
```

The GNU Debugger offers a rich debugging environment, although it is not specific to Go. It is possible to be extremely granular and even step through a program line by line.

Summary

This hour introduced you to a number of techniques for debugging Go programs. You were introduced to the log package and how logging can help as a proactive approach to debugging. You explored the fmt package as a way to output values of variables to the console and understood that this can be a pragmatic approach for simple debugging tasks. You were introduced to two third-party tools that provide richer, more interactive environments for debugging. First, you understood how Delve, a community project, supports pausing the execution of a program and setting breakpoints. Finally, you were introduced to the GNU Debugger, a mature Open Source tool that provides a similar capability to pause the execution of a program and step through it. Although this hour introduced you to some useful tooling for debugging, the best way to learn is to have a real bug and to debug it! With the tools that you have learned in this hour, you should have everything you need to get started.

Q&A

Q. Which of the debugging tools is right for me?

A. The level of debugging that you use will depend on the complexity of your program and your willingness to learn how to use a tool like Delve or gdb. For quick debugging, often using fmt to print the value of a variable can resolve a bug. As programs become more complex, however, a more fully featured debugger may be necessary.

Q. Will using `fmt` or `log` leave me with lots of debugging statements in my code?

A. Yes, you will have statements in your code. These can be potentially useful, or you can choose to remove them after debugging is complete. Some third-party logging tools support different modes, allowing an application to be run in debug mode to increase the level of logging. If you really do not want any debugging code in your program, consider using a debugger, like Delve or `gdb`.

Q. What role do tests play in debugging?

A. In Hour 15, you learned how to write tests in Go. If a bug is found, it is a good idea to write a failing test for it. As you debug your code, you can run the test to see if it is fixed. This has the added benefit that if the program code changes in the future and reintroduces the bug, there is a test to cover it.

Workshop

The workshop contains quiz questions and exercises to help you solidify your understanding of the material covered. Try to answer all questions before looking at the "Answers" section that follows.

Quiz

1. Why is logging a useful aid in debugging?

2. What is a breakpoint?

3. What are the advantages and disadvantages or using logging over a tool like Delve?

Answers

1. Logging can provide useful information when a bug is found in a program. As a program writes logs throughout the execution of a program, this can help with debugging before a bug is known because a log file will contain the state of a program when the bug happened. Occasionally, logs can provide an answer immediately.

2. A breakpoint allows the execution of a program to be paused at a particular point. Depending on the debugger, the entire program state can often be inspected including variable values, the call stack, and memory allocation. Breakpoints only pause execution temporarily, meaning a program can be continued.

3. Using a tool like Delve provides a rich debugging environment, but it takes some time to learn. It exposes the internals of Go and how the language interacts with the operating system. As such, there may be some new things to learn and pick up. It is likely that this will pay off in the long run, but for simple debugging, using logging or printing values to the terminal may be sufficient.

Exercises

1. Use Delve or `gdb` to interact with a Go program you have written. Set breakpoints at function or line numbers and step through the program. Run the `help` command to attempt to understand some of the capabilities of the debugger.

HOUR 17
Using Command-Line Programs

What You'll Learn in This Hour:

- ▶ Operating with inputs and outputs
- ▶ Accessing raw arguments
- ▶ Parsing command-line flags
- ▶ Customizing help text
- ▶ POSIX compliance
- ▶ Installing and sharing command-line programs

A *command-line program* (sometimes also called a command-line utility or tool) is a program designed to be run from a terminal. In this hour, you will learn how to create a command-line program with Go. You will understand how to parse arguments and move on to create subcommands.

Before graphical user interfaces (GUI), it was normal to interact with a computer via the command line. Today, command-line utilities continue to be a popular and practical way for programmers and systems administrators to interact with an underlying operating system. A programmer might want to create a command-line program to:

- ▶ Create a script that can be run automatically on a regular basis.
- ▶ Create a script to interact with files on an operating system.
- ▶ Create a script to perform system maintenance tasks.
- ▶ Avoid the unnecessary overhead of designing a graphical interface.

A command-line program normally performs an operation like managing files in a directory or taking some input data and returning some output data. A good example of this is the `sort` command that is present on Windows, Linux, and macOS. The `sort` command takes a file with words on each line and returns a sorted version. Suppose the following file `beatles.txt` exists containing the following text.

```
John
Paul
Ringo
George
```

By giving the file to the `sort` command as input data, it will return a sorted version of the file and print it to the terminal.

```
$ sort beatles.txt
George
John
Paul
Ringo
```

Command-line programs can be written in any programming language, and, providing that a script is executable, they are run (or executed) using a terminal. Command-line programs may also be run automatically by an operating system. Some examples of scripts that can be automatically run by an operating system include a program that is run:

▶ every minute to fetch data from a web service,

▶ every hour to remove temporary files,

▶ every day to back up a database,

▶ every month to complete system maintenance tasks,

▶ every year to remind you it is your birthday.

Operating with Inputs and Outputs

Before writing a command-line program, there is some theory to understand to ensure your script can interact with operating systems and other scripts. Command-line programs operate with inputs and outputs. Windows, macOS, and Linux agree on the terminology for these inputs and outputs, and Go uses these contentions. As such, it is useful to get familiar with the terms and codes for inputs and outputs. Table 17.1 shows a summary of exit codes and their meanings.

TABLE 17.1   Exit Codes and Their Meanings

Name	Code	Description
Standard Input	0	Contains input to the program
Standard Output	1	Contains output to display on the screen
Standard Error	2	Contains any error messages to display on the screen

Standard Input is data given to a command-line program. This can be a file, or just a string of text given to a program. In the `sort` example, the file `beatles.txt` is the standard input.

Standard Output is output from a program. In the `sort` example, this sorted data is printed to the terminal. Standard Error is any error from the program. The `sort` example contains no error, but if the file `beatles.txt` did not exist, an error message would be printed to Standard Error to say the file does not exist.

Long-running processes, like web servers, often log data to both Standard Input and Standard Output, and typically these are sent to log files. Much of the ecosystem around command-line programs is derived from programs using the standard streams of Standard Input, Standard Output, and Standard Error correctly. As such, even a passing understanding of how this works is useful.

Accessing Raw Command-Line Arguments

Go offers great support for creating command-line programs. It conforms to the idea of taking inputs and sending outputs, and often Go will automatically ensure that output is sent to the correct output stream. Data passed to a command-line program on the command line is known as arguments. At the most basic level, Go can read arguments to a command line for a program using the `os` package in the standard library, as shown in Listing 17.1.

LISTING 17.1   Accessing Command-Line Arguments

```
1:  package main
2:
3:  import (
4:      "fmt"
5:      "os"
6:  )
7:
8:  func main() {
9:      for i, arg := range os.Args {
10:         fmt.Println("argument", i, "is", arg)
11:     }
12: }
```

The `Args` method returns a slice of strings containing the name of the program and any arguments passed to it. In the example, `range` is used to iterate over the arguments and print them to the terminal. For this hour, instead of using `go run` to execute the program, it will first be built using `go build` and then run as an executable. This is to get used to the concept of a command-line program as an executable and to highlight some minor differences between platforms.

With the previous example saved in a file named `example01.go`, the file may be built and run. Running the `go build` command on Windows produces a file with `.exe` extension. Running the `go build` command on Linux or macOS produces an executable file with no extension. Note that there is a slight difference between executing files on Windows and on Linux/macOS. For running local executables on Linux/macOS, an executable in the current working directory must be prefixed by `./`. There is no requirement to add the prefix on Windows.

```
# Linux / macOS
$ go build example01.go
$ ./example01
argument 0 is ./example01

# Windows
$ go build example01.go
$ example01
argument 0 is example01
```

▼ TRY IT YOURSELF

Accessing Arguments

In this example, you will understand how to use arguments.

1. Open the file hour17/example01.go in a text editor and try to understand what the example is doing.

2. Build the program with `go build example01.go`.

3. Run the example:
   ```
   # Linux
   ./example01
   # Windows
   example01
   ```

4. You should see that the first argument is the name of the executable.

Parsing Command-Line Flags

While using the `os` package to receive command-line arguments is possible, Go provides the `flag` package in the standard library. This offers much over `os.Args`, including:

▶ The ability to specify the type of values passed as arguments

▶ The ability to set default values for a flag

▶ Automatically generated help text

A simple example demonstrating the flag package is shown in Listing 17.2.

LISTING 17.2   Parsing Command-Line Flags

```
 1:  package main
 2:
 3:  import (
 4:      "flag"
 5:      "fmt"
 6:  )
 7:
 8:  func main() {
 9:      s := flag.String("s", "Hello world", "String help text")
10:      flag.Parse()
11:      fmt.Println("value of s:", *s)
12:  }
```

The program may be explained as follows:

▶ A variable s is initialized and assigned to a value returned by flag.String.

▶ flag.String allows a command-line flag to be declared with a name, a default value, and some help text.

▶ flag.Parse is called so that the program may pass arguments once they have been declared.

▶ Finally, the value of s is printed. Note that the return value of flag.String is a pointer, so the * operator is used to dereference it and show the underlying value.

Building and running the example shows that the flag package has set a default value for the -s flag.

```
$ go build example02.go
$ ./example02
value of s: Hello World
```

Running the program again, a value can also be passed to -s.

```
$ ./example02 -s Goodbye
value of s: Goodbye
```

The `flag` package creates some help text automatically that will be returned by either passing any of the following:

- `-h`

- `--h`

- `-help`

- `--help`

The help text is formatted and provides the end user with the expected type of argument values.

```
$ ./example02 -h
Usage of ./example02:
  -s string
    String help text (default "Hello world")
```

For the remainder of this hour, the examples will be given for Linux/macOS. If you are on Windows, these are interchangeable. Simply omit . / before the executable when running it.

Working with the executable file from example01, it is possible to pass more than one argument. This can be achieved by typing the name of the executable, followed by each argument, separated by a space. These arguments are received by the program and printed to the terminal.

```
$ go build example01.go
$ ./example01 foo bar baz
argument 0 is ./example01
argument 1 is foo
argument 2 is bar
argument 3 is baz
```

Working with Types

The `flag` package parses flags based on declarations, and these map to the type system in Go. When writing a command-line program, it is important to think about the data that the program will be receiving and to map it to the correct type. Listing 17.3 shows flag parsing for a String, an Int, and a Boolean, and prints their values to the terminal.

LISTING 17.3   Flag Parsing for a String, Int, and Boolean

```
1:  package main
2:
3:  import (
4:      "flag"
5:      "fmt"
```

```
 6:  )
 7:
 8:  func main() {
 9:      s := flag.String("s", "Hello world", "String help text")
10:      i := flag.Int("i", 1, "Int help text")
11:      b := flag.Bool("b", false, "Bool help text")
12:      flag.Parse()
13:      fmt.Println("value of s:", *s)
14:      fmt.Println("value of i:", *i)
15:      fmt.Println("value of b:", *b)
16:  }
```

Building and running this example shows that values for the types are correctly set.

```
$ go build example03.go
$ ./example03
value of s: Hello world
value of i: 1
value of b: false
```

Using the same example, arguments may be passed to the executable to change these values. Note that for a Boolean type, simply declaring the option will set it to true.

```
$ ./example03 -s Goodbye -i 42 -b
value of s: Goodbye
value of i: 42
value of b: true
```

If a user of the command-line program passes a value that does not map to the required type, an error will be shown. In the following example, a string value "String" is passed to the -i flag. As this expects an integer value, an error is thrown. The default behavior of the flag package is to print the error followed by help text.

```
$ ./example03 -i String
invalid value "String" for flag -i: strconv.ParseInt: parsing "String": invalid
syntax
  Usage of ./example03:
    -b    Bool help text
    -i int
      Int help text (default 1)
    -s string
      String help text (default "Hello world")
```

Customizing Help Text

Although the flags package generates help text automatically, it is quite possible to override the default help format and provide custom help text. The `Usage` variable expects a function and is called whenever an error occurs while parsing flags. A simple implementation is as follows:

```
flag.Usage = func() {
    fmt.Fprintln(os.Stderr, "hello world")
}
```

Note that the `os` standard library package is used to print the message to Standard Error, as this message is shown when there is a parsing error, but the output is completely customizable. Returning to the previous example, a custom usage function can be added, as shown in Listing 17.4.

LISTING 17.4   Creating Help Text for a Command-Line Tool

```
 1:  package main
 2:
 3:  import (
 4:      "flag"
 5:      "fmt"
 6:      "os"
 7:  )
 8:
 9:  func main() {
10:      flag.Usage = func() {
11:          usageText := `Usage example04 [OPTION]
12:  An example of customizing usage output
13:
14:    -s, --s          example string argument, default: String help text
15:    -i, --i          example integer argument, default: Int help text
16:    -b, --b          example boolean argument, default: Bool help text`
17:          fmt.Fprintf(os.Stderr, "%s\n", usageText)
18:      }
19:
20:      s := flag.String("s", "Hello world", "String help text")
21:      i := flag.Int("i", 1, "Int help text")
22:      b := flag.Bool("b", true, "Bool help text")
23:      flag.Parse()
24:      fmt.Println("value of s:", *s)
25:      fmt.Println("value of i:", *i)
26:      fmt.Println("value of b:", *b)
27:  }
```

By using a raw string literal (anything between ` `` `), the formatting will be preserved. Building and running the program now shows the custom help text.

```
$ go build example04.go
$ ./example04 --help
Usage example04 [OPTION]
An example of customizing usage output

 -s, --s          example string argument, default: String help text
 -i, --i          example integer argument, default: Int help text
 -b, --b          example boolean argument, default: Bool help text
```

Setting Help Text in a Command-Line Program

In this example, you customize help text.

1. Open the file hour17/example04.go in a text editor and try to understand what the example is doing.

2. Build the program with `go build example04.go`.

3. Run the example with the –h option:

```
# Linux
./example04 -h
# Windows
example04 -h
```

4. Note that custom formatted help text is shown.

Creating Subcommands

Many command-line programs support subcommands. A good example of this is the `git` command. This has a top-level command `git` and then multiple sub-level commands that each have their own options and help text. Some examples of subcommands in `git` are as follows:

```
git clone
git branch
```

Running these commands with `--help`, it is possible to see that each subcommand has a different and independent option. The `flag` package is able to offer support for subcommands through `FlagSets`. This supports creating independent sets of flags that may, among other things, be used to create subcommands. Flagsets and flags assigned to them are as follows:

```
cloneCmd := flag.NewFlagSet("clone", flag.ExitOnError)
```

The first argument is the name and defines the command name. The second argument defines the error handline behavior.

- ▶ `flag.ContinueOnError`—if there is a parsing error, continue execution.
- ▶ `flag.ExitOnError`—if there is a parsing error, exit with a status code of 2.
- ▶ `flag.PanicOnError`—if there is a parsing error, panic.

Using `NewFlagSet`, independent sets of flags may be created. To work with the arguments received, a switch statement can be used. The beginning of this hour showed how `os.Args` contains raw arguments, and this may be used to switch flag sets. Note that as the index starts at 0, the index number is 1.

```
switch os.Args[1] {
    case "clone":
    // handle clone subcommand here
    case "branch":
    // handle branch subcommand here
    default:
    // handle everything else here
}
```

In the following example, a command-line tool will be created to offer two commands, uppercase and lowercase. These will accept a string from the `-s` or `--s` flag and return the text. Of course this is a trivial example, but the point is to demonstrate creating subcommands rather than complex logic.

```
uppercaseCmd := flag.NewFlagSet("uppercase", flag.ExitOnError)
lowercaseCmd := flag.NewFlagSet("lowercase", flag.ExitOnError)

switch os.Args[1] {
    case "uppercase":
        s := uppercaseCmd.String("s", "", "A string of text to be uppercased")
        uppercaseCmd.Parse(os.Args[2:])
        fmt.Println(strings.ToUpper(*s))
    case "lowercase":
        s := lowercaseCmd.String("s", "", "A string of text to be lowercased")
        lowercaseCmd.Parse(os.Args[2:])
        fmt.Println(strings.ToLower(*s))
    default:
        // handle everything else here
}
```

The snippet of code may be explained as follows:

- Two `FlagSets` are created, one for the uppercase command and one for the lowercase command.

- A switch statement reads in the first argument to the command.

- If the argument is uppercase, a string flag is initialized within the uppercase `FlagSet`. The remaining arguments after the first argument are then passed to the uppercase `FlagSet` and parsed.

- The value of s is passed to the `ToUpper` method of the strings package to uppercase it. If no value is provided by the user, an empty string is passed as the default value.

- The same is applied for the lowercase `FlagSet`.

- If the first argument is neither uppercase nor lowercase, the switch statement falls through to default, although nothing is implemented yet.

There is currently nothing implemented at the top level for this program. If, for example, the user executes the program with no arguments, there is nothing to handle this scenario. Looking at how the git command behaves, if the user executes the executable with no subcommand, some help text with information on each of the subcommands is shown. This may be achieved by setting the usage variable and calling it if the length of os.Args is 1. If the length is 1, only the executable has been called, as shown in Listing 17.5.

LISTING 17.5   Introducing Subcommands

```
 1:  package main
 2:
 3:  import (
 4:      "flag"
 5:      "fmt"
 6:      "os"
 7:      "strings"
 8:  )
 9:  func flagUsage() {
10:      usageText := `example05 is an example cli tool.
11:
12:  Usage:
13:  example05 command [arguments]
14:  The commands are:
15:  uppercase   uppercase a string
16:  lowercase   lowercase a string
17:  Use "example05 [command] --help" for more information about a command.`
18:      fmt.Fprintf(os.Stderr, "%s\n\n", usageText)
```

```
19:  }
20:
21:  func main() {
22:
23:      flag.Usage = flagUsage
24:      uppercaseCmd := flag.NewFlagSet("uppercase", flag.ExitOnError)
25:      lowercaseCmd := flag.NewFlagSet("lowercase", flag.ExitOnError)
26:
27:      if len(os.Args) == 1 {
28:          flag.Usage()
29:          return
30:      }
31:  }
```

Now if users simply type the command with no arguments, they will get some useful help text to start using the program. Listing 17.6 shows the full example.

LISTING 17.6   Using Subcommands in a Command-Line Program

```
 1:  package main
 2:
 3:  import (
 4:      "flag"
 5:      "fmt"
 6:      "os"
 7:      "strings"
 8:  )
 9:  func flagUsage() {
10:      usageText := `example05 is an example cli tool.
11:
12:  Usage:
13:  example05 command [arguments]
14:  The commands are:
15:  uppercase  uppercase a string
16:  lowercase  lowercase a string
17:  Use "example05 [command] --help" for more information about a command.`
18:      fmt.Fprintf(os.Stderr, "%s\n\n", usageText)
19:  }
20:
21:  func main() {
22:
23:      flag.Usage = flagUsage
24:      uppercaseCmd := flag.NewFlagSet("uppercase", flag.ExitOnError)
25:      lowercaseCmd := flag.NewFlagSet("lowercase", flag.ExitOnError)
26:
```

```
27:      if len(os.Args) == 1 {
28:          flag.Usage()
29:          return
30:      }
31:
32:      switch os.Args[1] {
33:          case "uppercase":
34:              s := uppercaseCmd.String("s", "", "A string of text to be
      uppercased")
35:              uppercaseCmd.Parse(os.Args[2:])
36:              fmt.Println(strings.ToUpper(*s))
37:          case "lowercase":
38:              s := lowercaseCmd.String("s", "", "A string of text to be
      lowercased")
39:              lowercaseCmd.Parse(os.Args[2:])
40:              fmt.Println(strings.ToLower(*s))
41          default:
42:              flag.Usage()
43:      }
44:  }
```

Building and executing the program, it is possible to see that text is returned correctly for each of the subcommands.

```
$ ./example05 uppercase -s "i want to grow up"
I WANT TO GROW UP
$ ./example05 lowercase -s "I DO NOT WANT TO GROW UP"
i do not want to grow up
```

POSIX Compliance

For the majority of command-line tools on Linux and macOS, the style of passing arguments follows a recommended POSIX standard. POSIX is a family of standards to maintain compatibility between operating systems. Many developers wish to consider this style, and the topic frequently comes up in discussions about Go's flag package. The POSIX recommendation and GNU extensions are documented here: https://www.gnu.org/software/libc/manual/html_node/Argument-Syntax.html.

Although Go's flag package differs from these recommendations, there are several third-party drop replacements for the standard library that map behavior to the POSIX recommendation.

Installing and Sharing Command-Line Programs

After you finish developing your command-line program, install it on your system so that it is accessible from anywhere, rather than just the folder where the binary exists from the `go build` command. It is important to follow the Go conventions so that Go tooling works. It is important that your `$GOPATH` is set correctly, and you are developing using the standard directory layout. Code should be placed in a subfolder within `src`.

```
.
├── bin
├── pkg
└── src
    └── github.com
```

If you followed the recommendation in Hour 1, you will be working with the `github.com` folder in a subfolder titled after your Github username. For me, this path is as follows. You will change `shapeshed` to your Github username.

```
$GOPATH/src/github.com/shapeshed/
```

Your Go projects reside within this folder. Create a folder called "helloworld" within this directory.

```
// Linux / macOS
$ mkdir -p $GOPATH/src/github.com/[your github username]/helloworld
// Windows
$ mkdir "%GOPATH%\src\github.com\[your github username]/helloworld"
```

Change to this directory and create a file called `helloworld.go`, with the content shown in Listing 17.7.

LISTING 17.7   Accessing Command-Line Arguments

```
1:  package main
2:
3:  import "fmt"
4:
5:  func main() {
6:      fmt.Println("Hurray! You are a Gopher!")
7:  }
```

Now the file may be installed with the `go install` command. Note the path should be relative to `$GOPATH`.

```
go install github.com/[your github username]/helloworld
```

If all went well, "helloworld" should now be available across your system.

```
helloworld
Hurray! You are a Gopher!
```

The advantage of following Go conventions is that you may now push your code to Github and let others easily install it with:

```
go get github.com/[your github username]/helloworld
```

TRY IT YOURSELF ▼

Installing a Command-Line Program

In this example, you install a command-line program.

1. Open the file hour17/example07.go in a text editor and try to understand what the example is doing.

2. Create a folder in your $GOPATH under your username:

```
// Linux / macOS
mkdir -p $GOPATH/src/github.com/[your github username]/helloworld
// Windows
mkdir "%GOPATH%\src\github.com\[your github username]/helloworld"
```

3. Copy the example07.go file into this folder.

4. Install the program:

```
go install github.com/[your github username]/helloworld
```

5. Run helloworld; if you see a message, you have successfully installed the program on your system.

Summary

During this hour, you learned the fundamentals of command-line programs and the difference between Standard Input, Standard Output, and Standard Error. You learned how to access raw arguments using the os package before understanding how to parse command-line arguments using the flag package. You learned how to customize help text, and then learned how to create subcommands within a command-line tool. Finally, you learned how to install and share a command-line tool.

Q&A

Q. How do I see the exit status of a command?

A. The exit status of a command may be seen on Windows using echo %errorlevel% and on macOS and Linux using echo $?. Try running some commands and checking the exit status.

Q. Why does Go treat -option and --option as the same?

A. Although single dash and double dash options are generally different, Go authors decided to make them the same.

Q. Is it safe to install a command-line program from someone else using go install?

A. Check the contents of a package before installing and running it. A Go program has a lot of access to your operating system, so be careful. Imagine that you are installing malicious code and try to do some research to make certain that it is safe. Do you understand what it does? Is the program widely used? Do you know other people that use it?

Workshop

The workshop contains quiz questions and exercises to help you solidify your understanding of the material covered. Try to answer all questions before looking at the "Answers" section that follows.

Quiz

1. If you have an error in your command-line program and want to show it to the user, which output should you send it to?

2. Why might you want to use a `NewFlagSet`?

3. Explain the difference between `go get` and `go install`.

Answers

1. Command-line scripts that want to write an error should use Standard Error. Sending text to standard error using the `fmt` and `os` packages may be achieved as follows:

   ```
   fmt.Fprintln(os.Stderr, "Something went wrong")
   ```

2. `NewFlagSet` may be used as a method to create subcommands within a command-line program. It may also be used to customize error-handling behavior.

3. `go install` is used to install local packages on your machine. These might be files that you have written or files you have gathered from the Internet or a fileserver. `go install` fetches files from a remote server (like Github) and installs them, like `go install` does. The commands are roughly equivalent, apart from the fact that `go get` downloads files as well.

Exercises

1. Examine the status codes of some common programs that you use on your operating system. Try to trigger an error and check the status code.

2. Extend `example05.go` to include custom help text for both subcommands. A solution is offered in the book's example files as `example06.go`.

3. Write a simple command-line program and publish it to Github. Invite a friend to install it.

Creating HTTP Servers

What You'll Learn in This Hour:

- ▶ Announcing the presence of your web server
- ▶ Examining requests and responses
- ▶ Working with handler functions
- ▶ Handling 404s
- ▶ Setting a header
- ▶ Responding with different content types
- ▶ Responding to different types of requests
- ▶ Receiving data from GET and Post requests

Go offers strong support for creating web servers that can serve web pages, web services, and files. During this hour, you will learn how to create web servers that can respond to different routes, different types of requests, and different content types. By taking advantage of Go's approach to concurrency, writing web servers in Go is a great option.

Announcing Your Presence with the "Hello World" Web Server

The `net/http` standard library package provides multiple methods for creating HTTP servers, and comes with a basic router. It is traditional to create a Hello World program to announce a basic presence to the world. The most basic HTTP server in Go is shown in Listing 18.1.

LISTING 18.1   Basic HTTP Server in Go

```
 1:   package main
 2:
 3:   import (
 4:       "net/http"
 5:   )
 6:
 7:   func helloWorld(w http.ResponseWriter, r *http.Request) {
 8:       w.Write([]byte("Hello World\n"))
 9:   }
10:
11:   func main() {
12:       http.HandleFunc("/", helloWorld)
13:       http.ListenAndServe(":8000", nil)
14:   }
```

Although the program is just 14 lines, plenty is going on.

► The net/http package is imported.

► Within the main function, a route / is created using the HandleFunc method. This takes a pattern describing a path, followed by a function that defines how to respond to a request to that path.

► The helloWorld function takes a http.ResponseWriter and a pointer to the request. This means that within the function, the request can be examined or manipulated before returning a response to the client. In this case, the Write method is used to write the response. This writes the HTTP response including status, headers, and the body. The usage of []byte initializes a byte slice and converts the string value into bytes. This means it can be used by the Write method, which expects a slice of bytes.

► The ListenAndServe method is used to start a server to respond to a client that listens on localhost and port 8000.

Although this is a short example, if you can begin to understand how a web server operates in Go, you will be well on your way to creating more complex programs.

Running a "Hello World" Web Server

In this example, you run a Hello World web server:

1. Open the file hour18/example01.go in a text editor and try to understand what the example is doing. If you need to, refer to the previous bullet points and step through the code.

2. From the terminal, run the program with `go run example01.go`.

3. Open a web browser at `http://localhost:8000`.

4. You should see "Hello World" in your web browser.

5. Congratulations! You just ran your first web server in Go.

Examining Requests and Responses

As this hour progresses, we will examine requests and responses that are being sent and received. The tool we use for this is `curl`.

`Curl` is a command-line tool for making HTTP requests, and is generally available on all platforms. On macOS, `curl` is pre-installed. On Linux, `curl` is often installed and is available through package managers. For Windows, `curl` is not pre-installed. For Windows users, installing GIT for Windows was recommended in an earlier chapter. If you have not done this, visit https://git-scm.com/download/win, open the download file, and install it. Once installed, you will have a new Start menu item: Git Bash. Open it.

To verify everything is installed correctly, follow these steps:

1a. On macOS or Linux, open a terminal.

1b. On Windows, open "Git Bash" from the Start menu.

2. Type `curl` and hit Return.

3. If `curl` is installed successfully, you will see the output shown in Figure 18.1.

FIGURE 18.1
Verifying `curl` is correctly installed.

Making a Request with `curl`

With `curl` installed, you can use it for developing and debugging web servers. Rather than using a browser, you can use `curl` to send a variety of requests to a web server and to examine the response. To make a request to the Hello World web server, open a terminal and run the server.

```
go run example01.go
```

On macOS or Linux, open another terminal tab or window. On Windows, switch to Git Bash. Run the following command. The `-is` options mean that headers are printed and that some unwanted output is ignored.

```
curl -is http://localhost:8000
```

If the command was successful, you will see a response from the web server that includes the headers and the response body.

```
HTTP/1.1 200 OK
Date: Wed, 16 Nov 2016 16:45:51 GMT
Content-Length: 12
Content-Type: text/plain; charset=utf-8

Hello World
```

The output may be explained as follows:

▶ The response uses the HTTP 1.1 protocol, and a 200 response was received.

▶ The `Date` header details when the response was sent.

▶ The `Content-Length` header details the length of the response. In this case, it is 12 bytes.

▶ The `Content-Type` header details the type of content and the encoding used. In this case, the response is `text/plain` encoded using `utf-8`.

▶ Finally, the response body is outputted. In this case, it is `Hello World`.

Routing in More Detail

The `HandleFunc` registers functions to respond to URL address mappings. In simplistic terms, `HandleFunc` sets up a routing table that allows the HTTP server to respond correctly.

```
http.HandleFunc("/", helloWorld)
http.HandleFunc("/users/", usersHandler)
http.HandleFunc("/projects/", projectsHandler)
```

In this example, whenever a request is made to /, the `helloWorld` function will be called. Whenever a request is made to /users/, the `usersHandler` function will be called, and so on.

Note the following points about the behavior of the router:

▶ The default router directs any request that it does not have a handler for to /.

▶ The route must match exactly; for example, a request to /users will go to /, as it is missing a trailing slash.

▶ The router has no concern over the type of request. It simply passes a request that matches a route to the handler.

Working with Handler Functions

While the Go router maps routes to functions, it is the handler functions that define how a request is handled and the response that is returned to the client. Many programming languages and web frameworks follow the pattern of passing a request and response through functions before returning the response. Go is similar in this respect. Handler functions are responsible for these common tasks:

▶ Reading or writing headers

▶ Examining the type of a request

▶ Fetching data from a database

▶ Parsing request data

▶ Authentication

Handler functions have access to the `Request` and the `Response`, so a common pattern is to complete everything needed for the request before writing the response back to the client. Once the response is written, no further processing on the response can take place. In the following example, the response is sent using the `Write` method. On the next line, a header is set on the response to be written. As the response has already been written, this will have no effect, but the code will compile. The key point: Write the response last.

```
func helloWorld(w http.ResponseWriter, r *http.Request) {
    w.Write([]byte("Hello World\n"))
    // This has no effect, as the response is already written
    w.Header().Set("X-My-Header", "I am setting a header!")
}
```

Handling 404s

The behavior of the default Handler is to pass any request that does not have a handler function defined to /. Returning to the first example, if a request is made to a non-existent page, the handler function for / is called, and a 200 along with the "Hello World" response is returned.

```
curl -is http://localhost:8000/asdfa
HTTP/1.1 200 OK
Date: Thu, 17 Nov 2016 09:07:51 GMT
Content-Length: 12
Content-Type: text/plain; charset=utf-8
```

As the route does not exist, a 404 Page Not Found should be returned. On the default route, a check can be added to return a 404 if the path is not / (see Listing 18.2).

LISTING 18.2 Adding a 404 Response

```
 1: package main
 2:
 3: import (
 4:     "net/http"
 5: )
 6:
 7: func helloWorld(w http.ResponseWriter, r *http.Request) {
 8:     if r.URL.Path != "/" {
 9:             http.NotFound(w, r)
10:             return
11:     }
12:     w.Write([]byte("Hello World\n"))
13: }
14:
15: func main() {
16:     http.HandleFunc("/", helloWorld)
17:     http.ListenAndServe(":8000", nil)
18: }
```

The modifications to the initial Hello World web server may be explained as follows:

- In the `helloWorld` handler function, the path is checked to see if it is `/`.

- If it is not, the `NotFound` method from the `http` package is called, passing the response and request. This writes a 404 response to the client.

- If the path does match `/`, then the `if` statement is ignored and the `Hello World` response is sent.

TRY IT YOURSELF ▼

Adding a 404 Response

In this example, you will understand how to add a 404 response.

1. Open the file hour18/example02.go in a text editor and try to understand what the example is doing. If you need to, refer to the previous bullet points and step through the code.

2. From the terminal, run the program with `go run example02.go`.

3. Using `curl`, make a request to a non-existent page. For example:

    ```
    curl -is http://localhost:8000/asdfa
    ```

4. You should see that the response is now a 404:

    ```
    HTTP/1.1 404 Not Found
    Content-Type: text/plain; charset=utf-8
    X-Content-Type-Options: nosniff
    Date: Thu, 17 Nov 2016 09:15:23 GMT
    Content-Length: 19

    404 page not found
    ```

Setting a Header

A common requirement when creating HTTP servers is to be able to set headers on a response. Go offers great support for creating, reading, updating, and deleting headers. In the following example, suppose that the server will send some JSON. By setting the `Content-Type` header, the server can inform the client that JSON data is being sent. Through the `ResponseWriter`, a handler function can add a header as follows:

```
w.Header().Set("Content-Type", "application/json; charset=utf-8")
```

Provided this is before the response is written to the client, the header will be added to the response. In Listing 18.3, the header is added before the JSON content is sent. Note that for simplicity the JSON is set as a string, but normally data would be read from somewhere and then encoded to JSON.

LISTING 18.3 Adding a Header to a Response

```
 1:  package main
 2:
 3:  import (
 4:      "net/http"
 5:  )
 6:
 7:  func helloWorld(w http.ResponseWriter, r *http.Request) {
 8:      if r.URL.Path != "/" {
 9:              http.NotFound(w, r)
10:              return
11:      }
12:      w.Header().Set("Content-Type", "application/json; charset=utf-8")
13:      w.Write([]byte(`{"hello": "world"}`))
14:  }
15:
16:  func main() {
17:      http.HandleFunc("/", helloWorld)
18:      http.ListenAndServe(":8000", nil)
19:  }
```

▼ TRY IT YOURSELF

Including an HTTP Header in a Response

In this example, you will understand how to add a HTTP header.

1. Open the file hour18/example03.go in a text editor and try to understand what the example is doing.

2. From the terminal, run the program with `go run example03.go`.

3. Using `curl`, make a request to the web server:

   `curl -is http://localhost:8000/`

4. You should see that the response contains a header setting the content type to: `application/json`.

   ```
   HTTP/1.1 200 OK
   Content-Type: application/json; charset=utf-8
   Date: Thu, 17 Nov 2016 09:28:44 GMT
   Content-Length: 18

   {"hello": "world"}
   ```

5. Congratulations! You just served JSON using Go.

Responding with Different Content Types

HTTP servers typically respond to clients with multiple content types. Some content types in common usage include `text/plain`, `text/html`, `application/json`, and `application/xml`. If a server supports multiple content types, a client may request a content type using an `Accept` header. This means the same URL can serve a browser with HTML or an API client with JSON. With a small modification, the example that you have been working through can now respond with multiple content types by examining the `Accept` header sent by the client, as shown in Listing 18.4.

LISTING 18.4   Responding with Different Content Types

```
 1:  package main
 2:
 3:  import (
 4:      "net/http"
 5:  )
 6:
 7:  func helloWorld(w http.ResponseWriter, r *http.Request) {
 8:      if r.URL.Path != "/" {
 9:              http.NotFound(w, r)
10:              return
11:      }
12:      switch r.Header.Get("Accept") {
13:      case "application/json":
14:              w.Header().Set("Content-Type", "application/json; charset=utf-8")
15:              w.Write([]byte(`{"message": "Hello World"}`))
16:      case "application/xml":
17:              w.Header().Set("Content-Type", "application/xml; charset=utf-8")
18:              w.Write([]byte(`<?xml version="1.0" encoding="utf-
    8"?><Message>Hello World</Message>`)
19:      default:
20:              w.Header().Set("Content-Type", "text/plain; charset=utf-8")
21:              w.Write([]byte("Hello World\n"))
22:      }
23:
24:  }
25:
26:  func main() {
27:      http.HandleFunc("/", helloWorld)
28:      http.ListenAndServe(":8000", nil)
29:  }
```

The amendments to the example may be explained as follows:

▶ In the `helloWorld` function, a switch statement is added that examines the `Accept` header from the client.

▶ Depending on the contents of the `Accept` header, a `switch` statement is used to set the response accordingly.

▶ If no header is found, the server defaults to sending a plain text response.

▼ TRY IT YOURSELF

Serving Different Content Types

In this example, you will understand how to serve different content types and how to request them using a client.

1. Open the file hour18/example04.go in a text editor and try to understand what the example is doing. If you need to, refer to the previous bullet points and step through the code.

2. From the terminal, run the program with `go run example04.go`.

3. Using `curl`, make a request to the web server that requests the content type `application/json` . Note that the `-H` option is used to set a header:

   ```
   curl -si -H 'Accept: application/json' http://localhost:8000
   ```

4. You should see that the response is of content type `application/json`:

   ```
   HTTP/1.1 200 OK
   Content-Type: application/json; charset=utf-8
   Date: Thu, 17 Nov 2016 09:28:44 GMT
   Content-Length: 18


   {"hello": "world"}
   ```

5. Using `curl`, make a second request to the web server that requests the content type `application/xml`:

   ```
   curl -si -H 'Accept: application/xml' http://localhost:8000
   ```

6. You should see that the response is of content type `application/xml`:

   ```
   HTTP/1.1 200 OK
   Content-Type: application/xml; charset=utf-8
   Date: Thu, 17 Nov 2016 09:45:24 GMT
   Content-Length: 68


   <?xml version="1.0" encoding="utf-8"?><Message>Hello World</Message>
   ```

Responding to Different Types of Requests

As well as being able to respond to requests for different content types, HTTP servers typically need to be able to respond to different types of requests. The types of requests that a client may make are defined in the HTTP specification and include GET, POST, PUT, and DELETE. To create a HTTP server in Go that responds to different types of requests, a similar technique to serve multiple content types may be used, as shown in Listing 18.5. In the handler function for a route, the request type can be checked and then a switch can determine how to handle the request.

LISTING 18.5   Responding to Different Types of Requests

```
 1:  package main
 2:
 3:  import (
 4:      "net/http"
 5:  )
 6:
 7:  func helloWorld(w http.ResponseWriter, r *http.Request) {
 8:      if r.URL.Path != "/" {
 9:              http.NotFound(w, r)
10:              return
11:      }
12:      switch r.Method {
13:      case "GET":
14:              w.Write([]byte("Received a GET request\n"))
15:      case "POST":
16:              w.Write([]byte("Received a POST request\n"))
17:      default:
18:              w.WriteHeader(http.StatusNotImplemented)
19:              w.Write([]byte(http.StatusText(http.StatusNotImplemented)) + "\n")
20:      }
21:
22:  }
23:
24:  func main() {
25:      http.HandleFunc("/", helloWorld)
26:      http.ListenAndServe(":8000", nil)
27:  }
```

The amendments to the server can be explained as follows:

▶ Instead of using content type to switch the response, the server uses the request method.

▶ The switch statement sends a response depending on the type of request.

▶ In this example, a plain text response is sent to indicate the type of request.

▶ If the method is not a GET or a POST, it falls through to the default. This sends a 501 Not Implemented HTTP response. The 501 code means the server does not understand or does not support the HTTP method sent by the client.

Running the server shows that both GET and POST requests may now be made. To change the request type using curl, the -X option is used.

▼ TRY IT YOURSELF

Understanding Different Types of Requests

In this example, you will understand how to respond to different types of requests, such as GET and POST.

1. Open the file hour18/example05.go in a text editor and try to understand what the example is doing. If you need to, refer to the explanation that follows Listing 18.5.

2. From the terminal, run the program with `go run example05.go`.

3. Using `curl`, make a request to the web server using a GET request. Note that the -X option is used to set the type of request:

   ```
   curl -si -X GET http://localhost:8000
   ```

4. You should see the server responding that it has received a GET request:

   ```
   HTTP/1.1 200 OK
   Date: Thu, 17 Nov 2016 10:02:49 GMT
   Content-Length: 23
   Content-Type: text/plain; charset=utf-8

   Received a GET request
   ```

5. Using `curl`, make a second request to the web server, this time making a POST request:

   ```
   curl -si -X POST http://localhost:8000
   ```

6. You should see the server responding that it has received a POST request:

   ```
   HTTP/1.1 200 OK
   Date: Thu, 17 Nov 2016 10:03:27 GMT
   Content-Length: 24
   Content-Type: text/plain; charset=utf-8

   Received a POST request
   ```

Receiving Data from GET and POST Requests

An HTTP client can send data to an HTTP server along with an HTTP request. Typical examples of this include:

- ▶ Submitting a form

- ▶ Setting options on data to be returned

- ▶ Managing data through an API interface

Getting data from a client request is simple in Go, but depending on the type of request it is accessed in different ways. For a GET, request data is usually set through a query string. An example of sending data through a GET request is making a search on Google. Here, the URL includes a search term as a query string:

```
https://www.google.com/?q=golang
```

A web server may then read in the query string data, using it to do something like fetch some data from a database before returning it to the client. In Go, the query string parameters for a request are available as a map of strings, and these can be iterated over using a range clause.

```
func queryParams(w http.ResponseWriter, r *http.Request) {
    for k, v := range r.URL.Query() {
        fmt.Printf("%s: %s\n", k, v)
    }
}
```

For a POST request, data is usually sent as the body of a request. This data may be read and used as follows:

```
func queryParams(w http.ResponseWriter, r *http.Request) {
    reqBody, err := ioutil.ReadAll(r.Body)
    if err != nil {
        log.Fatal(err)
    }

    fmt.Printf("%s", reqBody)
}
```

WARNING

Do Not Trust User Input

An aside on security for a moment: Data received on a server should be considered untrusted. An attacker may send a request that attempts to steal information, gain access to a server, or delete a database. All data coming into a server should be considered unsafe and should be filtered before use. For the purposes of these examples, data is used unfiltered, but when writing code for production use, ensure that the incoming data is sanitized before use.

A full code example can now be created to demonstrate handling data from different requests, which appears in Listing 18.6. This server builds on the previous example to show the data that is sent to the server. Running this example shows that data can be received for different types of requests. Of course, the server will probably want to do something more interesting with the data other than return it to the client.

LISTING 18.6   **Handling Data from Different Requests**

```go
 1:   package main
 2:
 3:   import (
 4:       "fmt"
 5:       "io/ioutil"
 6:       "log"
 7:       "net/http"
 8:   )
 9:
10:   func helloWorld(w http.ResponseWriter, r *http.Request) {
11:       if r.URL.Path != "/" {
12:               http.NotFound(w, r)
13:               return
14:       }
15:       switch r.Method {
16:       case "GET":
17:               for k, v := range r.URL.Query() {
18:                       fmt.Printf("%s: %s\n", k, v)
19:               }
20:               w.Write([]byte("Received a GET request\n"))
21:       case "POST":
22:               reqBody, err := ioutil.ReadAll(r.Body)
23:               if err != nil {
24:                       log.Fatal(err)
25:               }
26:
27:               fmt.Printf("%s\n", reqBody)
28:               w.Write([]byte("Received a POST request\n"))
29:       default:
30:               w.WriteHeader(http.StatusNotImplemented)
31:               w.Write([]byte(http.StatusText(http.StatusNotImplemented)))
32:       }
33:
34:   }
35:
36:   func main() {
37:       http.HandleFunc("/", helloWorld)
38:       http.ListenAndServe(":8000", nil)
39:   }
```

Receiving Data from GET and POST Requests

In this example, you will understand how to receive data from GET and POST requests.

1. Open the file hour18/example06.go in a text editor and try to understand what the example is doing.

2. From the terminal, run the program with `go run example06.go`.

3. Using `curl`, make a request to the web server using a GET request that includes some query parameters:

   ```
   curl -si "http://localhost:8000/?foo=1&bar=2"
   ```

4. In the terminal that is running the server, you should see the data has been received:

   ```
   foo: [1]
   bar: [2]
   ```

5. Using `curl`, make a second request to the web server, this time making a POST request:

   ```
   curl -si -X POST -d "some data to send" http://localhost:8000/
   ```

6. In the terminal that is running the server, you should see the data has been received:

   ```
   some data to send
   ```

Summary

This hour introduced you to creating HTTP servers with Go. You were introduced to how routing works with the HTTP package and understood how handler functions may be used to handle requests. You learned how to set a header on an HTTP response and then progressed to being able to respond to different types of requests. Finally, you learned how to receive data from HTTP client requests.

Q&A

Q. Is it possible to set variables in the routing pattern? I want to set something like `/products/:id`, where `:id` is a variable.

A. The `http` package by default uses `ServeMux` to handle routing, and neither variables nor regular expressions are supported. Some popular community-created routers offer variables and other features like request and content types. Generally, they integrate with the `http` package.

Q. I used framework libraries in other languages to create servers. Is anything similar available in Go?

A. Yes. There are framework libraries available in Go. For many cases, however, the `http` package provides everything needed.

Q. How do I create a HTTPS server?

A. The `http` package supports creating a server served over HTTPS (TLS) through the `ListenAndServeTLS` method. This works in the same way as `ListenAndServe`, but expects certificate and key files to be passed to it.

Workshop

The workshop contains quiz questions and exercises to help you solidify your understanding of the material covered. Try to answer all questions before looking at the "Answers" section that follows.

Quiz

1. What is the difference between an `HTTP GET` and a `POST` request?

2. In a handler function, what does `w.Write` do in terms of processing the response where `w` is a `ResponseWriter`?

3. Should you trust data submitted to an `HTTP` server?

Answers

1. A `GET` request requests data from a specified resource. A `POST` request submits data to a specified resource. A GET request may set data through query string parameters. A `POST` request sends data to the server as the message body.

2. Calling `Write` on a `ResponseWriter` causes the response to be sent to the client. This includes headers and the body content. Once sent, it is not possible to modify the response.

3. No. You should never trust data submitted by a client to a server. Data should be sanitized before use.

Exercises

1. Modify example04.go to be able to respond to a request for `HTML` with a simple `HTML` document. The `HTML` content type is `"text/html; charset=utf-8"`.

2. Modify example05.go to allow the server to support `DELETE` requests.

3. Read the documentation for the http package and try to understand some of the modifications you can make to a request and a response when writing a server.

Creating HTTP Clients with Go

What You'll Learn in This Hour:

▶ Understanding HTTP
▶ Making a GET request
▶ Making a POST request
▶ Gaining further control over HTTP requests
▶ Debugging HTTP requests
▶ Dealing with timeouts

Hypertext Transfer Protocol (HTTP) is the network protocol used to send and receive resources on the Internet. Among other things, it's used to transmit images, HTML documents, and JSON. In this hour, you learn how to create HTTP clients using Go. You will learn how to make different types of requests and how to debug your program during development.

Understanding HTTP

A good way to understand the structure of an HTTP request is to use `curl`. You used `curl` in Hour 18 to work with HTTP servers. It is also a useful client for working with HTTP clients! In the following command, the Google homepage is fetched. Do not be too concerned about the command or the syntax here. Of interest is the structure of an HTTP request.

```
$ curl -s -o /dev/null -v http://google.com
> GET / HTTP/1.1
> Host: google.com
> User-Agent: curl/7.43.0
> Accept: */*
>
< HTTP/1.1 302 Found
< Cache-Control: private
< Content-Type: text/html; charset=UTF-8
< Referrer-Policy: no-referrer
```

```
< Location: http://www.google.co.uk/?gfe_rd=cr&ei=ALMhWdzRK4qwcpmaoLAE
< Content-Length: 259
< Date: Sun, 21 May 2017 15:32:16 GMT
<
{ [259 bytes data]
* Connection #0 to host google.com left intact
```

The output of the `curl` command in verbose mode describes an HTTP request and response cycle between a server and a client. The log from the example details the request being made and a response being received. It may be explained as follows:

▶ Lines beginning with the > character denote the client request being sent.

▶ Lines beginning with the < character denote the response received.

▶ The client request details some headers being sent with the request that give the server some information about the client sending the request.

▶ The response details some headers detailing the content type of the response, the length of response in bytes, and the time the response was sent.

If you do not have access to `curl`, the nature of HTTP requests may also be examined through Google Chrome Developer Tools. Information on how to access Chrome DevTools is available at https://developer.chrome.com/devtools.

1. Open the Google Chrome web browser. If you need to install it, it may be downloaded from https://www.google.com/chrome/.

2. Open the Chrome DevTools per the instructions for your platform at https://developer.chrome.com/devtools. Chrome DevTools let you look under the hood of a browser while the page loads.

3. Open the BBC website by typing **http://www.bbc.co.uk** into the address bar and hitting Return.

4. As the page loads, the network tab will be filled with a number of HTTP requests and responses.

5. Click any of the items in the Name column.

6. A series of tabs open, showing the Headers tab. This details the request and response headers for one of the HTTP requests that make up the web page.

7. Examine the request and response headers. Can you identify any of the headers like the content type or length?

The point of introducing `curl` and Chrome DevTools is to show that for HTTP clients, it is worth having a basic understanding of the anatomy of the HTTP request. Go's HTTP client is fully featured. In the most basic form, it abstracts options away from the user and applies sane defaults. The Go HTTP client supports fine-grained control, so a stronger understanding of HTTP can be rewarding.

For more than trivial interactions with HTTP, it is well worth understanding the specification in more detail.

Making a GET Request

For simple GET requests, Go provides a shorthand method in the `net/http` package to make GET requests. Using this method means there is no need to be concerned about configuring the HTTP client or setting request headers. The default configuration is good, and if the requirement is to fetch some data from a remote server, it works well.

As shown in Listing 19.1, the client will be requesting the `ifconfig.co` homepage. This service reports the IP address of the client requesting the page.

LISTING 19.1   GET Request

```
 1:  package main
 2:
 3:  import (
 4:      "fmt"
 5:      "io/ioutil"
 6:      "log"
 7:      "net/http"
 8:  )
 9:
10:  func main() {
11:      response, err := http.Get("https://ifconfig.co/")
12:      if err != nil {
13:          log.Fatal(err)
14:      }
15:      defer response.Body.Close()
16:      body, err := ioutil.ReadAll(response.Body)
17:      if err != nil {
18:          log.Fatal(err)
19:      }
20:      fmt.Printf("%s", body)
21:  }
```

The example may be explained as follows:

▶ Using the `net/http` package, a GET request is made to `https://ifconfig.co/`.

▶ If there is an error from this request (e.g., no network), the error is logged, and the script exits.

▶ When all the data has been read by the client, the connection is closed.

▶ The response body is read into a variable so that it may be printed.

▶ If there is an error in reading the response body, the error is logged, and the script exits.

▶ The response body is printed.

Executing this program will make a request to the `ifconfig.co` service and return the IP address that the request was initiated from.

```
$ go run example01.go
68.235.53.83
```

▼ TRY IT YOURSELF

Making a GET Request to a Web Service

In this example, you make a GET request to a web service to discover your external IP address.

1. Open the file hour19/example01.go in a text editor and try to understand what the example is doing. If you need to, refer to the bullet points above and step through the code.

2. From the terminal, run the program with `go run example01.go`.

3. You should see your external IP address shown in the terminal.

Making a POST Request

For simple POST requests, the `net/http` standard library package also provides a shorthand method to make POST requests. The `Post` method supports setting a `Content-Type` and sending data.

In Listing 19.2, the client will be making a POST request to `https://httpbin.org/post`. The `httpbin` service is a tool for testing HTTP clients, and the `/post` endpoint returns data that was posted to it along with information on the client.

LISTING 19.2   POST Request

```
1:  package main
2:
3:  import (
4:      "fmt"
5:      "io/ioutil"
6:      "log"
7:      "net/http"
8:      "strings"
9:  )
10:
11: func main() {
12:     postData := strings.NewReader(`{ "some": "json" }`)
13:     response, err := http.Post("https://httpbin.org/post", "application/json",
    postData)
14:     if err != nil {
15:         log.Fatal(err)
16:     }
17:     defer response.Body.Close()
18:     body, err := ioutil.ReadAll(response.Body)
19:     if err != nil {
20:         log.Fatal(err)
21:     }
22:     fmt.Printf("%s", body)
23: }
```

The example can be explained as follows:

▶ A `postData` variable is initialized, and a JSON string is assigned as the value. This uses the `strings` standard library to format it as an `io.Reader` ready for transmission.

▶ A POST request is made using the `Post` method. The first argument is the URL to post to, the second is the `Content-Type` of the data, and the third is the data.

▶ If there is an error from this request (e.g., no network), the error is logged, and the script exits.

▶ When all the data has been read by the client, the connection is closed.

▶ The response body is read into a variable so that it may be printed.

▶ If there is an error in reading the response body, the error is logged, and the script exits.

▶ The response body is printed.

Running this program returns a response from the `httpbin` service indicating that data was posted as JSON successfully. It is possible to see the raw data that was posted and the data parsed out as JSON by the server.

```
$ go run example02.go
{
  "args": {},
  "data": "{ \"some\": \"json\" }",
  "files": {},
  "form": {},
  "headers": {
    "Accept-Encoding": "gzip",
    "Connection": "close",
    "Content-Length": "18",
    "Content-Type": "application/json",
    "Host": "httpbin.org",
    "User-Agent": "Go-http-client/1.1"
  },
  "json": {
    "some": "json"
  },
  "origin": "68.235.53.83",
  "url": "https://httpbin.org/post"
}
```

Gaining Further Control over HTTP Requests

To have further control over an HTTP request, a custom HTTP client should be used. The default HTTP client from the `net/http` package may be used, and the default settings are automatically applied unless they are overridden. Listing 19.3 is equivalent to Listing 19.1, but uses a custom HTTP client with default settings.

LISTING 19.3   **Using a Custom Client**

```
 1:  package main
 2:
 3:  import (
 4:      "fmt"
 5:      "io/ioutil"
 6:      "log"
 7:      "net/http"
 8:  )
 9:
10:  func main() {
11:      client := &http.Client{}
12:      request, err := http.NewRequest("GET", "https://ifconfig.co", nil)
```

```
13:        if err != nil {
14:            log.Fatal(err)
15:        }
16:
17:        response, err := client.Do(request)
18:        defer response.Body.Close()
19:        body, err := ioutil.ReadAll(response.Body)
20:        if err != nil {
21:            log.Fatal(err)
22:        }
23:        fmt.Printf("%s", body)
24:    }
```

The modifications to use a custom HTTP client may be explained as follows:

▶ Instead of using the shorthand `Get` method from the `net/http` package, a new HTTP client is created.

▶ The `NewRequest` method is used to issue a GET request to `https://ifconfig.co`.

▶ The `Do` method is used to send the request and handle the response.

Running this program yields the same results as the previous example:

```
$ go run example03.go
68.235.53.83
```

Using a custom HTTP client means that custom headers, basic authentication, and cookies may be set on a request. Given that the difference between the code needed to make a request with the shorthand method and a custom HTTP client is trivial, it is recommended that for anything other than trivial requirements, a custom HTTP client is used.

Debugging HTTP Requests

When creating HTTP clients, it can be useful to see the full flow of request and response headers and the data sent and received. This can be achieved using the `fmt` standard library package and logging out individual pieces of data, but the `net/http/httputil` also provides methods that make debugging HTTP clients and servers easy. The `DumpRequestOut` and `DumpResponse` methods from the `net/http/httputil` package provide a way to view requests and responses.

The previous example can be enhanced to support logging of the use of the `DumpRequestOut` and `DumpResponse` methods from `net/http/httputil`. These methods show the request and response headers, as well as the body returned.

Although it is possible to add and remove these methods for debugging, another option is to use an environment variable to turn debugging on and off. The `os` standard library package supports reading environment variables, and this allows debugging to be turned on and off easily. Listing 19.4 shows an HTTP GET request with debugging.

LISTING 19.4   Debugging a Request

```
1:   package main
2:
3:   import (
4:        "fmt"
5:        "io/ioutil"
6:        "log"
7:        "net/http"
8:        "net/http/httputil"
9:        "os"
10:  )
11:
12:  func main() {
13:       debug := os.Getenv("DEBUG")
14:       client := &http.Client{}
15:       request, err := http.NewRequest("GET", "https://ifconfig.co", nil)
16:       if err != nil {
17:            log.Fatal(err)
18:       }
19:
20:       if debug == "1" {
21:            debugRequest, err := httputil.DumpRequestOut(request, true)
22:            if err != nil {
23:                 log.Fatal(err)
24:            }
25:            fmt.Printf("%s", debugRequest)
26:       }
27:       response, err := client.Do(request)
28:       defer response.Body.Close()
29:
30:       if debug == "1" {
31:            debugResponse, err := httputil.DumpResponse(response, true)
32:            if err != nil {
33:                 log.Fatal(err)
34:            }
35:            fmt.Printf("%s", debugResponse)
36:       }
37:       body, err := ioutil.ReadAll(response.Body)
38:       if err != nil {
39:            log.Fatal(err)
40:       }
41:
42:       fmt.Printf("%s\n", body)
43:  }
```

Executing the program with debugging turned on now shows the request and response headers as well as the body response. Note that the program will print the response body twice, as this included debugging information.

```
# For OSX and Linux
$ DEBUG=1 go run example04.go
# For Windows
$ set DEBUG=1
$ go run example04.go

GET / HTTP/1.1
Host: ifconfig.co
User-Agent: Go-http-client/1.1
Accept-Encoding: gzip

HTTP/1.1 200 OK
Content-Length: 12
Connection: keep-alive
Content-Type: text/plain; charset=utf-8
Date: Tue, 15 Nov 2016 09:48:04 GMT
Server: nginx
Strict-Transport-Security: max-age=31536000; includeSubdomains; preload

68.235.53.83
68.235.53.83
```

The output now has some rich information on the request and response cycle. It is possible to see what is being sent to the server and what has been returned in terms of the headers and the data. When creating HTTP clients, this information can be useful in tracking down bugs or understanding why a response is being received. Suppose, for example, that it had been expected that a response would be received in JSON format. The debugging information shows that the server is returning a `Content-Type` of `text/plain`. Looking at the request headers, nothing is being set in terms of the type of data that the client wants. It is therefore no surprise that the server returned data in plain text.

To request JSON data, the client may be amended to set a header to request JSON. This can be added to the request as follows.

```
request.Header.Add("Accept", "application/json")
```

Now when a request is made, it is possible to see that JSON has been requested and successfully returned.

```
# For macOS and Linux
DEBUG=1 go run example05.go
# For Windows
set DEBUG=1
go run example05.go


GET / HTTP/1.1
Host: ifconfig.co
User-Agent: Go-http-client/1.1
Accept: application/json
Accept-Encoding: gzip


HTTP/1.1 200 OK
Transfer-Encoding: chunked
Connection: keep-alive
Content-Type: application/json
Date: Tue, 15 Nov 2016 10:33:48 GMT
Server: nginx
Strict-Transport-Security: max-age=31536000; includeSubdomains; preload
Vary: Accept-Encoding

88
{"ip":"68.235.53.83","ip_decimal":1156265299,"country":"United States","city":
"Chicago","hostname":"static-68-235-53-83.cust.tzulo.com"}
0

{"ip":"68.235.53.83","ip_decimal":1156265299,"country":"United States","city":
"Chicago","hostname":"static-68-235-53-83.cust.tzulo.com"}%
```

Using the `Accept` header, the client informs the server that it wants `application/json`, and the server returns data with the `Content-Type` header of `application/json`. Although most third-party APIs follow the HTTP specification, you may find that an API is implemented incorrectly or simply does not serve JSON. Using Go's debugging capabilities can quickly help to track down bugs and issues in this instance.

Dealing with Timeouts

An HTTP transaction takes a certain amount of time to receive a response. Once a client has sent a request to a server, it is impossible to know how fast the response will return. At a low level, a number of variables affect the speed of the response:

- ▶ Speed of a DNS lookup.

- ▶ Speed of opening a TCP socket to the server IP address.

- ▶ Speed of establishing a TCP connection.

- ▶ Speed of a TLS handshake if the connection is over TLS.

- ▶ Speed of sending data to the server.

- ▶ Speed of any redirects.

- ▶ Speed of the web server in returning the response.

- ▶ Speed of the data being returned to the client.

Do not be concerned if you don't understand what these stages mean. It is enough to know that the speed of an HTTP response is unpredictable. So, for example, a request to a web server might take 1000 milliseconds on one request and 10,000 milliseconds on another request. This is an issue for HTTP clients, as each connection allocates some memory and uses a socket on the underlying operating system. If connections are slow, a program can quickly see a memory leak or exhaust the resources available on the underlying operating system.

Using the default HTTP client, there is no timeout on a client request. This means that if a server does not respond, a request will wait or hang indefinitely. It is recommended that on any request, a timeout is set. If a request is not completed before a timeout, an error is returned.

```
client := &http.Client{
    Timeout: 1 * time.Second,
}
```

This configuration allows the client one second to complete the request. To demonstrate this, working with the previous example, a timeout setting can be applied to the client. In this case, a short timeout is applied so the timeout may be seen.

```
client := &http.Client{
    Timeout: 50 * time.Millisecond,
}
```

Running this program results in an error, as the server does not respond quickly enough.

```
$ go run example06.go
Get https://ifconfig.co: net/http: request canceled while waiting for connection
(Client.Timeout exceeded while awaiting headers)
exit status 1
```

▼ TRY IT YOURSELF

Setting a Timeout

In this example, set a timeout on a HTTP request:

1. Open the file hour19/example06.go in a text editor and try to understand what the example is doing.

2. From the terminal, run the program with `go run example06.go.`

3. You should see that an error is logged.

Even more fine-grained control on timeouts is available by creating a transport and passing it to a client. This allows detailed control on the various stages of a HTTP connection. For most cases, it is enough to use `Timeout` on the client to cover the entire HTTP transaction, but Go also exposes individual parts of an HTTP transaction via creating a transport if required.

```
tr := &http.Transport{
    DialContext: (&net.Dialer{
        Timeout:   30 * time.Second,
        KeepAlive: 30 * time.Second,
    }).DialContext,
    TLSHandshakeTimeout:   10 * time.Second,
    IdleConnTimeout:       90 * time.Second,
    ResponseHeaderTimeout: 10 * time.Second,
    ExpectContinueTimeout: 1 * time.Second,
}

client := &http.Client{
    Transport: tr,
}
```

Summary

In this hour, you learned about creating HTTP servers with Go. You were introduced to how routing works with the `http` package and understood how handler functions may be used to handle requests. You learned how to set a header on a HTTP response and then progressed to being able to respond to different types of requests. Finally, you learned how to receive data from HTTP client requests.

Q&A

Q. I'm new to HTTP, and it seems overwhelming. Is it normal to feel this way?

A. The finer details of HTTP can be overwhelming, particularly if you have not taken a computer science class. If you are just getting started with Go and development in general, it is enough to understand that HTTP defines one way for a client and server to interact. You can easily get started with HTTP by using Go's shorthand methods. As you start to create more HTTP clients and servers, you will become more familiar with HTTP. If you are likely to be creating services using HTTP, investing some time in understanding HTTP is worth it. Before you know it, you will be reading the specification.

Q. Can I make more than one HTTP request at once?

A. Yes. Using goroutines, multiple HTTP requests can be made to a client concurrently.

Q. Can I change how a program responds based on the HTTP status code returned?

A. Yes. The status code of a response is available within `Response.StatusCode`, so logic can switch based on how a server responds.

Workshop

The workshop contains quiz questions and exercises to help you solidify your understanding of the material covered. Try to answer all questions before looking at the "Answers" section that follows.

Quiz

1. What do the `Accept` and `Content-Type` headers do?

2. How would you set a custom header on a request?

3. When should you use the `net/http` `Get` and `Post` method, and when should you use `NewRequest`?

Answers

1. The `Accept` header tells a server what type or types of content the client is able to receive. The `Content-Type` header is sent by the server to indicate what type of data is being sent to the server. If a client asks the server for `application/json` using the `Accept` header, and the server supports it, data should be returned with the `Content-Type` header set to `application/json`.

2. If an HTTP client is created, a header may be set on the request as follows:

```
client := &http.Client{}
  request, err := http.NewRequest("GET", "http://www.example.com", nil)
  request.Header.Add("Connection", "close")
```

3. Depending on your level of experience with HTTP, the `Get` and `Post` methods provide a quick way of getting started. These methods can also be used with creating an HTTP client and specifying a timeout, as follows:

```
client := &http.Client{
            Timeout: 1 * time.Second,
}
resp, err := client.Get("http://example.com")
```

If you need control over headers and other elements of the request, the `NewRequest` method should be used.

Exercises

1. Create an HTTP client that makes a GET request to http://google.com/404. Print the response code. Is it 404?

2. Create an HTTP client that makes a POST request to https://httpbin.org/post. Post some data and examine the response to see that it was correctly posted.

3. Create an HTTP client that makes a GET request to https://httpbin.org/user-agent. Modify the 'User-Agent' header to be "GolangBot." Make a request and examine the `user-agent` value in the response. If it says "GolangBot," you just set the User Agent!

HOUR 20
Working with JSON

What You'll Learn in This Hour:

▶ Introducing JSON
▶ Using JSON APIs
▶ Using JSON with Go
▶ Decoding JSON
▶ Mapping data types
▶ Working with JSON received over HTTP

During this hour, you learn how to work with JSON in Go. You will learn how to encode and decode JSON and understand some of the differences between JavaScript and Go data types. You will understand how to use struct tags to have finer control over JSON and see how to fetch JSON from remote APIs using HTTP.

Introducing JSON

JavaScript Object Notation (JSON) is a data format for storing and exchanging data that is written using plain text and has a readable format. JSON can represent data as key value pairs or as arrays of data. JSON was originally created as a subset of JavaScript, but the data format is independent of the language; indeed, most languages support encoding and decoding data as JSON. JSON has become a de facto standard for storing and exchanging data on the Internet, and has largely taken over from XML (Extensible Markup Language). Although many modern data services still offer an XML format, the most common data format to be found on the Internet is JSON. If you are doing any programming that consumes or exposes services from the Internet, it is highly likely you will be using JSON.

Listing 20.1 shows a response from the Github API for the GET /user/:username resource. This is data provided to clients in text format to use as they wish. It is most likely that the data will be parsed by the receiving language (e.g., JavaScript, Ruby, C#) and then used.

LISTING 20.1   Example JSON Object

```
 1:  {
 2:      "login": "octocat",
 3:      "id": 1,
 4:      "avatar_url": "https://github.com/images/error/octocat_happy.gif",
 5:      "gravatar_id": "",
 6:      "url": "https://api.github.com/users/octocat",
 7:      "html_url": "https://github.com/octocat",
 8:      "followers_url": "https://api.github.com/users/octocat/followers",
 9:      "following_url": "https://api.github.com/users/octocat/following{/
     other_user}",
10:      "gists_url": "https://api.github.com/users/octocat/gists{/gist_id}",
11:      "starred_url": "https://api.github.com/users/octocat/starred{/owner}{/
     repo}",
12:      "subscriptions_url": "https://api.github.com/users/octocat/subscriptions",
13:      "organizations_url": "https://api.github.com/users/octocat/orgs",
14:      "repos_url": "https://api.github.com/users/octocat/repos",
15:      "events_url": "https://api.github.com/users/octocat/events{/privacy}",
16:      "received_events_url": "https://api.github.com/users/octocat/
     received_events",
17:      "type": "User",
18:      "site_admin": false,
19:      "name": "monalisa octocat",
20:      "company": "GitHub",
21:      "blog": "https://github.com/blog",
22:      "location": "San Francisco",
23:      "email": "octocat@github.com",
24:      "hireable": false,
25:      "bio": "There once was...",
26:      "public_repos": 2,
27:      "public_gists": 1,
28:      "followers": 20,
29:      "following": 0,
30:      "created_at": "2008-01-14T04:33:35Z",
31:      "updated_at": "2008-01-14T04:33:35Z"
32:  }
```

Listing 20.1 consists entirely of key value pairs, but a key can also have an array of values. The following example shows an array in JSON.

```
{
    "name":"George",
    "age":40,
    "children":[ "Bea", "Fin"]
}
```

Although an array exists in Go, slices are used more commonly to represent a group of elements. Somewhat confusingly, arrays can also be known as lists in other programming languages, but they all share a common definition of a group of single elements.

JSON has gained popularity because it is a flexible, understandable, and lightweight data format. Although XML offers schemas (strict ways of representing data), programmers are free to represent data however they want. JSON is typically more lightweight in terms of the number of bytes needed to represent the data. For sending data over a network like the Internet, this can mean that applications run slightly faster. Furthermore, the predominant programming environment of web browsers is JavaScript, and given that JSON is a subset of JavaScript, it is trivial to encode and decode data in JSON format.

Using JSON APIs

In recent years, many excellent JSON APIs have been created on the Internet. It is now possible to have access to a wealth of data on almost any subject using the Internet as a data exchange platform. Instead of connecting directly to a database, APIs allow programmers to request data in a range of formats and to use the data. Some examples of APIs include:

- ▶ New York City Transit. This provides train, bus, and rail schedules and even provides the status of escalators on the network.

- ▶ British Broadcasting Corporation. This provides TV and radio schedules, catalog details, and images.

- ▶ Github. This provides information on almost all the data available on github.com including users, organizations, repositories, commits, and issues.

- ▶ Dark Sky. This is a weather prediction service that is often more accurate than other services.

Application developers have used many of these APIs to create new and interesting products and services. There are many Dark Sky clients for Android, for example, and there is an emerging business model of being a data provider and allowing customers to consume the data however they like.

Using JSON with Go

Go is an excellent language for creating clients and servers that send and receive JSON. The standard library provides support for decoding and encoding data to JSON format through the `encoding/json` package.

The process of encoding means to convert data into an encoded form. For the purposes of this hour, this format is JSON. The `encoding/json` package provides the `Marshal` function for encoding Go data to JSON. Listing 20.2 shows an example of a Go struct that contains some data. You learned in Hour 7, "Using Structs and Pointers," how to define a struct, and how they are an excellent way to encapsulate data.

LISTING 20.2   Creating a Struct

```
 1:  package main
 2:
 3:  import "fmt"
 4:
 5:  type Person struct {
 6:      Name     string
 7:      Age      int
 8:      Hobbies []string
 9:  }
10:
11:  func main() {
12:      hobbies := []string{"Cycling", "Cheese", "Techno"}
13:      p := Person{
14:          Name:     "George",
15:          Age:      40,
16:          Hobbies: hobbies,
17:      }
18:      fmt.Printf("%+v\n", p)
19:  {
```

▼ TRY IT YOURSELF

Creating a Struct to Encode as JSON

In this example, you will create a struct to use later to encode as JSON.

1. Open hour20/example01.go from the code examples for this book.

2. Read the code and try to understand what it is doing.

3. From the terminal, run `go run example01.go`.

4. You will see a struct printed to the terminal:

   ```
   {Name:George Age:40 Hobbies:[Cycling Cheese Techno]}
   ```

Running this example shows that the struct has been initialized and contains data. To encode this data to JSON, use the `Marshal` function. This expects an interface and returns a string of bytes. As a struct may implement an interface, the struct can be passed directly to the `Marshal` function.

```
jsonByteData, err = json.Marshall(p)
```

After checking for an error, the byte slice can be converted into a string, and the data is converted to JSON text format.

```
jsonStringData := string(jsonByteData)
fmt.Println(jsonStringData)
```

Listing 20.3 shows a full example of a struct being converted to JSON format.

LISTING 20.3   Encoding a Struct as JSON

```
1:  package main
2:
3:  import (
4:      "encoding/json"
5:      "fmt"
6:      "log"
7:  )
8:
9:  type Person struct {
10:     Name     string
11:     Age      int
12:     Hobbies []string
13: }
14:
15: func main() {
16:     hobbies := []string{"Cycling", "Cheese", "Techno"}
17:     p := Person{
18:         Name:     "George",
19:         Age:      40,
20:         Hobbies: hobbies,
21:     }
22:     fmt.Printf("%+v\n", p)
23:     jsonByteData, err := json.Marshal(p)
24:     if err != nil {
25:         log.Fatal(err)
26:     }
27:     jsonStringData := string(jsonByteData)
28:     fmt.Println(jsonStringData)
29: }
```

▼ TRY IT YOURSELF

Encoding JSON

In this example, you will learn how to encode JSON.

1. Open hour20/example02.go from the code examples for this book.

2. Read the code and try to understand what it is doing.

3. From the terminal, run `go run example02.go`.

4. You will first see a struct printed to the terminal, then the encoded JSON version of the struct.

```
{Name:George Age:40 Hobbies:[Cycling Cheese Techno]}
{"Name":"George","Age":40,"Hobbies":["Cycling","Cheese","Techno"]}
```

Although the previous example successfully converted data to JSON format, there is one problem. The JSON key names all begin with uppercase letters. Although JSON has no official standard, the convention is to use CamelCase. Table 20.1 shows the difference between the Go variable names and the expected variable names in JSON.

TABLE 20.1   Go and JSON Key Names

Go	JSON
Name	name
Age	age
Hobbies	hobbies

Although you may think this is a small and maybe irritating point, many JavaScript libraries work from the assumption that data keys will be provided in CamelCase format. Failing to provide data in this format is likely to cause problems for developers using the data. Initially, it may seem a daunting task to have to parse all the keys and make them start with a lowercase letter, but thankfully the language designers have already solved this problem.

Structs can declare tags on data fields, and if there is a data tag for JSON, the encoder will use this value for the key. To map correctly to the CamelCase expectations of JSON is simply a case of tagging the fields of the struct correctly.

```
type Person struct {
    Name     string   `json:"name"`
    Age      int      `json:"age"`
    Hobbies  []string `json:"hobbies"`
}
```

Listing 20.4 shows a full example of using struct tags to create expected JSON keys.

LISTING 20.4   Using Struct Tags

```
 1:   package main
 2:
 3:   import (
 4:        "encoding/json"
 5:        "fmt"
 6:        "log"
 7:   )
 8:
 9:   type Person struct {
10:        Name     string    `json:"name"`
11:        Age      int       `json:"age"`
12:        Hobbies []string `json:"hobbies"`
13:   }
14:
15:   func main() {
16:        hobbies := []string{"Cycling", "Cheese", "Techno"}
17:        p := Person{
18:            Name:     "George",
19:            Age:      40,
20:            Hobbies: hobbies,
21:        }
22:        fmt.Printf("%+v\n", p)
23:        jsonByteData, err := json.Marshal(p)
24:        if err != nil {
25:            log.Fatal(err)
26:        }
27:        jsonStringData := string(jsonByteData)
28:        fmt.Println(jsonStringData)
29:   }
```

Running Listing 20.4 correctly encodes JSON keys as expected.

```
go run example03.go
{Name:George Age:40 Hobbies:[Cycling Cheese Techno]}
{"name":"George","age":40,"hobbies":["Cycling","Cheese","Techno"]}
```

Struct tags can also be used to omit empty fields in a struct from being encoded to JSON. By default, if a struct is initialized with empty values, the ensuing encoded JSON includes values that have been assigned according to Go's zero values.

```
p := Person{}
{"name":"","age":0,"hobbies":null}
```

To omit zero values from encoded JSON, struct tags can be used to indicate that the field may optionally be empty, and that it should not be included if it is empty. This appends `omitempty` after the JSON key name.

```
type Person struct {
    Name    string   `json:"name,omitempty"`
    Age     int      `json:"age,omitempty"`
    Hobbies []string `json:"hobbies,omitempty"`
}
```

Listing 20.5 shows an example of an empty struct being encoded to JSON.

LISTING 20.5   Omitting Empty Struct Fields

```
 1:  package main
 2:
 3:  import (
 4:      "encoding/json"
 5:      "fmt"
 6:      "log"
 7:  )
 8:
 9:  type Person struct {
10:      Name    string   `json:"name,omitempty"`
11:      Age     int      `json:"age,omitempty"`
12:      Hobbies []string `json:"hobbies,omitempty"`
13:  }
14:
15:  func main() {
16:      hobbies := []string{"Cycling", "Cheese", "Techno"}
17:      p := Person{
18:          Name:    "George",
19:          Age:     40,
20:          Hobbies: hobbies,
21:      }
22:      fmt.Printf("%+v\n", p)
23:      jsonByteData, err := json.Marshal(p)
24:      if err != nil {
25:          log.Fatal(err)
26:      }
27:      jsonStringData := string(jsonByteData)
28:      fmt.Println(jsonStringData)
29:  }
```

Omitting Empty Struct Fields

In this example, you will learn how to omit empty struct fields.

1. Open hour20/example04.go from the code examples for this book.

2. Read the code and try to understand what it is doing.

3. From the terminal, run `go run example04.go`.

4. You will see an empty JSON object printed to the terminal.

```
{}
```

Decoding JSON

Decoding JSON is also a common task for network programming. Data may be received from a database, an API call, or from configuration files. As raw JSON is just data in text format, it can be represented initially in Go as a string. The Unmarshal function expects a slice of bytes and an interface to decode the data to. Depending on how data is received, it may be possible to receive it as a slice of bytes. If this is not possible, it must be converted before passing it to the Unmarshal function.

```
var jsonStringData := `{"name":"George","age":40,"hobbies":["Cycling","Cheese",
"Techno"]}`
jsonByteData := []byte(jsonStringData)
```

Like encoding data to JSON, an interface must be defined for the data to be decoded to. Just like when encoding JSON, struct tags may be used to tell the decoder to map a key to a field.

```
type Person struct {
    Name    string   `json:"name"`
    Age     int      `json:"age"`
    Hobbies []string `json:"hobbies"`
}
```

Listing 20.6 shows a string of JSON data being converted to a slice of bytes and then decoded using json.Unmarshal.

LISTING 20.6   Decoding a Struct into JSON

```
1:  package main
2:
3:  import (
```

```
 4:        "encoding/json"
 5:        "fmt"
 6:        "log"
 7:    )
 8:
 9:    type Person struct {
10:        Name      string    `json:"name"`
11:        Age       int       `json:"age"`
12:        Hobbies   []string  `json:"hobbies"`
13:    }
14:
15:    func main() {
16:        jsonStringData := `{"name":"George","age":40,"hobbies":["Cycling",
    "Cheese","Techno"]}`
17:        jsonByteData := []byte(jsonStringData)
18:        p := Person{}
19:        err := json.Unmarshal(jsonByteData, &p)
20:        if err != nil {
21:            log.Fatal(err)
22:        }
23:        fmt.Printf("%+v\n", p)
24:    {
```

Running Listing 20.6 shows that the JSON string has successfully been converted to an instance of a `Person` struct.

```
go run example05.go
{Name:George Age:40 Hobbies:[Cycling Cheese Techno]}
```

▼ TRY IT YOURSELF

Decoding JSON from a String

In this example, you will learn how to decode JSON from a string.

1. Open hour20/example05.go from the code examples for this book.

2. Read the code and try to understand what it is doing.

3. From the terminal, run `go run example05.go`.

4. You will see the JSON string decoded to a struct.

```
{Name:George Age:40 Hobbies:[Cycling Cheese Techno]}
```

Mapping Data Types

When encoding and decoding JSON, it is important to consider how data types are represented in both Go and JavaScript. In Hour 2, "Understanding Types," you learned that Go is a strongly typed language. JavaScript is a loosely typed language, meaning that data types of variables are not explicitly declared. Compare how Go and JavaScript declare `string` and `int` variables.

```
// JavaScript
var i = 4;
var s = "string";

// Go
var i int = 4
var s string = "string"
```

Note that Go explicitly declares the data type while JavaScript does not. As JSON is a subset of JavaScript, it follows the same approach of not needing to declare data types. This leads to some tricky data transformation problems between loosely and strongly typed languages. The following data types are available to use in JSON:

- ▶ Boolean

- ▶ Number

- ▶ String

- ▶ Array

- ▶ Object

- ▶ Null

Listing 20.7 shows some examples of JSON with all of these data types.

LISTING 20.7   JSON Data Types

```
 1:  {
 2:       "exampleBoolean": false,
 3:       "exampleNumber": 4,
 4:       "exampleString": "string",
 5:       "exampleArray": ["one", "two", "three"],
 6:       "exampleObject": {
 7:            "foo": "bar"
 8:       },
 9:       "exampleNull": null
10:  }
```

Unfortunately, these do not map directly onto the data types in Go, so the `encoding/json` package makes an explicit transformation between data types. Table 20.2 shows the mapping between JSON and Go data types.

TABLE 20.2   Go and JSON Data Types

JSON	Go
Boolean	bool
Number	float64
String	string
Array	[]interface{}
Object	map[string]interface{}
Null	nil

When creating structs to decode or encode JSON, be aware of these data types, as the `encoding/json` package will throw an error if data types are mismatched. Listing 20.8 shows an example of a JSON string being decoded into a struct. What do you think will happen?

LISTING 20.8   Mapping Data Types Between JSON and Go

```
 1:  package main
 2:
 3:  import (
 4:      "encoding/json"
 5:      "fmt"
 6:      "log"
 7:  )
 8:
 9:  type Switch struct {
10:      On    bool    `json:"on"`
11:  }
12:
13:  func main() {
14:      jsonStringData := `{"on":"true"}`
15:      jsonByteData := []byte(jsonStringData)
16:      s := Switch{}
17:      err := json.Unmarshal(jsonByteData, &s)
18:      if err != nil {
19:          log.Fatal(err)
20:      }
21:      fmt.Printf("%+v\n", s)
22:  }
```

Running this example results in an error, because the true value is actually a string in JSON, as it is surrounded by quote marks. The Go decoder tries to unmarshal this value into a Go Boolean value, but since the value is a string this is not possible, and a fatal error is thrown.

```
go run example06.go
2017/08/27 17:07:13 json: cannot unmarshal string into Go struct field Switch.on of
type bool
exit status 1
```

Working with JSON Received over HTTP

When retrieving JSON via an HTTP request in Go, data will be received as a stream rather than a string or a slice of bytes. As such, a different method from the `encoding/json` package should be used for this scenario. For this example, the Github API will be used. This is a good example, as it provides well-formatted JSON, and there is no need to authenticate against some of the endpoints. In Hour 19, "Creating HTTP with Go," you learned about how to create an HTTP client to retrieve data over the HTTP protocol. This is directly applicable for retrieving data from a JSON API.

```
res, err := http.Get("https://api.github.com/users/shapeshed")
if err != nil {
log.Fatal(err)
}
defer res.Body.Close()
```

As the data is a stream, the `NewDecoder` function from the `encoding/json` package can be used. This expects an `io.Reader`, which conveniently is the type returned by `http.Get`, and returns a Decoder type. This type decodes the data into a struct. As before, the decoder expects a struct, so an instance of the struct must be created and passed to the `Decode` method. Listing 20.9 shows a full example of a call being made to the Github API and the data being decoded into a Go struct. As before, it is possible to use struct tags to map fields in a JSON response to fields in a struct if desired.

LISTING 20.9   Fetching JSON over HTTP

```
1:  package main
2:
3:  import (
4:      "encoding/json"
5:      "fmt"
6:      "log"
7:      "net/http"
8:  )
9:
```

```
10:   type User struct {
11:       Name string `json:"name"`
12:       Blog string `json:"blog"`
13:   }
14:
15:   func main() {
16:       var u User
17:       res, err := http.Get("https://api.github.com/users/shapeshed")
18:       if err != nil {
19:           log.Fatal(err)
20:       }
21:       defer res.Body.Close()
22:       err = json.NewDecoder(res.Body).Decode(&u)
23:       if err != nil {
24:           log.Fatal(err)
25:       }
26:       fmt.Printf("%+v\n", u)
27:   }
```

Summary

During this hour, you learned how to work with JSON in Go. You saw how to encode a struct as JSON and how to use struct tags to support custom JSON keys and optionally empty values. You learned how to decode JSON and the differences between JavaScript and Go data types. Finally, you saw how to retrieve JSON from an API using HTTP.

Q&A

Q. Do I have to create a struct to encode and decode JSON, or can this be figured out for me?

A. Yes, you need to create a struct to encode or decode JSON. Although this may seem tedious, particularly for large JSON objects, like the Github example you saw, it does lead to more robust and fault-tolerant code. If you can map JSON types on Go types, you get the benefit of type safety as well as using JSON as a data exchange format. There are several services online that can automatically create Go structs from JSON data.

Q. Why is everyone choosing JSON over other data transfer formats, like XML?

A. JSON has shown itself to be a flexible, easy to learn, and expressive data format. The rise of JavaScript as the language of the web means that JSON services are easy to consume within a browser. JSON is also smaller than other formats, meaning it can be transferred and stored efficiently.

Q. Does the `encoding/json` package provide any way to validate data being encoded to and from a struct?

A. No. The `encoding/json` package does not provide validation. You can choose to write methods on the struct that could be called, but there is nothing available as part of the encoder. There are several third-party struct validation libraries available.

Workshop

The workshop contains quiz questions and exercises to help you solidify your understanding of the material covered. Try to answer all questions before looking at the "Answers" section that follows.

Quiz

1. To which Go type does a JavaScript number map?

2. Do all fields in a JSON object have to be decoded into a struct?

3. Which struct tag should be used if a field can be optionally empty? What will happen if the field is empty?

Answers

1. A JavaScript number maps to a float64 in Go.

2. No. It is possible to define a struct to only include fields that you are interested in. Struct tags can be used to map JSON fields to Go struct fields.

3. If a field can be optionally empty, the `omitempty` struct tag should be added. When decoding, this will omit the field from the tag if the value is empty.

Exercises

1. Find an API of a service that you are interested in and create a HTTP client to consume some data from it. Refer to Hour 19 if necessary. Retrieve some JSON data and decode it into a struct. Some examples of APIs that might be interesting include Dark Sky, Reddit, and Github.

Working with Files

What You'll Learn in This Hour:

▶ Importance of files

▶ Reading and writing files with the `ioutil` package

▶ Writing to a file

▶ Listing a directory

▶ Copying a file

▶ Deleting files

▶ Using files to manage configuration

During this hour, you will learn about working with files in Go. You will learn how to read, create, and delete files and understand how to list a directory. You will be introduced to the differences between using the `ioutil` convenience functions and the `os` package. Finally, you will see how to use files to manage configuration.

Importance of Files

Files might not seem like much; they just are just data on a hard disk. But, in fact, files offer a programmer configuration management, storing the state of a program, and even reading data from the underlying operating system.

On Unix-type operating systems (Linux and macOS), one of the defining features is the idea that everything is a file. This means that in terms of the operating system, everything from keyboards to printers can be addressed as if it were a file. Unix goes even further in this design and exposes system information through a virtual filesystem. This means it is possible to read system data as if it were a file.

The `cat` command in Unix allows the contents of a file to be read and printed to the terminal. Because Unix exposes system data as a file, the `cat` command can be used to extract information on the underlying system. One of these virtual files is `/proc/loadavg`, which shows the current load on the system.

```
cat /proc/loadavg
0.31 0.25 0.26 1/227 15992
```

Run the command again, and the values change, showing that the data is giving a real-time view into the load on a machine.

```
cat /proc/loadavg
0.47 0.30 0.28 2/229 16571
```

Using the `watch` command that is available on most Unix-type systems, a real-time view can be created of the system load where the screen is refreshed every 2 seconds as the `/proc/loadavg` file is read and then written to the screen.

```
watch cat /proc/loadavg
Every 2.0s: cat /proc/loadavg
0.32 0.30 0.28 1/232 18308
```

In one line of code, a real-time view of the load on a system can be created! This is all because of the way Unix treats everything as if it were a file. Files are not always dumb pieces of data. Often, they can be used to create programs that can react to the state of an operating system simply by reading a file.

Reading and Writing Files with the `ioutil` Package

Working with files is a such a common requirement that the `ioutil` package is offered as part of the standard library to provide a shorthand for many of the operations involved in reading and writing files. In fact, this package is mostly just a wrapper for the `os` module, providing shorter code and removing the need to handle cleanup operations. If any of the following operations are needed and fine-grained control is not needed, the `ioutil` package is a good option:

- ► Reading a file
- ► Listing a directory
- ► Creating a temporary directory
- ► Creating a temporary file
- ► Creating a file
- ► Writing to a file

Reading a File

One of the most common file operations is reading. The `ioutil` package provides the `Readfile` function to do this, and it expects a filename to be passed to it. The function returns the contents of the file as a slice of bytes. This means that if the file contents are to be used as a string, the slice of bytes needs to be converted to a string type. Listing 21.1 shows a file being read and the contents printed to the terminal.

LISTING 21.1   Reading a File and Printing Content to the Terminal

```
 1:   package main
 2:
 3:   import (
 4:        "fmt"
 5:        "io/ioutil"
 6:        "log"
 7:   )
 8:
 9:   func main() {
10:        fileBytes, err := ioutil.ReadFile("example01.txt")
11:        if err != nil {
12:             log.Fatal(err)
13:        }
14:
15:        fmt.Println(fileBytes)
16:
17:        fileString := string(fileBytes)
18:        fmt.Println(fileString)
19:   }
```

Listing 21.1 can be explained as follows:

▶ The `Readfile` function from the `ioutil` package is used to read a file.

▶ This returns a slice of bytes, and this is printed to the terminal.

▶ A string is then created from the byte slice.

▶ The string value is printed to the terminal to show the text content of the file.

TRY IT YOURSELF ▼

Reading a File in Go

In this example, you will understand how to read a file in Go.

1. Open hour21/example01.go from the code examples for this book.

2. At the terminal, type `go run example01.go`.

3. You should see the contents of the file printed to the terminal.

Creating a File

The `ioutil` package also provides a convenience function for creating files through the `WriteFile` function. Although the `WriteFile` function is designed to write data to a file, it can also be used to create a file. The `WriteFile` function expects a filename, a byte slice of data to write to the file, and the permissions that should be applied to the file.

Permissions on files are derived from Unix permissions. These map to three user levels – the owner of the file, anyone who is in the same group as the file, and everyone else. In working with files, understanding permissions on files is an important aspect of security, because setting incorrect permissions on a file can mean that data could be read by someone that shouldn't be able to read it.

Go uses the numeric notation of Unix permissions, and many functions that work with files expect a permissions value to be passed as an argument. Table 21.1 shows the numeric notation and the symbolic notation.

TABLE 21.1   File Permissions

Symbolic Notation	Numeric Notation	Explanation
`----------`	`0000`	No permissions
`-rwx------`	`0700`	Read, write, and execute only for the owner
`-rwxrwx---`	`0770`	Read, write, and execute for the owner and the group
`-rwxrwxrwx`	`0777`	Read, write, and execute for the owner, the group, and others
`---x--x--x`	`0111`	Execute for everyone
`--w--w--w-`	`0222`	Write for everyone
`--wx-wx-wx`	`0333`	Write and execute for everyone
`-r--r--r--`	`0444`	Read for everyone
`-r-xr-xr-x`	`0555`	Read and execute for everyone
`-rw-rw-rw-`	`0666`	Read and write for everyone
`-rwxr-----`	`0740`	Read, write, and execute for the owner and read for the group

The symbolic notation shows a visual representation of the numeric notation. There are ten characters in a symbolic notation. The left-most value represents whether the file is a regular file, directory, or something else. The – character means that it is a regular file. The next three values define the permissions the owner has on the file. The next three values represent the permissions that the group has on the file, and the last three values represent the permissions that everyone else has.

Referencing Table 21.1, a file with 0777 permissions means that everyone has full permissions on the file, and all of the values in the equivalent symbolic notation are present. Conversely, a file with 0700 permissions means that only the owner of the file can do anything with the file. Generally, the default mode for files on Unix type systems is 0644, meaning the owner can read and write, but everyone else can only read. If you are creating files on a filesystem, some thought should be given to the permissions used to create a file. If you are unsure, following the default Unix permissions of 0644 is a good default.

Listing 21.2 shows a file being created on a filesystem with 0644 permissions.

LISTING 21.2   Creating a File on a System with 0644 Permissions

```
 1:   package main
 2:
 3:   import (
 4:        "fmt"
 5:        "io/ioutil"
 6:        "log"
 7:   )
 8:
 9:   func main() {
10:        b := make([]byte, 0)
11:        err := ioutil.WriteFile("example02.txt", b, 0644)
12:        if err != nil {
13:             log.Fatal(err)
14:        }
15:   }
```

Listing 21.2 can be explained as follows:

▶ The `WriteFile` function expects a slice of bytes, so an empty slice of bytes is initialized and assigned to the variable `b`.

▶ The `WriteFile` function is called and given the name of the file, the empty byte slice, and the permissions that should be set on the file.

▶ If there is no error, the file will be created.

Passing an empty slice of bytes to the `WriteFile` method is somewhat of a trick to take advantage of using the shorthand functions available in the `ioutil` package. Because the behavior of the `WriteFile` function is to create the file if it does not exist, it can also be used to create an empty file.

Running the example shows that an empty file has been created with the correct permissions.

```
go run example02.go
ls -l
-rw-r--r--  1 go go  172 Aug 29 09:44 example02.go
-rw-r--r--  1 go go    0 Sep  2 12:32 example02.txt
```

▼ TRY IT YOURSELF

Creating a File in Go

In this example, you will understand how to create a file in Go.

1. Open hour21/example02.go from the code examples for this book.

2. At the terminal, type go run example02.go.

3. You should see that a new file, example02.txt, has been created.

Writing to a File

As you might expect, the WriteFile function can also be used to write to a file. In Listing 21.2, you saw how to create an empty file by passing an empty byte slice. To write to a file is simply a case of passing some values instead of an empty byte slice. To write a string to a file, this must first be converted to a slice of bytes. Listing 21.3 shows a string of text being written to a file. If the file does not exist, it will be created.

LISTING 21.3   **Text String Being Written to a File**

```
 1:  package main
 2:
 3:  import (
 4:      "fmt"
 5:      "io/ioutil"
 6:      "log"
 7:  )
 8:
 9:  func main() {
10:      s := "Hello World"
11:      err := ioutil.WriteFile("example03.txt", []byte(s), 0644)
12:      if err != nil {
13:          log.Fatal(err)
14:      }
15:
```

Writing to a File in Go

In this example, you will understand how to write to a file in Go.

1. Open hour21/example03.go from the code examples for this book.

2. At the terminal, type `go run example03.go`.

3. You should see that a new file, `example03.text`, has been created.

4. Open this file. You will see that some text has been written to it.

Listing a Directory

In working with a file system, it is necessary to understand the directory structure in order to work with files. The `ioutil` package also provides a convenience function for this in the `ReadDir`, expects to be given a directory as a string, and returns a list of directories sorted by filename. The filenames are a `FileInfo` type and offer the following pieces of information:

▶ **Name**: the name of the file

▶ **Size**: the size in bytes of the file

▶ **Mode**: a representation of permissions in bits

▶ **ModTime**: when the file was last modified

▶ **IsDir**: whether the file is a directory

▶ **Sys**: underlying data source

Listing 21.4 shows a directory being listed and the permissions and filename being printed.

LISTING 21.4 Listing a Directory and Printing the Permissions and Filename

```
1:  package main
2:
3:  import (
4:      "fmt"
5:      "io/ioutil"
6:      "log"
7:  )
8:
9:  func main() {
```

```
10:        files, err := ioutil.ReadDir(".")
11:        if err != nil {
12:            log.Fatal(err)
13:        }
14:
15:        for _, file := range files {
16:            fmt.Println(file.Mode(), file.Name())
17:        }
18:    }
```

▼ TRY IT YOURSELF

Listing a Directory in Go

In this example, you will understand how to list a directory in Go.

1. Open hour21/example04.go from the code examples for this book.

2. At the terminal, type `go run example04.go`.

3. You should see a directory listing printed to the terminal.

Copying a File

The `ioutil` package offers some of the common operations needed when working with files. However, as operations become more complex, the `os` package should be used. The `os` package operates at a slightly lower level, and as such expects that files are explicitly closed after opening them. Reading the source code of the `os` package shows that many of the functions in the `ioutil` package are wrappers around the `os` package and remove the requirements to explicitly close files.

To copy a file is therefore a case of gluing together a few functions from the `os` package. Programmatically, the process is as follows:

1. Open the file that should be copied.

2. Read the contents.

3. Create and open the file that the contents should be copied into.

4. Write to the new file.

5. Close both files.

Listing 21.5 shows a full example of reading from an existing file and copying the contents to a new one.

LISTING 21.5   Copying a File's Content into a New File

```
 1:  package main
 2:
 3:  import (
 4:      "fmt"
 5:      "log"
 6:      "os"
 7:  )
 8:
 9:  func main() {
10:      from, err := os.Open("./example05.txt")
11:      if err != nil {
12:          log.Fatal(err)
13:      }
14:      defer from.Close()
15:
16:      to, err := os.OpenFile("./example05.copy.txt", os.O_RDWR|os.O_CREATE, 0666)
17:      if err != nil {
18:          log.Fatal(err)
19:      }
20:      defer to.Close()
21:
22:      _, err = io.Copy(to, from)
23:      if err != nil {
24:          log.Fatal(err)
25:      }
26:  }
```

Listing 21.5 can be explained as follows:

▶ The Open function from the os module is used to read a file from the disk.

▶ A defer statement is used to close the file once the script has finished all other executions.

▶ The OpenFile function is used to open a file. The first argument is the name of the file to be opened or created if it does not exist. The second argument represents the flags to be used on the file. In this case, it is read and write and should be created if it does not exist. Finally, the permissions on the file are set.

▶ Another defer statement is used to close this file after the other execution has finished.

▶ The Copy function is then used from the io package. This copies from the source file and writes it to the destination.

Copying a File in Go

In this example, you will understand how to copy a file in Go.

1. Open hour21/example05/example05.go from the code examples for this book.

2. At the terminal, type `go run example05.go`.

3. You should see a new file has been created in the folder that contains the same contents as example05.txt.

Deleting Files

Among programmers, deleting files is often considered a bad thing. Once a file is gone, *it is gone*, and a bug in code that deletes files can lead to catastrophic results, especially if there are no backups. It is considered good practice to "soft delete" data where possible, so that it can be recovered if there was a bug in the code or if someone changes his or her mind. There are times when expunging a file or folder is really required, and the os package makes this trivial with the Remove function. Be warned: there is no warning or ability to recover the file when using this, so be careful.

Listing 21.6 shows a file being deleted.

LISTING 21.6   Deleting a File

```
 1:   package main
 2:
 3:   import (
 4:       "log"
 5:       "os"
 6:   )
 7:
 8:   func main() {
 9:       err := os.Remove("./deleteme.txt")
10:       if err != nil {
11:           log.Fatal(err)
12:       }
13:   }
```

TRY IT YOURSELF

Deleting a File in Go

In this example, you will understand how to delete a file in Go.

1. Open hour21/example06/example06.go from the code examples for this book.

2. In the folder, you should see a file called `deleteme.txt`.

3. At the terminal, type `go run example06.go`.

4. Verify that the file `deleteme.txt` has been deleted.

Using Files to Manage Configuration

A common use of files in programming is to manage configuration. As code may be used in different contexts, a file can often be used to set different configuration parameters that can be used to start a program. In a development process, as an application moves through development, staging, and production environments, using a file can be an effective way to manage the differences between environments. Example of this include:

▶ The URL of a web service

▶ Access keys

▶ Port numbers

▶ Environment variables

Using JSON Files

In Hour 20, "Working with JSON," you learned how to work with JSON. JSON represents an effective, standard way to declare configuration that can be stored as a file and read as necessary. Another advantage of declaring configuration as a file is that it can be added to version control and incorporated in automated build processes. As you learned in Hour 20, JSON is a simple way of declaring keys and values that can be decoded into a Go struct and then used.

```
{
  "name": "George",
  "awake": true,
  "hungry": false
}
```

By storing JSON in a file, a Go program can read this file and use it as configuration data. Listing 21.7 shows a JSON file being read and decoded into a configuration struct.

LISTING 21.7   Using JSON for Configuration

```
 1:   package main
 2:
 3:   import (
 4:       "encoding/json"
 5:       "fmt"
 6:       "io/ioutil"
 7:       "log"
 8:   )
 9:
10:   type Config struct {
11:       Name    string `json:"name"`
12:       Awake   bool   `json:"awake"`
13:       Hungry bool    `json:"hungry"`
14:   }
15:
16:   func main() {
17:       f, err := ioutil.ReadFile("config.json")
18:       if err != nil {
19:           log.Fatal(err)
20:       }
21:       c := Config{}
22:       err = json.Unmarshal(f, &c)
21:       if err != nil {
22:           log.Fatal(err)
23:       }
24:       fmt.Printf("%+v\n", c)
25:   }
```

The example makes use of the ReadFile function that you saw earlier in this hour and decodes the contents of the file into a struct in the same way as Hour 20. In very few lines of code and using only the standard library, a program can now be configurable depending on the context it is running in. If more configuration is needed, the Go struct can be extended and more fields added to the JSON object.

▼ TRY IT YOURSELF

Reading Configuration from a JSON File

In this example, you will understand how to read configuration from a JSON file.

1. Open hour21/example07/example07.go from the code examples for this book.

2. In the folder, you will see a JSON file containing some configuration.

3. At the terminal, type go run example07.go.

4. You will see the configuration being read from the JSON file and printed to the console.

Using TOML Files

TOML (Tom's Obvious, Minimal Language, https://github.com/toml-lang/toml) is a file format that was specifically designed for configuration files and is popular in the Go community. It supports a more expressive format than JSON and maps more easily to Go types than JSON. While JSON is designed for serializing data, TOML is designed specifically for configuration files. As such, TOML has some advantages over JSON in that it is easier to read and has some features, like comments, that JSON does not have. At a basic level, the syntax is straightforward and can be used to specify keys and values in the same way that JSON does.

```
Name = "George"
Awake = true
Hungry = false
```

TOML is not part of Go in the same way that JSON is not, and it can be used with any language. There is no TOML package in the standard library, and although it would be possible to write some code to parse a TOML file, there are some excellent third-party packages available. The most popular one at the time of writing is the package by BurntSushi available at https://github.com/BurntSushi/toml. This makes it trivial to use TOML as a configuration file format with Go. Since it is not part of the standard library, the package must be installed.

```
go get github.com/BurntSushi/toml
```

The package provides a `DecodeFile` function that expects a filename and a struct to decode the TOML into. Listing 21.8 shows a TOML file being decoded into a configuration struct.

LISTING 21.8   Using TOML for Configuration

```
 1:  package main
 2:
 3:  import (
 4:      "fmt"
 5:      "log"
 6:
 7:      "github.com/BurntSushi/toml"
 8:  )
 9:
10:  type Config struct {
11:      Name    string
12:      Awake   bool
13:      Hungry  bool
14:  }
15:
16:  func main() {
17:      c := Config{}
```

```
18:        _, err := toml.DecodeFile("config.toml", &c)
19:        if err != nil {
20:            log.Fatal(err)
21:        }
22:        fmt.Printf("%+v\n", c)
23:    }
```

The lines of code to read configuration from a file are even shorter than JSON, and given that TOML is a more expressive and readable configuration format, it is clear why the library is so popular.

▼ TRY IT YOURSELF

Reading Configuration from a TOML File

In this example, you will understand how to read configuration from a TOML file.

1. Open hour21/example08/example08.go from the code examples for this book.

2. In the folder, you will see a TOML file containing some configuration.

3. At the terminal, type `go run example08.go`.

4. You will see the configuration being read from the TOML file and printed to the console.

Whether or not you choose to use a third-party package is personal preference, but some thought should be given to how you choose between writing code yourself or using a third-party package. Code in the standard library has a high chance of being interoperable with future Go releases, and the Go project takes stability seriously. With third-party packages there can be no guarantee of quality or continuity, because a developer may stop maintaining a package and move onto other things. Generally, popular projects in the Go community are well maintained and provide extremely high quality packages that can save a huge amount of time.

For the case of deciding whether to use JSON and standard libraries or TOML and a third-party package, there is no right answer. If you prefer the expressiveness of TOML, adding a well-maintained dependency to your project is not a bad thing. If, however, you can express your configuration in a JSON file, you have one less dependency to manage.

Summary

This hour introduced you to working with files in Go. You understood the difference between the `ioutil` package and the `os` and how the former offers several shorthand convenience methods for working with files. You learned about permissions and some of the implications around security. Finally, you saw how to use both JSON and TOML files to manage configuration.

Q&A

Q. Why does the `ioutil` package not have functions for things like copying files?

A. Go has a worthy goal of keeping the core libraries small and lightweight. Furthermore, there are large number of differences between operating systems that make creating a generic copy method difficult. As such, there are no convenience methods for copying files, and the `os` package should be used.

Q. Does Go check whether a file exists before operating on it?

A. No. As a programmer, you are required to check that a file exists before using it. If a file does not exist, an error will be thrown.

Q. How should I decide on which file permissions to set on a file?

A. If you are unsure about what permissions to set on a file, you should be conservative and set the lowest possible access. The default Unix permissions of 0644 are a good default. Offering a permissive permission level like 0777 means that if for some reason a server is compromised, an attacker can do anything with the file, including deleting it.

Workshop

The workshop contains quiz questions and exercises to help you solidify your understanding of the material covered. Try to answer all questions before looking at the "Answers" section that follows.

Quiz

1. If a file on an operating system has permissions set to 0700, will Go be able to read it?

2. What are some of the advantages of using TOML over JSON?

3. What are implications of using a third-party package?

Answers

1. This is a tricky question! A Go program is executed in the context of the user that you are logged in as. A file with 0700 permissions is limited to the owner of the file. If the file owner is the same as the user executing the Go process, it will be readable. If it is not the same, it will not be accessible.

2. TOML is a data format written specifically for configuration files. As such, it supports comments in files, which can help with readability and maintainability. Go data types are also represented more closely in TOML format.

3. Third-party packages can save a huge amount of time and provide high quality, well-maintained code. They do introduce a hard dependency into your project, however, so choosing a project that could disappear in a few months could lead to a lot more work. The Go community has some extremely talented developers who produce some excellent packages. If you do some research on things like how long the package has been in existence and how actively it is maintained, you can have a reasonable level of confidence.

Exercises

1. Imagine that you are writing a small program to print information on your first pet. Create a struct to describe your pet and create a configuration file using either JSON or TOML to describe your pet. Explore how you can represent different data types like arrays, integers, and floats using JSON and TOML.

Introducing Regular Expressions

What You'll Learn in This Hour:

▶ Defining Regular Expressions

▶ Getting familiar with regular expression syntax

▶ Using Regular Expressions for validation

▶ Using Regular Expressions to transform data

▶ Parsing data with Regular Expressions

Regular Expressions are a mystical, magical subset of most programming languages that offer a powerful way to pattern match and parse data. They can be initially complex to understand, but it is well worth devoting some time to learning them; they can be expressive and powerful. If you can master Regular Expressions, you will find that they become a powerful part of your programming toolkit. This hour introduces you to Regular Expressions in Go and some of the ways you can use them.

Defining Regular Expressions

A *Regular Expression* describes a search pattern that can be used to interact with data. Although Regular Expressions are difficult to learn, they can be extremely powerful. Regular Expressions support tasks like data validation, searching for data, and manipulating large bodies of text. Using expression searching and pattern matching can be vastly more efficient than other techniques, but learning Regular Expressions can be daunting. They are similar to a mini programming language, and, therefore, mastering them takes some time. It is possible, however, to use Regular Expressions as a beginner and take advantage of their power.

One use of Regular Expressions is to take a string of text and look for a match against a Regular Expression. This is often described as *looking for a needle in a haystack*. A concrete example is looking for the word "chocolate" in the sentence "Chocolate is my favorite!" Although you might consider that "chocolate" is in the sentence, a Regular Expression check is case sensitive, so depending on the expression it may be found or not.

Regular Expressions in Go are provided by the `regex` package, which implements Regular Expression search and pattern matching. The package implements the RE2 syntax and is the same general syntax used by Perl and Python. It can operate on strings or bytes.

To look for a needle in a haystack, the `MatchString` function is provided. This takes a Regular Expression pattern and a string and returns true or false depending on whether there is a match. Listing 22.1 shows an example of looking for the word *chocolate*.

LISTING 22.1   Looking for a Needle in a Haystack

```
1:   package main
2:
3:   import (
4:       "fmt"
5:       "log"
6:       "regexp"
7:   )
8:
9:   func main() {
10:      needle := "chocolate"
11:      haystack := "Chocolate is my favorite!"
12:      match, err := regexp.MatchString(needle, haystack)
13:      if err != nil {
14:          log.Fatal(err)
15:      }
16:      fmt.Println(match)
17:  }
```

Running this example prints false, indicating there is no match. Why is this? Because Regular Expressions are case sensitive, the string "chocolate" is not found.

▼ TRY IT YOURSELF

Searching for a String

In this example, you will understand how to use Regular Expressions to search for a string.

1. In your terminal, navigate to the hour22/ folder.

2. At the terminal, type `go run example01`.

3. You will see that the Regular Expression evaluates to false.

To make the search case insensitive, the Regular Expression must be updated to match a case insensitive search for the word. This uses some special syntax to indicate the search should be case insensitive.

```
needle := "(?i)chocolate"
```

The special syntax at the start of the string instructs the Regular Expression engine to ignore case sensitivity. Running this example returns `true`, as the string is found.

```
go run example02.go
true
```

Case Insensitivity

In this example, you will understand how to make Regular Expression searches case insensitive.

1. In your terminal, navigate to the hour22/ folder.

2. At the terminal, type `go run example02`.

3. You will see that the Regular Expression evaluates to `true`.

Getting Familiar with Regular Expression Syntax

A detailed explanation of Regular Expression syntax is beyond the scope of this book, but you are likely to use some common syntax definitions in creating Regular Expressions. Table 22.1 shows some of the most common characters.

TABLE 22.1   Common Regular Expression Syntax

Character(s)	Meaning
.	Matches any character except a line break
*	Matches the previous character zero or more times
^	Signifies the start of a line
$	Signifies the end of a line
+	Matches one or more times
?	Matches zero or one times
[]	Matches any character with the brackets
{n}	Matches n times
{n,}	Matches n or more times
{m,n}	Matches at least m times and at most n times

To help explore Regular Expression syntax, suppose that a username needs to be validated before it is inserted into a database. Before writing a Regular Expression, it is a good idea to write down the conditions for which it must test. In this case, the string should match according to the following rules:

▶ It should be longer than four characters but no longer than twelve characters.

▶ It should include nothing other than alphanumeric characters.

▶ Characters may be uppercase or lowercase.

Think about trying to write some code to test this without using a Regular Expression. It would be possible, but it would take a *lot* of code. By using Regular Expressions, this can be achieved in a single line:

```
^[a-zA-Z0-9]{5-12}$
```

It might seem magical that this can be achieved in so few characters. The previous line can be explained as follows:

▶ The ^ character indicates that the match should start from the beginning of the string.

▶ The character set within the square brackets [] represents any character that should be matched.

▶ The numbers within the curly brackets {} represent that the match should occur at least 5 times and not more than 12 times.

Using Regular Expressions for Validation

Regular Expressions can be used as a way to validate input data to a program, and they represent an efficient way to parse and understand data. To assign a Regular Expression to a variable, it must first be parsed. Two functions are provided for this:

▶ Compile returns an error if the Regular Expression fails to compile.

▶ MustCompile panics if it cannot compile the Regular Expression.

Which one you prefer depends on the context it is used in, but generally MustCompile is favored.

```
re := regexp.MustCompile("^[a-zA-Z0-9]{5,12}")
```

Listing 22.2 shows a Regular Expression being used to check usernames.

LISTING 22.2 Using Regular Expressions to Validate Data

```
 1:  package main
 2:
 3:  import (
 4:      "fmt"
 5:      "regexp"
 6:  )
 7:
 8:  func main() {
 9:      re := regexp.MustCompile("^[a-zA-Z0-9]{5,12}")
10:      fmt.Println(re.MatchString("slimshady99"))
11:      fmt.Println(re.MatchString("!asdf£33£3"))
12:      fmt.Println(re.MatchString("roger"))
13:      fmt.Println(re.MatchString("iamthebestuseofthisappevaaaar"))
14:  }
```

Running Listing 22.2 evaluates each of the strings and prints true or false depending on whether there is a match. In a real programming context, this could be used to check whether a username can be safely inserted into a database.

```
go run example03.go
true
false
true
true
```

Using Regular Expressions to Transform Data

In the previous example, some of the usernames were invalid because of length or invalid characters being used. Another common programming task is to clean data so that it can safely be used. Regular Expressions can also be used for this task to match a pattern and perform a substitution. In Listing 22.2, you saw how a Regular Expression can be used to check that a username conforms to a particular pattern. An improvement to this would be to clean usernames as they are received, so that if they do not match the Regular Expression, they can still be used.

Looking at the rules for a username, the names must be no more than 12 characters. To clean names that are too long, a string can be truncated to only be 12 characters. This string can then be evaluated against the Regular Expression to see if it contains invalid characters. If invalid characters are found, they can be substituted with another valid character.

It is not uncommon to build little data pipelines like this to cleanse data, and Regular Expressions are an extremely handy tool in doing so. Listing 22.3 shows a list of usernames being evaluated to see if they match the rules for a username. If a username is found to be too long, it is truncated. If invalid characters are found, they are swapped for another character.

LISTING 22.3   Transforming Data with Regular Expressions

```
 1:  package main
 2:
 3:  import (
 4:      "fmt"
 5:      "regexp"
 6:  )
 7:
 8:  func main() {
 9:      usernames := [4]string{
10:          "slimshady99",
11:          "!asdf£33£3",
12:          "roger",
13:          "Iamthebestuserofthisappevaaaar",
14:      }
15:
16:      re := regexp.MustCompile("^[a-zA-Z0-9]{5,12}")
17:      an := regexp.MustCompile("[[:^alnum:]]")
18:
19:      for _, username := range usernames {
20:          if len(username) > 12 {
21:              username = username[:12]
22:              fmt.Printf("trimmed username to %v\n", username)
23:          }
24:          if !re.MatchString(username) {
25:              username = an.ReplaceAllString(username, "x")
26:              fmt.Printf("rewrote username to %v\n", username)
27:          }
28:      }
29:  }
```

Running this program shows that the username "Iamthebestuserofthisappevaaaar" is successfully truncated to "Iamthebestus" and the username "!asdf£33£3" is cleaned so that invalid characters are replaced with an "x".

```
go run example04.go
rewrote username to xasdfx33x3
trimmed username to Iamthebestus
```

TRY IT YOURSELF

Using Regular Expressions to Transform Data

In this example, you will understand how to use Regular Expressions to transform data.

1. In your terminal, navigate to the hour22/ folder.

2. At the terminal, type `go run example04`.

3. You will see that the input strings are trimmed and converted to conform with the Regular Expression.

Parsing Data with Regular Expressions

Once you become familiar with the idea that Regular Expressions operate on strings or bytes, there are many opportunities to use Regular Expressions to extract and manipulate data. Although Go has an HTML parser for this example, a Regular Expression will be used to extract data from a web page. This is typically known as scraping a page. Scraping HTML pages is bad for a number of reasons.

▶ HTML is not an equivalent for a data API.

▶ There is no guarantee that HTML structure will not change, meaning scripts can break.

▶ The owner of the data has not explicitly given consent to use the data.

Nonetheless, there are times when scraping HTML can be the only option. Because HTML is a text document, a Regular Expression can be used to extract relevant pieces of information. For the purposes of this example, the UK Government Petitions site will be used. This is a site where citizens of the UK can create and sign petitions. If a petition gets enough signatures, the Government guarantees that it be discussed in Parliament. This is a good idea in principle, but typically issues raised by citizen petitions get kicked into the long grass. Suppose that we are interested in programmatically retrieving the latest list of petitions, maybe to see what people in the UK care about.

Using a browser, the structure of the HTML document at https://petition.parliament.uk/petitions can be viewed. Viewing this page, all of the petition titles are contained with h3 HTML tags. A Regular Expression can be written to write a pattern to match this!

The following matches text within h3 tags:

```
re := regexp.MustCompile("\\<h3\\>.*\\</h3\\>")
```

You learned about creating HTTP clients in Hour 19, "Creating HTTP Clients with Go." A simple HTTP client can be used to fetch the HTML page and then search for h3 tags within it. Listing 22.4 shows the UK Government Petitions page being fetched and h3 tags being extracted from the page using a Regular Expression.

LISTING 22.4   Using Regular Expressions to Extract Data

```
 1:  package main
 2:
 3:  import (
 4:      "fmt"
 5:      "io/ioutil"
 6:      "log"
 7:      "net/http"
 8:      "regexp"
 9:  )
10:
11:  func main() {
12:      resp, err := http.Get("https://petition.parliament.uk/petitions")
13:      if err != nil {
14:          log.Fatal(err)
15:      }
16:      defer resp.Body.Close()
17:      body, err := ioutil.ReadAll(resp.Body)
18:      if err != nil {
19:          log.Fatal(err)
20:      }
21:
22:      src := string(body)
23:
24:      re := regexp.MustCompile("\\<h3\\>.*\\</h3\\>")
25:      titles := re.FindAllString(src, -1)
26:
27:      for _, title := range titles {
28:          fmt.Println(title)
29:      }
30:  }
```

The `FindAllString` function is used to look for all occurrences of a Regular Expression within a string, and these occurrences are then printed to the terminal. Running Listing 22.4 successfully prints the petitions to the terminal.

```
<h3><a href="/petitions/131215">EU Referendum Rules triggering a 2nd EU
Referendum</a></h3>
<h3><a href="/petitions/171928">Prevent Donald Trump from making a State Visit to
the United Kingdom.</a></h3>
<h3><a href="/petitions/108072">Give the Meningitis B vaccine to ALL children, not
just newborn babies.</a></h3>
```

It would be great if the HTML surrounding the petition titles could be removed. A Regular Expression can be used for this, too! The following matches HTML tags:

```
rHTML := regexp.MustCompile("<[^>]*>")
```

The opening angled bracket "<" signifies the start of an HTML tag. The square brackets then signify any character that is not a closing bracket through the use of the caret character to negate the search. The asterisk signifies that any number of these characters can be matched. Finally, a closing angled bracket indicates that the HTML tag is closed. Using this Regular Expression, the titles of petitions can have the HTML tags removed. Listing 22.5 shows the HTML being parsed, cleaned, and the titles being written to the terminal.

LISTING 22.5   Parsing, Cleaning, and Writing Titles to a Terminal with Regular Expressions

```
1:  package main
2:
3:  import (
4:      "fmt"
5:      "io/ioutil"
6:      "log"
7:      "net/http"
8:      "regexp"
9:  )
```

```
10:
11:  func main() {
12:      resp, err := http.Get("https://petition.parliament.uk/petitions")
13:      if err != nil {
14:          log.Fatal(err)
15:      }
16:      defer resp.Body.Close()
17:      body, err := ioutil.ReadAll(resp.Body)
18:      if err != nil {
19:          log.Fatal(err)
20:      }
21:
22:      src := string(body)
23:
24:      re := regexp.MustCompile("\\<h3\\>.*\\</h3\\>")
25:      rHTML := regexp.MustCompile("<[^>]*>")
26:      titles := re.FindAllString(src, -1)
27:
28:      for _, title := range titles {
29:          cleanTitle := rHTML.ReplaceAllString(title, "")
30:          fmt.Println(cleanTitle)
31:      }
32:  }
```

Running this example retrieves the data and prints it to the terminal.

```
go run example06.go
EU Referendum Rules triggering a 2nd EU Referendum
Prevent Donald Trump from making a State Visit to the United Kingdom.
Give the Meningitis B vaccine to ALL children, not just newborn babies.
Block Donald J Trump from UK entry
Stop all immigration and close the UK borders until ISIS is defeated.
```

▼ TRY IT YOURSELF

Cleaning Data with Regular Expressions

In this example, you will understand how to clean data with Regular Expressions.

1. In your terminal, navigate to the hour22/ folder.

2. At the terminal, type `go run example06`.

3. You will see a list of petitions without HTML tags printed to the terminal.

Thanks to the Regular Expressions, it is possible to see that in late 2017, people in the UK are concerned about Brexit, Donald Trump, vaccinations for children, and immigration. A script like this could be automated and this data fed into a sentiment engine to help understand what the people of the UK are really interested in.

In reality, for scraping HTML, it is recommended that Go's `html` package is used, because it is likely to be more performant than Regular Expressions, but working with HTML is a good way to showcase some features of Go's Regular Expressions.

Summary

This hour introduced you to Regular Expressions, a powerful way to perform pattern matching and substitution. You learned how to search for a needle in a haystack and were introduced to some common Regular Expression syntax. You then saw an example where Regular Expressions were used to validate data and a further example where Regular Expressions were used to cleanse data. Finally, you saw how to parse text data using Regular Expressions to extract interesting data.

Q&A

Q. Are there any resources where I can learn more about Regular Expression syntax?

A. Regular Expression syntax is difficult to learn. That's why there are several books available specifically on Regular Expressions and a number of excellent browser-based Regular Expression testers. These can be an excellent way to test Regular Expressions and improve knowledge.

Q. Are Regular Expressions more or less efficient than using the strings package?

A. The strings package contains some functions for searching for a needle within a haystack. It does not support complex pattern matching, though. Generally, Regular Expressions are likely to be slower. You learned in Hour 15 about performance testing. This would be a perfect scenario to use for benchmarking to see which code runs faster!

Q. Do people ever commit Regular Expression syntax to memory?

A. Some people are naturally gifted at constructing Regular Expressions and carry around the entire syntax of Regular Expressions in their heads. For most mere mortals, constructing complex Regular Expressions is often a case of referring to documentation and testing patterns.

Workshop

The workshop contains quiz questions and exercises to help you solidify your understanding of the material covered. Try to answer all questions before looking at the "Answers" section that follows.

Quiz

1. What is the difference between the `Compile` and `MustCompile` functions?

2. How would you make a Regular Expression case insensitive?

3. Which Regular Expression character signifies the end of a line?

Answers

1. The `Compile` method returns an error if the Regular Expression cannot be parsed. If the `MustCompile` function fails to parse the Regular Expression, it will cause a panic.

2. The `i` flag makes a Regular Expression case insensitive.

3. The `$` signifies the end of a line.

Exercises

1. Construct a Regular Expression that matches any string 1–10 characters long and includes only numbers. You may want to use an online Regular Expression builder.

2. Construct a Regular Expression that matches any string that includes only capital letters. You may want to use an online Regular Expression builder to help you.

HOUR 23
Programming Time in Go

What You'll Learn in This Hour:

- ▶ Programming the element of time
- ▶ Putting your program to sleep
- ▶ Setting a timeout
- ▶ Using a ticker
- ▶ Representing time in a string format
- ▶ Working with `Time` structs
- ▶ Adding and subtracting time
- ▶ Comparing different `Time` structs

This hour introduces you to time in Go. You will understand how to show the current time and use tickers and timeouts. You will learn how Go parses strings into time and will see how to access things like the day and month once a time has been parsed. You will also learn how to compare one time with another one. By the end of this hour, you will have a good understanding of how to work with time in Go.

Programming the Element of Time

Time is an important element in programming. It can be used as part of a computation process, to synchronize servers, and to take measurements. Go offers the `time` package in the standard library, providing functions and methods to interact with the current time and to take time measurements.

In programming, time is typically referred to as "real time," "elapsed real time," or "wall clock." The term "wall clock" can be thought of a clock on a wall. It can have differences based on time zones or regional adjustments, and every 24 hours it resets to zero hours. This kind of variance with time zones, regional adjustments, and the 24-hour clock is not ideal for programming, so the concept of a monotonic clock also exists. A monotonic clock measures time in a constant way without any variance so can be used for timing events reliably.

To print the current time on a machine using Go, the Now function can be used. Listing 23.1 shows an example of discovering the current time.

LISTING 23.1   Printing Current Time

```
 1:   package main
 2:
 3:   import (
 4:        "fmt"
 5:        "time"
 6:   )
 7:
 8:   func main() {
 9:        fmt.Println(time.Now())
10:   }
```

Running this program prints the current time on a machine. Depending on the locale settings on your machine, you may see the time printed in a different format.

```
go run example01.go
2017-09-03 13:38:04.608932763 +0100 BST
```

Where does this time come from? Does Go have a magical clock that it consults? In fact, it comes from the underlying operating system. Depending on how accurate the time on your underlying operating system is, this can be useful or not. On most operating systems, the user can set the time.

On Linux, for example, it is possible to time travel and set the time way in the future. With the following command, time can be set to New Year's Day in 2050.

```
sudo date +%Y%m%d -s "20500101"
```

Running Listing 23.1 again shows that the code is being run in a totally different time.

```
go run example01.go
2050-01-01 00:01:19.186167091 +0000 GMT
```

As you can see, time is prone to many variables, including the operating system having the incorrect time. For this reason, one of the first things that many systems administrators do is to install a service that synchronizes time with a network clock. The Network Time Protocol (NTP) is a networking protocol for synchronizing across a network. Computers that use NTP are more likely to agree on time, but locally, they may still apply time zone differences.

In computing, the difference between time zones can be negated by referring to Coordinated Universal Time (UTC). UTC is a time standard rather than a time zone and allows computers anywhere in the work to have a common reference without having to work out relative time zones.

Many operating systems use NTP by default and set the time on behalf of the user. If you are deploying software to a server, accurate time must be established. As such, it is recommended that an NTP service is installed.

TRY IT YOURSELF ▼

Printing Time to the Terminal

In this example, you will understand how to access the current time through Go.

1. In your terminal, navigate to the hour23/ folder.

2. At the terminal, type `go run example01`.

3. You will see the current time on your computer printed to the terminal.

4. Try changing the time on your machine and running the example again.

Putting Your Program to Sleep

Now that you have an understanding of the complexity of time in programming, it's time to sleep. *Sleeping* in a computer program means pausing the execution of a program. Nothing happens while a program sleeps. In Go, if a Goroutine sleeps, other parts of the program can continue though. Listing 23.2 show an example a program that sleeps for 3 seconds and wakes up. Once the program wakes up, it prints to the console.

LISTING 23.2   Sleeping for 3 Seconds

```
 1:  package main
 2:
 3:  import (
 4:      "fmt"
 5:      "time"
 6:  )
 7:
 8:  func main() {
 9:      time.Sleep(3 * time.Second)
10:      fmt.Println("I'm awake")
11:  }
```

▼ TRY IT YOURSELF

Using Sleep to Pause a Process

In this example, you will understand how to get your process to sleep for 3 seconds.

1. In your terminal, navigate to the hour23/ folder.

2. At the terminal, type `go run example02`.

3. You will see the process sleep for 3 seconds and then print a message to the terminal.

Using sleep is a useful technique in halting execution for a short while. It can be used to wait for something else to complete or to pause the program. For more than trivial, temporary pauses, Goroutines are a better way to manage execution flow.

Setting a Timeout

Hour 12 introduced you to channels, and you saw how a select statement can have a timeout. This uses the `time` package to send a message to channel after a certain amount of time. The `After` function can be used to execute something after a certain amount of time. Listing 23.3 shows an example of using the `After` function to trigger a timeout after a certain amount time.

LISTING 23.3   Triggering a Timeout with `After`

```
 1:  package main
 2:
 3:  import (
 4:      "fmt"
 5:      "time"
 6:  )
 7:
 8:  func main() {
 9:      fmt.Println("You have two seconds to calculate 19 * 4")
10:      for {
11:          select {
12:          case <-time.After(2 * time.Second):
13:              fmt.Println("Time's up! The answer is 74. Did you get it?")
14:              return
15:          }
16:      }
17:  }
```

Running this example shows a message for 2 seconds before printing the answer and exiting.

```
go run example03.go
You have two seconds to calculate 19 * 4
Time's up! The answer is 74. Did you get it?
```

Using a Timeout

In this example, you will understand how to set a timeout.

1. In your terminal, navigate to the hour22/ folder.

2. At the terminal, type `go run example03`.

3. You will see a message appear posing a math question.

4. After 2 seconds, another message appears, and the process will exit.

Using a Ticker

A *ticker* allows code to be repeatedly executed after a certain amount of time. This can be useful for scenarios where jobs need to be run at regular intervals on a long-running process.

Listing 23.4 shows a ticker being used to display the time every 5 seconds.

LISTING 23.4   Displaying Time with a Ticker

```
 1:  package main
 2:
 3:  import (
 4:      "fmt"
 5:      "time"
 6:  )
 7:
 8:  func main() {
 9:      c := time.Tick(5 * time.Second)
10:      for t := range c {
11:          fmt.Printf("The time is now %v\n", t)
12:      }
13:  }
```

Using a Ticker to Display Current Time

In this example, you will understand how to use a ticker.

1. In your terminal, navigate to the hour22/ folder.

2. At the terminal, type `go run example04`.

3. You will see the current time written to the terminal every 5 seconds.

Representing Time in a String Format

You learned that time on computers can have a huge amount of variance. There is also variance in how time is represented in string format. Table 23.1 shows different time standards and their string representations.

TABLE 23.1   String Representations of Time

Type	String
ANSIC	Mon Jan _2 15:04:05 2006
UnixDate	Mon Jan _2 15:04:05 MST 2006
RubyDate	Mon Jan 02 15:04:05 -0700 2006
RFC822	02 Jan 06 15:04 MST
RFC822Z	02 Jan 06 15:04 -0700
RFC850	Monday, 02-Jan-06 15:04:05 MST
RFC1123	Mon, 02 Jan 2006 15:04:05 MST
RFC1123Z	Mon, 02 Jan 2006 15:04:05 -0700
RFC3339	2006-01-02T15:04:05Z07:00
RFC3339Nano	2006-01-02T15:04:05.999999999Z07:00

Often, data will be stored in a database according to one of these standards and can be delivered as a string. In order for Go to use the string as a time object, it must be parsed. Go has support for time standards and also supports defining custom time formats for dates that do not conform with standards.

Listing 23.5 shows a time string in RFC3339 format being parsed into a Time struct and printed to the terminal.

LISTING 23.5   Parsing a String

```
 1:   package main
 2:
 3:   import (
 4:        "fmt"
 5:        "log"
 6:        "time"
 7:   )
 8:
 9:   func main() {
10:        s := "2006-01-02T15:04:05+07:00"
11:        t, err := time.Parse(time.RFC3339, s)
```

```
12:        if err != nil {
13:             log.Fatal(err)
14:        }
15:        fmt.Println(t)
16:   }
```

Running this example shows that the time string has successfully been parsed:

```
go run example05.go
2006-01-02 15:04:05 +0700 +0700
```

TRY IT YOURSELF ▼

Parsing a String

In this example, you will understand how to parse a string.

1. In your terminal, navigate to the hour22/ folder.

2. At the terminal, type `go run example05`.

3. You will see the string has been parsed into a Time struct.

Working with Time Structs

Once a time string has been parsed into a Time struct, there a number of useful methods for working with a Time struct. Listing 23.6 shows some of the methods that are available on a Time struct.

LISTING 23.6   Available Methods on a Time Struct

```
 1:  package main
 2:
 3:  import (
 4:       "fmt"
 5:       "log"
 6:       "time"
 7:  )
 8:
 9:  func main() {
10:       s := "2006-01-02T15:04:05+07:00"
11:       t, err := time.Parse(time.RFC3339, s)
12:       if err != nil {
13:            log.Fatal(err)
14:       }
```

```
15:        fmt.Printf("The hour is %v\n", t.Hour())
16:        fmt.Printf("The minute is %v\n", t.Minute())
17:        fmt.Printf("The second is %v\n", t.Second())
18:        fmt.Printf("The day is %v\n", t.Day())
19:        fmt.Printf("The month is %v\n", t.Month())
20:        fmt.Printf("UNIX time is %v\n", t.Unix())
21:        fmt.Printf("The day of the week is %v\n", t.Weekday())
22:    }
```

Running this example shows some of the different methods available on a `Time` struct.

```
go run example06.go
The hour is 15
The minute is 4
The second is 5
The day is 2
The month is January
UNIX time is 1136189045
The day of the week is Monday
```

Adding and Subtracting Time

The `Add` method adds time onto the existing time and assigns the value to a variable.

```
s := "2006-01-02T15:04:05+07:00"
t, err := time.Parse(time.RFC3339, s)
if err != nil {
    log.Fatal(err)
}
nt := t.Add(2 * time.Second)
```

The `Sub` method subtracts time from the existing time and assigns the value to a variable.

```
s := "2006-01-02T15:04:05+07:00"
t, err := time.Parse(time.RFC3339, s)
if err != nil {
    log.Fatal(err)
}
nt := t.Sub(2 * time.Second)
```

Comparing Different `Time` Structs

Often, you will need to know whether one event happened before, after, or at the same time as another one. The `time` package supports this with the `Before`, `After`, and `Equal` methods. All of these return a Boolean field and compare two `Time` structs. Listing 23.7 shows these methods being used to evaluate the difference between two dates.

LISTING 23.7   Comparing Time

```
 1:  package main
 2:
 3:  import (
 4:      "fmt"
 5:      "log"
 6:      "time"
 7:  )
 8:
 9:  func main() {
10:      s1 := "2017-09-03T18:00:00+00:00"
11:      s2 := "2017-09-04T18:00:00+00:00"
12:      today, err := time.Parse(time.RFC3339, s1)
13:      if err != nil {
14:          log.Fatal(err)
15:      }
16:      tomorrow, err := time.Parse(time.RFC3339, s2)
17:      if err != nil {
18:      log.Fatal(err)
19:      }
20:      fmt.Println(today.After(tomorrow))
21:      fmt.Println(today.Before(tomorrow))
22:      fmt.Println(today.Equal(tomorrow))
23:  }
```

Running this example shows that the times are evaluated correctly.

```
go run example07.go
false
true
false
```

 TRY IT YOURSELF ▼

Comparing Time

In this example, you will understand how to compare time.

1. In your terminal, navigate to the hour22/ folder.

2. At the terminal, type `go run example07`.

3. You will see the time being compared and true or false statements being written to the terminal.

Summary

This hour introduced you to the `time` package in Go. You understood that time can have many variables including time zones, regional offsets, and time being set to something completely different. You learned about Network Time Protocol, a way to synchronize time on computers. You were introduced to different standards that exist for formatting time and learned how Go can parse many of these formats. You saw how to sleep a program and use a ticker before exploring the methods available on a `Time` struct for reading data, adding and subtracting time, and comparing `Time` structs.

Q&A

Q. Can I have any confidence in time on computers?

A. In this hour, you saw how it is easy to set a computer to an incorrect time. As such, you should be beware that time can easily be wrong. Computers might be set to the wrong time zone or may have drifted far away from the actual time. If you control a server, ensure that something like the Network Time Protocol is installed.

Q. Which of the time formats should I use?

A. There have been many different efforts to standardize time, and even before computers, Greenwich Mean time was used to provide a common time reference across the world. The ISO 8601 format is used in UTC and is well implemented across the web. RFC3339 is an extension to ISO 8601. The two are both good to use. If in doubt, the ISO 8601 standard is widely supported.

Q. Should I use UTC or GMT as Internet Time?

A. Computers and the Internet now refer to UTC as a common time standard. GMT is in fact a time zone. Time zones are theoretically subject to time adjustments while time standards are not. Although mainstream society commonly refers to GMT as a time standard, computing and scientific communities now use UTC.

Workshop

The workshop contains quiz questions and exercises to help you solidify your understanding of the material covered. Try to answer all questions before looking at the "Answers" section that follows.

Quiz

1. What is the difference between a wall clock and a monotonic clock?

2. How can you reduce the variance in time on a computer and ensure consistency?

3. What does sleeping a Goroutine do? Does it stop other Goroutines from executing?

Answers

1. A wall clock is subject to time zones and adjustments and is not really suitable for measurements. A monotonic clock is constant so is suitable for measurements.

2. Using something like NTP (Network Time Protocol) means that time will be synchronized with time servers on the Internet and can also check for time drifts.

3. Sleeping pauses the execution of a Goroutine meaning nothing happens. Other Goroutines can continue execution.

Exercises

1. Write a program to compute the number of days before Christmas next year.

2. Assuming tea time is at 1600 hours, write a program to display whether it is before or after tea time.

3. Write a program to display your age by comparing the current time with the time of your birthday.

HOUR 24
Deploying Go Code

What You'll Learn in This Hour:

- ▶ Understanding targets
- ▶ Reducing the size of binaries
- ▶ Using Docker
- ▶ Downloading binary files
- ▶ Using `go get`
- ▶ Releasing code with package managers

By this time, you have probably written some software that you are ready to share with the world. This hour introduces you to compiling Go code for different environments and minimizing the size of binary files. You will then learn how to ship a binary in a Docker container and understand the security considerations of offering binaries as downloads.

Understanding Targets

One of the great things about Go is that it can run on many different operating systems and architectures. An *operating system* is something like Windows or macOS, and *architecture* describes the architecture of the computer processor that is used to run programs. The difference in architecture affects the number of calculations a processor can perform and the amount of memory that it can support. Generally, most computers that are sold today are 64-bit, but there are some environments where 32-bit is normal. By programming in Go, there is a reasonable chance that code will run on most common platforms with little or no modifications.

If you are unsure of the environment you are on, and you have Go installed on a machine, the go env command gives full information on the operating system and architecture.

```
go env
GOARCH="amd64"
GOBIN=""
GOEXE=""
GOHOSTARCH="amd64"
GOHOSTOS="linux"
GOOS="linux"
GOPATH="/home/go/go"
GORACE=""
GOROOT="/usr/lib/go"
GOTOOLDIR="/usr/lib/go/pkg/tool/linux_amd64"
GCCGO="gccgo"
CC="gcc"
GOGCCFLAGS="-fPIC -m64 -pthread -fmessage-length=0 -fdebug-prefix-map=/tmp/
go-build674078985/tmp/go-build -gno-record-gcc-switches"
CXX="g++"
CGO_ENABLED="1"
PKG_CONFIG="pkg-config"
CGO_CFLAGS="-g -O2"
CGO_CPPFLAGS=""
CGO_CXXFLAGS="-g -O2"
CGO_FFLAGS="-g -O2"
CGO_LDFLAGS="-g -O2"
```

In this example, the computer is a 64-bit Linux machine. By default, the compiler will compile for the operating system and architecture that it is run on. So, if you know you are working on a 64-bit Linux machine and you are deploying to a 64-bit Linux server, there is nothing to do. If, however, a program should be compiled for a different operating system and architecture, this needs to be declared.

▼ TRY IT YOURSELF

Discovering Your Go Environment

In this example, you will understand your Go environment, including its operating system and architecture.

1. Open a terminal.

2. At the terminal, type go env.

3. You should see your Go environment printed to the console. Can you identify your operating system and architecture?

To specify target platforms, the go compiler accepts an operating system and architecture as environment variables. The GOOS environment variable is used to specify the operating system. The GOARCH environment variable is used to specify the architecture of the system. The build for a 32-bit Linux is as follows:

```
GOOS=linux GOARCH=386 go build example01.go
```

To build for a 64-bit Windows machine, run the following:

```
GOOS=windows GOARCH=amd64 go build example01.go
```

You do not need to be on a 32-bit Linux machine or a 64-bit Windows machine to compile binaries for these platforms. For example, compiling the Windows binary results in a `.exe` file that can be run on Windows.

TRY IT YOURSELF ▼

Compiling to Different Targets

In this example, you will understand how to cross-compile Go binaries.

1. In a terminal, navigate to the hour24/ folder in the code examples for this book.

2. Compile a binary for 64-bit Windows using `GOOS=windows GOARCH=amd64 go build example01.go`.

3. Compile a binary for 64-bit Linux using `GOOS=linux GOARCH=amd64 go build example01.go`.

Go supports a vast combination of operating systems and architectures, as shown in Table 24.1.

TABLE 24.1   Go-Supported Platforms and Architectures

Platform	Architecture
android	arm
darwin	386
darwin	amd64
darwin	arm
darwin	arm64
dragonfly	amd64

(Continued)

Platform	Architecture
freebsd	386
freebsd	amd64
freebsd	arm
linux	386
linux	amd64
linux	arm
linux	arm64
linux	ppc64
linux	ppc64le
linux	mips
linux	mipsle
linux	mips64
linux	mips64le
netbsd	386
netbsd	amd64
netbsd	arm
openbsd	386
openbsd	amd64
openbsd	arm
plan9	386
plan9	amd64
solaris	amd64
windows	386
windows	amd64

The broad array of operating systems and architectures that Go compiles to is one of the strengths of Go as a programming language, and as a Go programmer you can cross compile to these targets.

Reducing the Size of Binaries

Releasing Go code is simple. By compiling a single binary, there are no dependencies to be concerned about, and everything needed to run a program is included in the binary file. In a language like Node.js or Ruby, deploying an application to production means assembling all the dependencies and shipping a bundle of files. Using a compiled language like Go greatly simplifies this process.

Suppose that the Hello World program you saw in Hour 1, "Getting Started," is ready for release. The program can be compiled to create a binary.

```
go build example01.go
```

Looking at the output of this command, a binary file has been created.

```
-rwxr-xr-x  1 go go 1.5M Sep  2 15:37 example01
-rw-r--r--  1 go go   73 Sep  2 15:37 example01.go
```

The file size is 1.5MB for a program that simply prints a line to the console. Why is this? The reason is that Go has to include everything it needs to execute the program, including the Go run-time. Using a language like Ruby or Node.js, the run-time is installed on the server, so only the files that need to be executed need to be shipped. Although the binary size seems relatively large, the advantages are that it will run anywhere on the architecture it was compiled for with no dependencies.

Some compile flags can reduce the size of compiled binaries. These omit the symbol table, debug information, and the DWARF symbol table. It is not necessary to understand what these are. It is enough to know that these are not needed once the binary is ready for release.

```
GOOS=linux go build -ldflags="-s -w" example01.go
```

Compiling with these flags reduces the size of the binary to 1001KB. That's a third smaller!

```
-rwxr-xr-x  1 go go 1001K Sep  2 15:50 example01
-rw-r--r--  1 go go   73 Sep  2 15:37 example01.go
```

Shipping a file of 1001KB is acceptable in an age when Internet connections are over 100MB, but if size continues to be an issue, there is another technique that can be used. A scenario where this might come into play is on a small hardware device like a Raspberry Pi, router, or Internet of Things (IoT) device. These devices typically have limited storage. In this scenario, a tool called upx (https://upx.github.io/) can be used. The upx tool is generally available in Linux package managers. It works by compressing the binary. This, of course, means that the binary must be decompressed when it is run. Although decompression is fast, this means that startup times will be slightly slower. Running the upx tool on the 1001KB again reduces the file size.

```
                Ultimate Packer for eXecutables
              Copyright (C) 1996 - 2017
UPX 3.94        Markus Oberhumer, Laszlo Molnar, & John Reiser    May 12th 2017
        File size         Ratio       Format       Name
  --------------------    ------    -----------    -----------
    1024512 ->  382592   37.34%    linux/amd64    example01
Packed 1 file.
```

Using `upx`, the Hello World program has been reduced to just 374KB. Not bad from the 1.5MB that it started at!

```
-rwxr-xr-x  1 go go 374K Sep  2 16:00 example01
-rw-r--r--  1 go go   73 Sep  2 15:37 example01.go
```

Depending on the context of the environments that code is being shipped to, small binaries are more or less important. If you are shipping a web server through infrastructure where you know the network speeds are excellent, a binary size of 20MB is not an issue. If you are shipping some firmware onto a device with little storage, it is going to be important. If you are shipping a command-line tool that will be downloaded from package managers, the size of the file is moderately important.

To summarize, understanding the intricacies of compilers and why file sizes are large is not necessary for the majority of programmers. For most cases, spending time obsessing over binary sizes is a distraction, and the defaults are fine. The Go team continues to work on reducing the binary size, and each major release sees binary sizes decreasing.

Using Docker

Docker is a modern alternative to running applications within virtual machines and offers a lightweight way to ensure applications run in the same environment, regardless of the operating system environment they are executed in. Docker uses containers to allow applications to have a sandboxed environment within an operating system without the overhead of a full virtual machine.

In recent years, Docker and, more generally, containers have grown in popularity. They offer a lightweight way to provide consistency, and because they can be run in a standard way, a rich and vibrant ecosystem has emerged around them. Most cloud providers now offer a container-based service where Docker containers can be hosted and run. The standardization has led to a large amount of tooling emerging around containers that make it easy to package and ship code. You may have heard of the term "DevOps." This is really about helping software teams to release and ship code quickly, safely, and smoothly. Along with other tools, Docker can help in this process. Using Docker, deployment pipelines can be created that mean developers can just push some code into a code repository, and a few minutes later it will automatically and magically be released into production.

Because a Go binary includes everything it needs to run in a single file, some might argue that using Docker for Go projects is overkill. Certainly, for ensuring consistency, this is true. A Go binary is either executed on the right operating system and architecture, or it is not. But the tooling that has emerged around Docker to "ship" containers warrants an argument to use Docker to package and release Go code.

Docker is widely available for Linux, Windows, and macOS, is generally available in Linux distribution package managers, and has downloads for most platforms. Detailed installation instructions are available at https://docs.docker.com/engine/installation/.

The Go Project maintains official Docker images that allow code to be compiled and run within Docker containers. Often, these images are used to test code in automated environments, but they can also be used to ship code. Although a detailed description of Docker and how to use it is beyond the scope of this hour, suppose that a simple Go web server exists that is ready to ship into production. The program is a simple web server that responds to a request with "Hello World." Listing 24.1 shows the program to be deployed.

LISTING 24.1   Example Web Server

```
 1:  package main
 2:
 3:  import "net/http"
 4:
 5:  func helloWorld(w http.ResponseWriter, r *http.Request) {
 6:      w.Write([]byte("Hello World.\n"))
 7:  }
 8:
 9:  func main() {
10:      http.HandleFunc("/", helloWorld)
11:      http.ListenAndServe(":8000", nil)
12:  }
```

Listing 24.2 shows a Docker file that copies this Go code into a container, compiles it, and exposes a port. This image can now be run on a local machine, pushed to a remote Docker registry, or run on any infrastructure that supports Docker.

LISTING 24.2   Docker file

```
 1:  FROM golang:1.9
 2:  COPY example02.go /
 3:  RUN go build -o /example02 /example02.go
 4:  EXPOSE 8000
 5:  ENTRYPOINT ["/example02"]
```

To build the image on a local machine, run the following:

```
docker build -t hello-go .
```

Some output from the Docker daemon is shown as it builds the image.

```
Sending build context to Docker daemon  3.072kB
Step 1/5 : FROM golang:1.9
---> 5e2f23f821ca
Step 2/5 : COPY example02.go /
---> Using cache
---> 121fb5f77ae8
Step 3/5 : RUN go build -o /example02 /example02.go
---> Using cache
---> 319fffb93040
Step 4/5 : EXPOSE 8000
---> Running in dc43db2be7f1
---> fd638d7376d5
Removing intermediate container dc43db2be7f1
Step 5/5 : ENTRYPOINT /example02
---> Running in f0325da83631
---> 9807df129deb
Removing intermediate container f0325da83631
Successfully built 9807df129deb
Successfully tagged hello-go:latest
```

Once the image is built, the container can be run on the local machine.

```
docker run -p 8000:8000 hello-go:latest
```

This command binds port 8000 from the container to the host machine, meaning it can be accessed. Opening a browser at `http://localhost:8000/` shows the application responding with the "Hello World" text.

To stop the application, open another terminal and run:

```
docker ps
```

You see the application listed with an id number. Using this number, run the following to kill the docker container:

```
docker stop <container_id>
```

Downloading Binary Files

Because a Go binary has everything it needs to run on a platform, it is not uncommon to see Go projects distributed as downloadable files from the Internet. Users of the files can choose the correct download for their environment, download the file, and run it. This is a lightweight and easy way to share a program, since it is very easy to upload and share files on the Internet.

Distributing and Downloading Files via the Internet

This approach has very weak guarantees that the code is what it says it is, and that it has not been tampered with. It would be quite possible, for example, for an attacker to put some code out on the Internet and invite anyone to download it. When the code is downloaded and run, it wipes the hard drive.

There are two common approaches to verifying the identity of a downloadable file. The first is to host the file on an https connection with a valid certificate for an identity. This allows a certificate authority to verify the owner of a site when a user connects to it. The second common approach is to provide a checksum of the file. This acts as a fingerprint on the file.

The fingerprint of any file can be shown by running the relevant checksum against the file. This can be seen by compiling code and viewing the checksum. Suppose that the simple Hello World program in Listing 24.1 is to be distributed on the Internet. Once a binary has been generated, a checksum can be viewed.

```
go build example03.go
sha1sum example03
40abf828e2c873dd7f57d91e4cc30cb923d5486f   example03
```

For macOS, the command is `shasum`; for Windows, the File Checksum Integrity Verifiter can be downloaded to allow checksum verifications.

TRY IT YOURSELF ▼

Generating a Checksum for a File

In this example, you will understand how to generate a checksum for a file.

1. In a terminal, navigate to the hour24/ folder in the code examples for this book.

2. At the terminal, run `go build example03.go`.

3. Run a checksum on the binary file `sha1sum example03`.

4. You should see a hash string printed to the terminal.

The checksum acts as a unique fingerprint, and publishing the checksum on the download site along with the file offers some guarantees that the file is the same one that has been uploaded. Suppose that the download server had been compromised by an attacker, and the download had been replaced with a download that includes malicious code. Listing 24.3 shows the code that has replaced it.

LISTING 24.3   Malicious Web Server

```
1:   package main
2:
3:   import "fmt"
4:   func main() {
5:       fmt.Println("Hello world!")
6:       fmt.Println("I am a hacker. I am going to delete everything.")
7:       fmt.Printf("%+v\n", u)
8:   }
```

Compiling this code and running a checksum on the file results in a different hash:

```
go build example04.go
sha1sum example04
42ea77ae08ef8ef5d0dcf0a58ce61aaa0a618364   example04
```

As an end user, this would be a big red warning sign to not run this software. If you plan to distribute Go software through downloadable files, it is a good idea to ensure that a checksum is published so that users can check the validity of the file. Furthermore, if you download Go binaries, or any software from the Internet, check that the checksum values provided match those of your download.

A good example of a project that follows this pattern is Terraform. *Terraform* is an open source project written in Go. It allows users to configure Cloud Services so that there are repeatable infrastructure environments to deploy code into. On the Terraform download page, there are binaries available for a range of platforms and architectures. There is also a link to the checksum file for these downloads. Users can therefore download the binary file and check it against the list of published checksums.

Using `go get`

A lightweight but effective way of distributing code is by using the `go get` command. In Hour 21, you saw how to install third-party packages. The `go get` command may also be used to install command line tools too, and even official tooling uses this approach. This light touch approach is extremely effective. The source for a tool can be shared on a site like Github and can then be installed with a single command. For example, installing `dep`, the dependency management tool, is as follows:

```
go get -u github.com/golang/dep/cmd/dep
```

After the package has been downloaded, the command will be available.

```
dep -help
dep is a tool for managing dependencies for Go projects
```

Especially for sharing command-line tools, using `go get` is an excellent way to share software. It is tightly integrated into the Go workflow and has the added benefit that if there is a desire to review the source code or documentation, a copy of the code is available locally. In Hour 9,

"Working with Strings," you learned how to publish code in this way, and it represents another way to publish your code.

Releasing Code with Package Managers

Although sharing a file on the Internet is an easy way to share a Go program, most operating systems have official or unofficial package managers for distributing code. This allows end users to install software in a consistent manner. Many package managers also support additional security, like automatically performing checksum comparisons or enforcing that developers digitally sign packages. Some popular package managers and their platforms include:

▶ Homebrew (https://brew.sh/) - macOS

▶ Chocolatey (https://chocolatey.org/) - Windows

▶ Apt (https://wiki.debian.org/Apt) - Debian, Ubuntu

▶ Yum (http://yum.baseurl.org/) - Fedora, Red Hat, Centos

▶ Pacman (https://www.archlinux.org/pacman/) - Arch Linux

All of these package managers share a way for the end user to install software in a consistent, safe manner. If you are looking to distribute Open Source software to a wider community, it is recommended that software is published to package managers.

Summary

This hour introduced you to some of the ways that you can use the Go programs you create. You understood that Go is capable of compiling to many different platforms and architectures, representing another strength of the Go programming language. You saw how to optimize the size of binary files and how to use a tool like upx to further shrink the file size of a binary. You were introduced to Docker as a way to share Go programs before understanding how to share binary files by offering them for download from the Internet. You were introduced to some security concerns and ways to mitigate them. Finally, you were introduced to package managers, a common way to provide a consistent and safe experience when installing software.

Q&A

Q. How should I share my software? Should I email it? Should I offer it for download? Should I use Docker?

A. There is no easy answer. If you are deploying a web application, using Docker is a good option. If you are sharing, a command line tool offering the file as a download or through go get are good options. If you are writing firmware, you will probably need an entirely different process. Of importance is that the receiver of the file can verify the integrity of the file. Sending or publishing a checksum is good, and, depending on the level of assurance you need, you may also wish to consider digitally signing the file.

Q. Are there really no dependencies with a Go binary?

A. No. That's one of the strengths of using a statically linked binary. If the binary is compiled for the correct target, there is nothing else that is needed to run the file.

Q. Docker seems like more complexity. Is it really worth learning?

A. If you are creating command line applications and system tools with Go, then learning Docker is probably not needed. If you are creating servers or anything that is deployed in the context of other applications, Docker is definitely worth understanding. It is likely that if you are working in a software team and deploying web products, Docker will be in use or is being considered. Many large software companies, including Google, use containers to manage their infrastructure.

Workshop

The workshop contains quiz questions and exercises to help you solidify your understanding of the material covered. Try to answer all questions before looking at the "Answers" section that follows.

Quiz

1. How would you discover the architecture of some hardware that you want to run Go code on?

2. Can you compile a binary to be run on a Windows machine from a Linux machine?

3. Should you trust Go binaries that you download from the Internet?

Answers

1. If Go is installed on the machine, running `go env` will give a large amount of information about the environment, from which you can gather the `GOOS` and `GOARCH` environment variables. If Go is not installed, most operating systems provide a way to establish the underlying architecture, and hopefully the operating system will be obvious by turning the machine on.

2. Yes. This is known as cross-compiling. Generally compiling on the same platform that you are targeting will be faster though!

3. By default, you should not trust binary files downloaded from the Internet. If you have confidence in the identity of the site, then trust can, and should, be established before executing the file.

Exercises

1. Find a friend that uses a different operating system from you. Compile a binary that can run on your friend's machine. Use a checksum to verify the file as you transfer it between operating systems.

Index

A

Accept header, 251-252, 268, 271

access log, 213-214

addition function, 15

Add method, 324

address, 35-38, 89-90

addUp function, 41

after, triggering timeout with, 320

Alarm struct, 92

Apache web server, 152

APIs, 273, 275, 285

append builtin function, 75, 80-81

architecture, 329, 331-332, 340

Args method, 229

arguments

    accessing, 230

    defined, 229

    number of, 51

    passing, 239

    passing functions as, 50, 52

    raw command-line, 229-230

    variable number of, 45

arithmetic operators, 59

arrays

    data types held by, 25

    definition and overview of,
      21-22, 71, 78

    elements, accessing, 81

    initializing, 72-73

    resizing, 81

    using, criteria for, 80

    working with, 71-73

ASCII encoding standard, 122

assignment operator, 119, 126

associative array (term), 78

automating workflow, 196-197

B

bad data, 213

BBC homepage, 143

benchmarking, 207-209, 211

binaries, 332-334, 340

binary files, downloading, 336-338

bits (defined), 18

blocking and flow control, 161-163

blocking code, 144-145, 154

blocks, 33-34, 40

Booleans and Boolean statements

    constructing, 68

    converting to and from,
      23-24

    evaluating, 55, 57, 59

    if statements and, 54

    implementing, 17-18

    logical comparisons used
      in, 59-60

    time applications, 324

brace brackets, 34

breakpoint, 222-223, 225-226

breakpoint (defined), 226

buffer, 120-121, 127, 207-209

buffered channels, 159-161

buffered messages, 171

bugs, 176, 213

builtin function, 80

bytes buffer, 121, 127

byte slice, 291

bytes package, 175

C

C (programming language), 3

C++ (programming language), 3-4

Camel Case, 189, 278

case, default, 61-62

case, selecting execution of, 166

case for identifiers, 183

case sensitivity, 219, 306-307

cat command, 289-290

Changelog file, 182

Channels, 155-161, 164-171

chat, 142

checksum, generating, 337

Chrome DevTools, 260-261

Chrome web browser, 3, 142-143

C-like languages, 89

code

 compiling, 4, 14, 196

 documenting, 192-196

 examples of, 2

 executing concurrently, 154

 formatting, 185-187, 198

 releasing, 339

 running, 198

 sharing, 8

 style, improving, 191

 writing *versus* third-party packages, 182

command, exit status of, 241

command-line arguments, 240-241

command-line flags, 230-232

command-line programs, 227-230, 232-234, 240-242

comments, writing, 192-193

commission rate, 40

communication, 158, 171

comparison operators, 58-59

compile method, 316

compiler, 4, 14, 17, 113

compiler error, 16-17, 213

compile-time errors, 16-17, 29, 31

compiling to different targets, 331

computer processor, 20

concurrency, 1, 139-141, 141-143, 155-156, 170

concurrent operations, 145-147, 161

configuration, 299-300, 301-302

constants, 38-39, 40

constructor function, 92-93

content-type header, 271

content types, 251-252

continue command, 222-223

Continuous Integration environments, 196

Coordinated Universal Time (UTC), 319, 326

copy function, 77

crash, 136, 138

cross-compiling, 340

curl, 245-247, 259-261

current time, 317-319, 321

custom HTTP client, 264-265

D

dash, single *versus* double, 242

data

 bad, 213

 cleaning, 314

 extracting, 312

 finding, 313

 incoming, filtering, 255

 parsing, 311-315

 printing, 218-219

 reading, 142, 154

 transforming, 309-311

 validation of, 308-309

database drivers, 182

databases, 13, 15, 141, 154

data elements, exporting, 100

data record, 83

data structures, 24

data type

 accessing, 84

 arrays holding more than one, 25

 of Channels, 170

 defined, 13

 mapping, 283-285

 method set associated with, 103

 names referencing, 189

 in struct, 100

debugging

 adding lines during, 218-219

 definition and overview of, 213

 delve, using for, 221-224

 fmt package, using for, 219, 222

 GNU Debugger, using for, 224-225

 of HTTP requests, 266-268

 logging role in, 214, 216

 test role in, 226

 tool, selecting, 225

 of web servers, 246

DecodeFile function, 301

default case, 61-62

default value, 91-93, 100

defer (defined), 53

defer statement, 66-69, 297

delve, 221-226

dependencies, 178-180, 183, 340

Developer Tools, 142-143

dictionary (term), 78, 80

directory, listing, 290, 295-296

disasters, handling, 129

disk, reading from, 140, 142, 154

distributed programming, 1

Docker, 334-336, 339-340

documentation, 195-198

dot notation

    data accessing with, 84, 90, 101

    sphere, working with, 104

    values, assigning with, 85-87

dynamically typed languages, 13-14, 26

E

echo function, 222-223, 225

elapsed real time (term), 317

elements, forming collection of, 21

else if statement, 57-58, 60-61, 68

else statement, 55-57

encoding/json package, 285, 287

encoding standards, 122

English-language special characters, 116, 122-123

environment, 8, 329-331, 340

Errorf method, 133

error log, 213

errors

    checking, 137

    creating, 132-133

    formatting, 133-134

    handling, 15, 129-131, 137-138

    logging, 214-215

    returning from function, 134-135

    type, understanding, 132

    and usability, 135-136

    writing, 242

errors package, 132-133

exit codes and meanings, 228

exiting, preventing process from, 163

F

fatal error, 215

file

    as block, 35, 40

    configuration, managing with, 299-300

    copying, 296-298, 303

    creating, 290, 292-294

    deleting, 298-299

    downloading, 336-338

    existence, checking on, 303

    importance of, 289-290

    managing in directory, 227

    name, 295-296

    reading, 130-131, 140, 290-291

    reformatting, 187

    writing logs to, 216-217

    writing to, 290, 294-295

file permissions, 213, 292-294, 295-296, 303

FindAllString function, 313

flag package, 232-235, 239

FlagSets, 237

floats, 20-21

flow control, 161-163

fmt package, 133, 219-222, 225-226

for loop, 167-169, 171

for statement, 62-66

4-bit integers, 18-19, 26

404s, 248-249

framework libraries, 257

FreeBSD, 4

French, Renee, 10

func keyword, 42

function

    arguments and types, modifying for, 51

    creating and calling, 43-44

    definition and overview of, 41-42

    errors, returning from, 134-135

    method compared to, 101, 105, 113

    passing as argument, 52

    passing as value, 49-50

    results, returning, 42-45

functional tests, 200

function arguments, 164

function signature, 41, 46-47

G

gdb, 224-225

GET requests, 255-258, 261-262, 266, 272

git command, 235

Github account, 8

Github API, 273, 285

GMT, 326

GNU Debugger, 224-225

GOARCH environment variable, 331

go build, 9-11, 229-230

go clean, 9

Go (Golang) description and
overview, 1, 3-4

godoc, 192-197

GoDoc site, 197

go env command, 329-330, 340

gofmt

conventions, 197

golint compared to, 190-191

overview of, 186-187

plugins running on, 188

remembering to use, 196

go get command, 177-179, 183,
338-339

Go Gopher, 10-11

go install, 242

go keyword, 151-152

golint, 190-192, 196

"Goodbye Cruel World" value, 223,
225

Google, 3-4

Google Chrome Developer Tools,
260

GOPATH variable, 6-8

Go projects, directory structure
for, 6-7

Goroutines

advantages of, 139, 153-154

Channels compared to, 171

communications between,
155-156

communication with, 159, 168

concurrent operations,
handling with, 145, 161

defining, 152

execution, pausing, 327

flow control alternatives to, 163

HTTP requests, aid in making,
271

latency, managing with,
147-152

managing, 156-157

go run, 9-11

go set, 242

go test command, 201

got want pattern, 203-204

graphical user interfaces (GUI), 227

greeting, returning, 202-204

Greeting function, 204-206

Griesemer, Robert, 3

guessing game, 218-219

H

Half function, 135

HandleFunc method, 244, 247

Handler, 248-249

handler functions, 247-249

hash (term), 78, 80

header, setting, 249-250

"Hello World" file, 240-241

HelloWorld function, 244, 252

"Hello World" program, 8-9, 173

"Hello World" value, 223

"Hello World" web server,
243-249

help text, 234-239

html package, 315

HTTP (Hypertext Transfer Protocol)

complexity of, 271

definition and overview of,
259-261

JSON received over, 285-286

scraping, 311-312, 315

HTTP clients, 267, 271-272

HTTP header, 250

http package, 257

HTTP requests, 259-261,
264-268, 271

HTTP servers

creating, 243-245, 249-250,
253-254

data and requests sent to,
255-258

response to clients, 251

HTTPS server, 258

I

identifiers, uppercase versus
lowercase letters starting, 183

idiomatic Go

defined, 185

error handling and, 130-131

golint aid in learning, 191

interface naming, 198

idiomatic variable, 33

if statement, 53-55, 69, 219

import statement, 174, 176

incorrect type, passing, 16-17

index, accessing array element
with, 81

init statement, 63-64

inner blocks, 34

inputs and outputs, 228-229

installing Go, 4-8

integers, 15-16, 18-20, 45-46

integration tests, 200

interfaces, 109-113, 189, 198

international characters, 122-123, 127

interpreted string literals, 115, 116-117, 127

ioutil package, 290-298, 303

J

Java (programming language), 10, 138, 152, 192-193

javadoc, 192-193

JavaScript (programming language), 4, 13, 15, 286-287

JSON

   advantages of, 286

   APIs, 275

   data posted as, 264

   data types, 283-285

   decoding, 281-282, 286

   description and overview of, 273-274

   encoding, 286

   fields, mapping, 287

   files, 299-300

   HTTP, received over, 285-286

   HTTP server sending, 249-250, 259

   requesting data as, 267-268

   string, 263

   TOML compared to, 301, 303

   using with Go, 275-281

K

key names, 278

L

languages, non-English, 126, 204-206

languages, programming, 9, 13, 89, 155-156

   See also specific language, e.g.: Python (programming language)

latency, 147-152

lexical (defined), 33-34

lexical scoping, 33-34

LICENSE file, 182

Linux, 4-5, 7-8, 340

list command, 225

ListenAndServe method, 244, 258

ListenAndServeTLS method, 258

logging, 213-217, 226

logical operators, 59-60

log package, 215-216, 226

looking for a needle in a haystack, 305-306

looping, 62-63

lowercase, 124, 174, 183, 188, 278

M

macOS, 4, 5, 7-8

main package, 174

make builtin function, 80

Makefile, 196-197

malicious web server, 338

maps, 78-80

Marshal function, 275-276

MatchString function, 306

mathematical operations, 13, 21

math package, 189-190

memory, 25, 39, 155-156

memory address, 35-38

messages and messaging

   advantages of, 156

   to Channels, 157-160, 171

   between Goroutines, 170

   response to, 167

methods, 101-103, 105-109, 113-114

method sets, 103-105

monotonic clock (concept), 317

multiplayer games, 142

multiple defer statements, 67-69

multiple values, function returning, 44-45, 51

multiple variables, 220

MustCompile function, 316

MySQL database, 112-113

N

named return values, 46-48

names, key, 278

names beginning with uppercase letter, 100

naming conventions, 188-190

nesting structs, 89-91, 99

.NET, 178

net/http package, 243-244, 261-262, 264

network, 141, 154

network latency, 147-150, 152

network programming, 1, 51

Network Time Protocol (NTP), 318-319, 326-327

NewAlarm function, 92

NewDecoder function, 285

NewFlagSet, 236, 242

new keyword, 87-88

NewRequest method, 272

Nginx, 152, 213-214

Node.js, 3, 152, 178, 186

non-blocking code, 147

NotFound method, 249

numbers, determining if odd or even, 42

numeric notation, 292-293

numeric types, 18-19, 21, 25

O

object-oriented language, 112

omitempty struct tag, 287

OpenFile function, 297

Open function, 297

Open Source blogging engine, 214

Open Source Licenses, 182

Open Source projects, 186, 197

operating system, 227, 329

operators, 68

OR logical operator, 69

os package, 230, 234, 303

outer blocks, 34

P

package level block, 40

package managers, 178, 339

packages, 173-182

panic, using, 136-138

parallelism, 141-142

Pascal Case, 189

pausing process, 320, 327

permissions, 213, 292-296, 303

Pi constant, 174

Pike, Rob, 3, 4, 10, 122, 138, 142, 154

Plan 9 operating system, 3

platform, 331-332

pointer, 35-38, 96-100, 105-109

pointer reference, 106-109, 113

polymorphism (defined), 113-114

POSIX compliance, 239

postData variable, 263

POST requests, 255-258, 262-264, 272

post statement, 63-64

PowerOn method, 109-111

Printf function, 220

private values, 95

process, running indefinitely, 162-163

programming languages, 9, 13, 89, 155-156

See also specific language, e.g.: Python (programming language)

program speed, factors affecting, 140-141, 151-152

public values, 95

Python (programming language), 3-4, 13, 178

Q

Quickfix menu, 191

R

range clause, 64-66

raw command-line arguments, 229-230

raw string literals, 117-118, 235

Readfile function, 130-131, 291

README file, 182

real time (term), 317

receiver function, 160

recursive functions, 48-49, 51

reflect package, 22-23, 26

regex package, 306

regular expressions

case sensitivity in, 315

data, parsing with, 311-315

data, transforming with, 309-311

definition and overview of, 305-307

end of line, character signifying, 316

strings package compared to, 315

syntax, 307-308, 315

validation, using for, 308-309

Remove function, 298

request, setting on custom header, 271

requests, types of, 253-254, 256

requests and responses, examining, 245-247

response, status code of, 271

response speed, factors affecting, 269

responseTime function, 148

ResponseWriter, 258

return values, 134, 138

Reverse function, 176

Robot interface, 109-112

robots.txt file, 214

routing, 247, 257

Ruby (programming language), 4, 178

rune literals, 116-118

runtime errors, 213

S

sayHello function, 14-15

Schaaf, Herman, 127

scope (defined), 33

security issues, 183, 255, 337, 338, 340

select statement, 164-171

sequential tasks, 139-142

server security issues, 255-258

SGOPATH, 177, 183

short functions, 51

shorthand variables, 29-30

short variable, 32, 40

short variable assignment, 88-90

signed integers, 19-20

single result, function returning, 42-44

64-bit floats, 21

64-bit integer, 20

sleeping, 319-320, 327

slice

    adding elements to, 74-76, 81

    of bytes, 291

    copying elements from, 77

    defined, 73, 78

    deleting elements from, 76, 80

    length limit, 80

    methods associated to, 114

    numbers variables containing, 45

    testing, use in, 206

    using, criteria for, 80-81

    working with, 73-74

slowFunc function, 144-146, 158

slowFunc method, 158-159

software, sharing, 339-340

sort comand, 227-228

source code, 39

space, trimming, 125-126

special characters, 116, 122-123, 127

Specification, 199

spheres, 103-104

Sqrt function, 189-190

square root, 190

Standard Error, 242

Standard Input (defined), 229

Standard Output (defined), 229

statically typed languages, 14, 26

strconv package, 23-24

string literals, 115-118, 127

strings

    array elements, assignment to, 72

    concatenating, 118-121, 126-127, 207-209

    converting to and from, 21, 23, 120, 174

    creating, 121, 127, 291

    definition and overview of, 15, 21, 122-123, 126

    format, representing time in, 322-323

    lowercase, changing, 124, 174

    number types distinguishing from, 25

    parsing, 322-323

    as programming building block, 115

    searching for, 306-307

    variable initializing with type of, 27-28

    working with, 123-126

    written to file, 294

strings package, 125, 174-175, 195, 315

stringutil package, 176, 179

strongly typed languages, 13-14, 26

struct

    checking type of, 94-95

    comparing, 93-95

    copying, 96-99, 100

    creating, 99, 206, 276, 286

    data encoded to and from, 287

    data type in, 100

    decoding to JSON, 281-282

    default value, creating for, 91-93

    definition and overview of, 83-85

    empty, encoding to JSON, 280-281

    empty fields, omitting, 280-281, 287

    encoding as JSON, 276-278

    equivalence, testing for, 94

    exporting, 100

    initializing, 84-89

    nesting, 89-91, 99

    tags, 278-280, 287

    time, 323-325

    values, printing, 220-221

subcommands, 235-239

Sub method, 324

subslice, 80

substring, searching for, 124-125

switch statements, 60-62, 68, 164

systems programming, 1

T

tab, representation of, 127

table tests, 204-207

targets, 329-332

tax code, 40

temporary directory, 290

temporary file, 290

Terraform, 338

Test-Driven Development (TDD), 200-201, 211

test files, placement of, 211

testing, 199-204, 209-210, 226

testing package, 201-204

tests, running, 201-202, 204-207, 210

tests, writing, 210

text editor, 8, 11, 188, 196

text string, 294

third-party dependencies, 178-180, 183

third-party Go plugins, 188

third-party packages, 175-180, 182-183, 303

third-party tools, 183

Thompson, Ken, 3, 122

ticker, using, 321

time, 317-319, 322-326

timeout, 167, 171, 269-270, 272, 320-321

time package, 324

timers, 155, 157, 167

time.Sleep method, 144, 146, 154

time structs, 323-325

time zone differences, 319, 326

32-bit floats, 21

32-bit integer, 20

titles, writing to terminal, 313-314

ToLower function, 174-175

TOML files, 301-303

ToUpper method, 237

triangle, 105-107

type keyword, 84

types

    checking, 22-23, 26

    converting between, 21, 23-24, 174

    number of, 51

    overview of, 14-17

    working with, 232-233

U

Unicode encoding scheme, 122

Unit Tests, 200

universe block, 40

UNIX operating system, 3, 197, 224, 289

The Unix Programming Environment (Thompson), 3

unsigned integer (defined), 26

uppercase, 100, 183, 188, 197

usability, errors and, 135-136

User Story, 199

UTF-8 encoding scheme, 3, 122, 126-127

V

V8 JavaScript engine, 3

validation of data, 308-309

value

    accessing, 83, 85

    assigning to data type, 85

    assigning to variable, 28-29, 35

    changing, 7, 83, 96-97

    default, 91-93, 100

    error as, 138

    functions having multiple, 44-45, 51

    passing function as, 49-50

    passing variable as, 36-37

    private *versus* public, 95

    return, 134, 138

    using, 100

value reference, 96-99, 106-107, 113

variable

    checking type of, 22-23

    declaring, 29-30, 32-33, 38-40

    definition and overview of, 27-29

    inferring type of, 39

    multiple, 220

    scope, using, 33-35

    struct, initializing using, 86-87

    zero value for, 30-31

variatic functions, 45-46, 75

var keyword, 71, 74, 78, 86

vendor folder, 179-180, 183

Vim text editor, 191

W

wall clock (term), 317, 327

weather applications, 140

web browsers, 142-143

web servers

    developing and debugging, 246

Western characters, 123

Windows, 4, 5-7

WordPress site, login page of, 214

Write, calling, 258

WriteFile function, 292-294

X

XML, 286

Z

0644 permissions, 293

0700 permissions, 303

zero value, 22, 30-31, 66, 91, 100

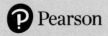

Register Your Product at informit.com/register

Access additional benefits and **save 35%** on your next purchase

- Automatically receive a coupon for 35% off your next purchase, valid for 30 days. Look for your code in your InformIT cart or the Manage Codes section of your account page.
- Download available product updates.
- Access bonus material if available.*
- Check the box to hear from us and receive exclusive offers on new editions and related products.

Registration benefits vary by product. Benefits will be listed on your account page under Registered Products.

InformIT.com—The Trusted Technology Learning Source

InformIT is the online home of information technology brands at Pearson, the world's foremost education company. At InformIT.com, you can:

- Shop our books, eBooks, software, and video training
- Take advantage of our special offers and promotions (informit.com/promotions)
- Sign up for special offers and content newsletter (informit.com/newsletters)
- Access thousands of free chapters and video lessons

Connect with InformIT—Visit informit.com/community

the trusted technology learning source

Addison-Wesley · Adobe Press · Cisco Press · Microsoft Press · Pearson IT Certification · Prentice Hall · Que · Sams · Peachpit Press

 Pearson